Classroom
Management
Techniques

74, 75, 183, 184,
214 - 218, 270 - 73
284 - 97

196 - 198
163 - 166
169 - 172
211 - 213

40 - 47
56 - 65
108 - 118
199 - 206

Cambridge Handbooks for Language Teachers

This series, now with over 40 titles, offers practical ideas, techniques and activities for the teaching of English and other languages providing inspiration for both teachers and trainers.

Recent titles in this series:

Classroom Management Techniques

Jim Scrivener

Consultant and editor: Scott Thornbury

 CAMBRIDGE
UNIVERSITY PRESS

CAMBRIDGE
UNIVERSITY PRESS

University Printing House, Cambridge CB2 8BS, United Kingdom

Cambridge University Press is part of the University of Cambridge.

It furthers the University's mission by disseminating knowledge in the pursuit of education, learning and research at the highest international levels of excellence.

www.cambridge.org
Information on this title: www.cambridge.org/9780521741859

© Cambridge University Press 2012

First published 2012
4th printing 2014

A catalogue record for this publication is available from the British Library

Library of Congress Cataloguing in Publication data
Scrivener, Jim.
 Classroom management techniques / Jim Scrivener ; consultant and editor, Scott Thornbury.
   p.   cm.
 Includes bibliographical references and index.
 ISBN 978-0-521-74185-9 (pbk.)
1. Classroom management. I. Thornbury, Scott, 1950- II. Title.
 LB3013.S42 2012
 371.102'4–dc23

                                                                2011039587

ISBN 978-0-521-74185-9 Paperback

Contents

Thanks and acknowledgements

I'd like to thank the following for all their work, advice and help towards creating this book: Nóirín Burke, Roslyn Henderson, Jane Walsh, Debbie Goldblatt, Andy George, Nick Hardcastle and especially Scott Thornbury and Verity Cole for their careful, thought-provoking editing. This book is dedicated to all the teachers and trainers who worked in Palace Court in the good old days. You know when that was and who you are. I learned it all from all of you.

The idea for analysing what a practitioner can do in terms of interventions comes from John Heron, particularly from Six Category Intervention Analysis. Some of the categories in Chapter Four are inspired by the original six categories.

The authors and publishers acknowledge the following sources of copyright material and are grateful for the permissions granted. While every effort has been made, it has not always been possible to identify the sources of all the material used, or to trace all copyright holders. If any omissions are brought to our notice, we will be happy to include the appropriate acknowledgements on reprinting.

Ken Wilsen for the extracts on pp.15, 201, taken from

http://kenwilsenelt.wordpress.com;

The estate of Theodore Roethke for the text on p.73 taken from *Straw for the Fire: From the Notebooks of Theodore Roethke*, 1972. Published by Doubleday;

Crown House Publishing for the text on pp.103–105 taken from *The Teacher's Toolkit–Raise Classroom Achievement with Strategies for Every Learner* by Paul Ginnis, 2002. Reproduced with permission of Crown House Publishing.

Introduction

◢ What is classroom management?

Your classroom management is the way that you manage students' learning by organising and controlling what happens in your classroom …

• Or the way that you consciously decide *not* to organise and control.
• Or the way that you delegate or relinquish such control to the learners.

It is also what happens (or doesn't happen) when you avoid or remain ignorant about these choices.

The classroom management choices you make play a large part in creating the individual working atmosphere of your class – how it feels to be in a room with you as a teacher. Whether it is an enjoyable, engaging place to be learning or whether it is dull, uninvolving and uninspiring. They reflect what you believe about teaching and learning, about learners and their potential and about the relationship of teacher to learner. They reveal how everyone relates to the class as a whole and to the hierarchy of the learning institution you are a part of.

Behind each selection of a technique is an intention – the thing that you want to happen.

A teacher who always keeps the students in whole-class mode and never makes use of pair work or group work of any kind may be a teacher who believes in such 'traditional' educational approaches, or one that has never thought about or questioned them very much. Or perhaps this sort of teacher is afraid of losing control over things or thinks that whole-class teaching is what the school or students expect and demand.

Similarly, at another extreme, a teacher who runs lessons in which the students always take the lead and decide what they want to do and how they want to do it may be working in such a way based on definite beliefs. Or perhaps that is simply what they have always done – and they will continue to do so – in the absence of clear ideas about how things might be done differently.

◢ Classroom management is independent of methodology

This book is not about one method of teaching. The techniques in this book underlie all methods. You may be following a task-based approach, the grammar-translation method, a communicative approach, a coursebook-driven course, or any way of teaching. The techniques discussed here should be usable and effective, whichever method you use.

Having said that, there is a definite set of beliefs and values informing the ideas proposed: an assumption that the most effective teaching and learning is going to happen when learners are actively involved, interested and engaged in their work. This is more likely to come about in situations where the learners are asked about, and have at least some direct influence or say in, what they study and how they do it. This presupposes a classroom where teacher and learners can work together and talk or listen to each other in a respectful and supportive manner – and much of good classroom management is to do with creating the conditions where such an atmosphere is likely to exist.

■ A wide definition

You may have noticed that the definition I am giving to classroom management is considerably wider than the way this term is often used in secondary education, where it typically refers to ways of keeping order in class and specifically to discipline-related problems. Discipline is certainly one area of classroom management, but it is only one, and, interestingly, many of the biggest problems associated with keeping order are often best answered by dealing with other, seemingly separate, issues of classroom management. For example, in many contexts, if you make significant improvements in how well you encourage all students (rather than just the fastest two or three) to participate in classroom interaction, then this is very likely to have significant knock-on effects to how engaged students are in your lessons – which then affects how well they behave.

■ Classroom management is complex

There is no way that a book such as this can solve the organisational problems of specific classes in all the different contexts of the world. Within any individual problem, there are many distinct characteristics that will make each situation unique (to do with location, cultural norms, people involved, time available, preceding events, relationships, moods and many other factors).

This means that I can't ever tell you what to do. There is no fixed book of guidelines that can ever tell you how to respond in a particular situation. All effective teaching requires an active moment-by-moment processing of the current situation and a flexible ever-changing reflection as to what might be the best thing to do next.

Some of the decisions we make will be just right and useful; others will be ineffective or even disastrous. That's normal for any teacher taking risks in the process of learning how to be a better teacher. We have to learn, slowly over time, which sort of responses seem to be suitable for certain types of situations. We also have to ensure that we don't let any of those responses set in concrete – for the answer that works one week may fall completely flat next week. Good classroom management involves learning from experience, but never allowing that experience to put you into automatic pilot.

■ Classroom management is simple

Having said that classroom management is complex, I also want to emphasise that, in lots of ways, it is also deliciously simple.

There are many small, easy-to-learn, concrete, practical techniques that can be read about, tried out, practised, improved and then used as part of any teacher's repertoire of classroom skills – and in most cases, having more of these at your fingertips will make you a better teacher. It's as clear-cut as that.

I would go so far as to assert that if most teachers in the world could get really good at just five or six of the key techniques, then the quality of education worldwide would hugely improve. Experienced teachers often take higher and higher qualifications, involving more and more in-depth study of aspects of education and become very knowledgeable classroom practitioners. Yet many remain ignorant of, or poor at, some absolutely foundation-level practical techniques that could and would, in a matter of minutes, completely transform their teaching. In such cases, one supportive 45-minute lesson observation of them at work in class, followed by insightful feedback and suggestions, might have a very profound and immediate effect on their classroom practice.

◼ Why do we need classroom management?

In our everyday lives – at home, on the phone, on a tram, in a café, on the Internet and in other contexts – we ask questions, talk, explain things, interact, organise, take control, give instructions, listen to each other and so on. When we become teachers, we might suppose that many of these normal natural skills transfer directly from the *world* to the *class*.

The classroom, however, is not the same as the outside world. Our habitual or intuitive responses, formed in the outside world, may let us down and, paradoxically, may lead to outcomes that are actually the opposite of what we had hoped for.

In order to help create the most engaging and useful learning environment, we need to learn new techniques, or perhaps relearn familiar ones, so that they are effective in a classroom environment; for example, how to talk to a group of people, how to give an instruction, how to organise seating, how to hand things out, how to listen to someone who has a problem, how to respond to a person who is talking too quietly and so on. These are all techniques that need to be thought about, tried out, reflected on and refined (maybe quite a number of times) before they become appropriate, effective, normal and instinctive.

◼ Who is this book for?

This book is intended for you if you are a teacher of English as a foreign, second or other language. The ideas proposed are suitable for a wide range of different face-to-face classrooms and educational contexts. You might:

• Be a native or a non-native speaker.
• Be newly qualified or experienced.
• Teach within the state or private sector.
• Teach children or adults.
• Teach multilingual or monolingual classes.
• Work in a country where English is a first, second or foreign language.

- Teach students studying general English, CLIL or specialising for example in business English, academic English or any other specific purpose.
- Use any methodology or approach.
- Use any kind of coursebook, resources and materials – or none.

In looking at classroom management, we are looking for the fundamental organisational issues that underlie what you can do successfully in class, wherever and however you do your teaching, whatever your starting point.

This book can't solve your immediate local classroom-management problem for you. But it can show you some techniques that have been effective for a number of different people, in a variety of contexts and situations. You can read these, decide which might be useful for you, try the ideas out and add them to your suitcase of possible classroom actions, for use as, and when, appropriate. They won't all work for you in your classrooms, but many of them will, and the ones that don't work can suggest a starting point for reflection and working out your own solutions.

■ What's in this book?

Classroom Management Techniques is organised in seven chapters:

1 **The classroom**   This chapter looks at the teaching/learning space and how best to organise it and exploit what it offers.
2 **The teacher**   We look at who the teacher is in the classroom, how he or she can encourage the most learning and what changes the teacher might be able to make to his or her own actions, reactions and behaviour.
3 **The learners**   We ask who the students are and how the teacher can work with both the group and the individuals.
4 **Key interventions**   This chapter provides a detailed look at fourteen different ways that teachers can behave, speak and do things in the classroom.
5 **Facilitating interaction**   Getting students to communicate in English, with the teacher and with each other, forms a significant part of any language teacher's job. This chapter offers lots of practical advice to get more, and better quality, interaction.
6 **Establishing and maintaining appropriate behaviour**   Discipline involves not just applying sanctions after bad behaviour, but a whole way of working that might encourage the desired good behaviour. This chapter looks at the issue from both angles.
7 **The lesson**   The last chapter considers a range of issues directly associated with in-lesson teaching, including ways of running tasks and approaches to materials and resources.

For most people, this is probably not a book to read from cover to cover (though that could be helpful, especially for newer teachers or teachers in training). For this reason, I have included many cross-references so that you can go to parts of the book that you may not have read, but which contain related teaching suggestions. These references are all given in the form 'Chapter x Unit x', where 'chapter' refers to the seven major chapters of the book, and 'unit' refers to the numbered subsections within those chapters.

I think that there are two main ways that you might approach the material:

• When you face a classroom management problem in your current teaching, you could look in here for possible techniques, strategies and approaches to try out. Even if you don't feel that any of the ideas are directly relevant or suitable for your particular situation, you may still find that reading about similar problems and solutions helps you to clarify your own thoughts and generate your own solutions.
• When you feel that you want to develop professionally and are looking for ways to move your teaching forward, you could research some of the practical ideas and suggestions, select one or two and then try them out in your classes.

At the end of each section I include some 'Questions for reflection' to help you relate the material to your own practice and to think a little more widely about some of the issues.

1 The classroom

1 Different classroom layouts

> *I always work in the same room with the same layout. It feels a little boring. I wonder if a shake-up would wake my class up a little.*

Aim
To experiment with different arrangements of seats and tables/desks.

Introduction
The way your classroom is arranged has a direct impact on what you can do and how you do it. The traditional classroom layout with rows of fixed desks all facing the front may be appropriate for teacher-fronted explanations, board work and quiet individual work, but is arguably less suitable for communicative or task-based work.

A teacher needs to keep in mind the possibility of occasionally changing the seating arrangements. Sometimes this will happen because you need to do so for a specific activity. At other times, change for its own sake may be justification enough. From the learners' perspective, having a new view, new eye contact, and new people next to them may, in a small way, help to keep their interest alive and motivation higher.

Some classrooms have furniture that is fixed to the floor, and, in such cases, one can only play around with how that is used. However, many rooms have seats and desks that can be moved – though it might seem noisy or troublesome to do so.

→ See Chapter 1 Unit 3 *Avoiding chaos when rearranging the room* for ideas on how to avoid such disruption.

Techniques: Classroom layouts

Here are a number of suggestions for rearrangements. Try one or more of these.

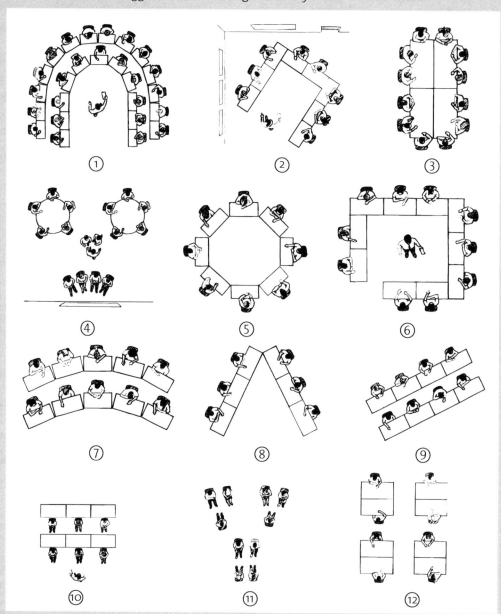

Smaller classes (up to about 20 learners)

1 Semi-circle or U

This allows learners to make eye contact and communicate with each other. There can be a number of rows if needed.

2 Tipped U

In reducing the rigid right angles of most classrooms, this can feel more informal, yet still provide desk space. A variation is to widen out the angle of the arms.

3 One large table

Pull the tables together to form a large table, and sit learners round it. This may increase the feeling of cooperating together on a single task.

4 Zones

If you have the luxury of a large enough classroom and there are spare chairs, you can arrange different areas within the room – a line of seats up front, facing the board; others around tables at the back of the room; a shared open-discussion / mingling area in the middle. During certain stages of a lesson, students may be able to move from zone to zone, depending on what they need to do.

5 Full circle

This is a very democratic arrangement allowing everyone to see everyone else. Notice the learners' expectation that you will sit in the frontmost seat. Try sitting somewhere off-centre, and notice what difference it makes to attitudes and interaction.

All sizes of class

6 Rectangular

Arrange rows of desks and seats around all four edges of the room, or closer in, allowing space to walk behind the seats.

7 Curved rows

Rather than the typical straight-line rows, try curving the lines a little, perhaps facing a long wall of the room (rather than the narrower front wall).

8 Arrowhead

A shape made up of diagonal rows with the arrow pointing towards the back of the class. This permits more eye contact. It also allows more open space at the front of the room (perhaps for mingling activities, or for getting students to come up and read or perform).

9 Diagonal

Keep the traditional rows, but angle them a little so that they leave a large diagonal space in one corner at the front. This is another way of creating a little more working space at the front of the class.

10 Reverse

If there is enough space in your room, try putting the tables *behind* the chairs. This means that students can face you without the intervening barrier. When they need to write at length or have another need for the tables, they can simply turn their chairs round and work with their backs to the teacher.

11 No tables

Or try working groups without any tables. You'll find that this frees up a lot of space in the room, which you can then exploit for speaking activities, games, simulations and so on.

12 Facing
Turn desks to face each other, rather than all facing the front.

13 Islands
Group learners round tables. Learners can work closely together with others, but can also get up and visit other groups without difficulty.

14 Change focus
For one or two lessons when you will not need to use the board much, ask the learners to move their seats (and possibly desks) to change the whole focus of the class to face the side or the back of the room. This is arguably a case of 'change for change's sake', but sometimes a new view can also change how people think, speak and react.

Technique: Seeing the room from a student's perspective

After the students have all gone home, take a few minutes to view your classroom from their viewpoint. Choose three or four random student desks at different places round the class, and sit in them for a minute or so. Imagine watching yourself up front at the board. Is the view clear? What might cause problems? What makes each place pleasant or uncomfortable? Based on what you experience, reflect on what changes you could make to the room to improve it.

These are some of the considerations you may need to think about:
a How cramped are people? Do they have sufficient personal space and elbow room?
b Can people get up and move around easily? Do people have to push past others to get out?
c Are there clear passageways or corridors that allow movement? Is it easy for the teacher to get to any part of the room quickly and without asking people to move things?
d Are sight lines to the front, the board and to other students good for each student?
e Are there any fittings that get in the way (e.g. windows, cupboards, doors, heaters , etc.) or make particular seats uncomfortable?
f Are doors or emergency exits fully accessible? Are there any trip hazards (e.g. from where students place their bags)?

Questions for reflection

- Have you always used the default room arrangement? If so, is it because it is really the best one for you and your students, or is it just because it was there?
- Are you worried that changing the seating arrangement might also have unexpected knock-on effects, for example, to do with how the teacher is listened to or how you are perceived by students?
- What positive student comments can you imagine a rearrangement leading to?

→ For classroom layouts for specific group work activities, see Chapter 1 Unit 2 *Setting up the room for specific activities.*

◾ 2 Setting up the room for specific activities

I'd like to organise my room differently – to make some familiar activities more exciting.

Aim

To create layouts of seating and desks that facilitate and encourage communication in some common activities.

Introduction

If students always do the same or similar tasks in the same seats (perhaps with the same people), there is a danger of *sameness* about everything, and hence boredom and lack of commitment. One activity blends into the next.

Techniques: Layouts for specific activities

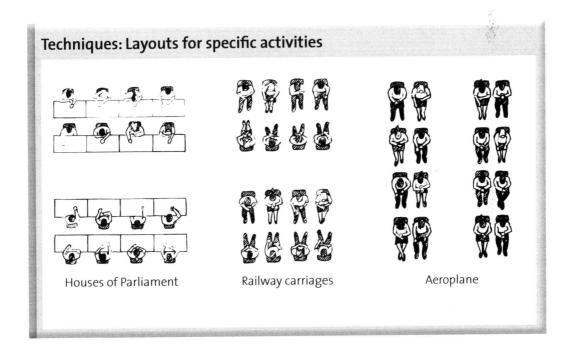

Houses of Parliament   Railway carriages   Aeroplane

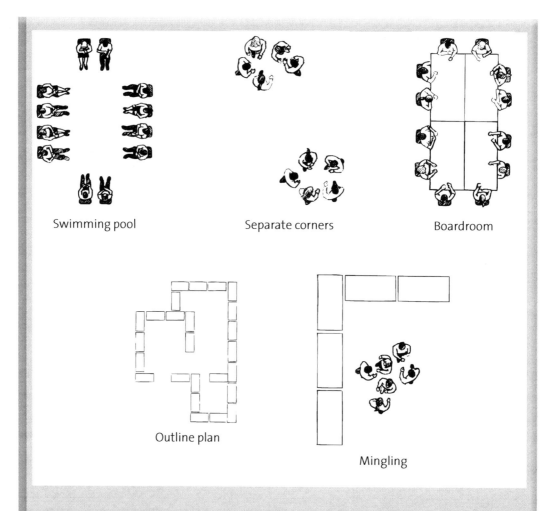

Swimming pool Separate corners Boardroom

Outline plan

Mingling

1 Debates or discussions

If these involve two (or more) opposing viewpoints, try a 'Houses of Parliament' divide, with two ranks of seats (perhaps without desks/tables) facing each other. This isn't suitable for general use, as it deliberately seeks to stir argument and disagreement: *us* versus *them*.

2 Social interaction and conversational activities

Try making 'railway carriages', i.e. separate blocks that have four or five seats facing a similar four or five. Similarly, make an 'aeroplane'. Or a lounge in a 'hotel'. Or a 'restaurant'. Or arrange seats in a rectangle around an imaginary 'swimming pool'.

3 Planning

Some activities (designing solutions, making plans, simulations, mock elections, etc.) require students to work together in groups to prepare their own ideas before coming back together for a meeting or discussion. The more dramatic the separation of the different groups in the preparation stage (e.g. into separate corners of the room), the more it might encourage a team spirit and an urge to compete against the other team.

4 Meetings, presentations and oral report backs

Pull all the desks or tables together to make a single large 'boardroom' table which everyone sits round.

5 Role plays and simulations set in offices, houses and other buildings

Arrange seats or tables to create the *outline plan* of a number of different connected room shapes, corridors, doorways, communal areas, etc. Establish clearly what each shape is: waiting room, surgery, reception desk, lobby with coffee machine, office and so on. Learners can take the roles of people doing different things in all the separate locations.

6 Mingling

When you have a task where learners must mingle, meet and talk with a number of different people, clear the desks/tables to one side of the room to create a 'party space'. Turn on some suitable loud music (if this is possible) as this will help to create an atmosphere and may encourage the quieter ones to speak up, realising that they are less likely to be overheard. You could even serve imaginary drinks!

Questions for reflection

- Which of the classroom layouts in this unit would you like to try tomorrow with your students? What activity would you use them with?
- Are there any layouts here that you would never consider using? Why?

■3 Avoiding chaos when rearranging the room

> *I often want to rearrange the classroom, but I can't find a way to do it that isn't noisy, disruptive and chaotic. My adult students seem to become unsettled and have trouble settling and focussing on the following task, My younger students seem to take advantage of any chance to misbehave and make a lot of noise.*

Aim
To change classroom seating arrangements with the minimum of disruption.

Introduction
If you want to frequently rearrange the room, it's important that you can do it as quickly, quietly and efficiently as possible. If your students do this in a noisy or unhelpful way, it can put you off ever making a new arrangement, to the detriment of activities and variety.

Learners in a classroom often feel rather powerless. Unhelpful, time-wasting or disruptive behaviour may arise from a sense of having no involvement or personal investment in what is being done. All the important and unimportant decisions are taken for them, and there is little they can influence. This, in turn, may lead to bad behaviour and noise when they get a small chance to express themselves – such as when the room is rearranged. By giving responsibility, even for small things, we can sometimes address this issue before it becomes a problem. Learners may feel more involved and may start to take some responsibility for what happens in class. There may even be a degree of pride in seeing their own ideas in operation and successfully carried out.

Technique: Using the learners' ideas
1 Explain to the class that you would like to use a different seating arrangement for the next task, but you feel that they may misbehave or do it slowly and noisily. Allow a few seconds for this to sink in; then ask your students for their advice, i.e. whether you should rearrange or not, and, if so, how best to do it.
2 Have a brief discussion, making sure that you mainly listen to them and echo their ideas (rather than selling or imposing your own solutions). If they suggest a good way of doing the rearrangement, ask if this will really reduce the expected problems. Explain that you will take the chance of following their idea, and that if it is successful, you can do lots more such rearrangements in the future. Make sure they understand that this depends on them.
3 Do the rearrangement, and before going on to the task that required the rearrangement, lead a short feedback discussion about how successful it was. If it worked, tell them that clearly and unambiguously. Collect any suggestions for doing it better next time.

Technique: Rearrangement options

Here are some ideas that learners may come up with, or which you could suggest:

1 Learners agree to do all the rearrangement completely silently. This will involve picking up furniture, rather than dragging, shoving, pushing or pulling. (You might want to take a minute to teach the verb 'pick up'!)
2 Get volunteers, or appoint one or two of the class, to take specific organisational roles. For example, 'Your job is to make sure that all the chairs are moved over to the side wall here and stacked neatly' or 'Monitor what is happening, and remind people to keep the noise down!'
3 Move all learners to one side or corner of the room, and select just a small number to do the actual moving. (These could be different people each time you need a move, adding an element of competition about which team does it best; timing the teams is also a possibility.)
4 Plan the moves like a military campaign, rather than all at once, and then give the instructions to do them in stages, waiting for each to be completed before going on to give the next one. For example: (1) Pick up your chair, (2) Bring your chair over here and stack it, (3) Go back to your table, (4) Push your table to the side of the room, etc. Tell students to stop moving and be quiet after they have finished each step.
5 Or ... get in early, and do all the rearrangement yourself before the class arrives!

Questions for reflection

• Have a look at this story from Ken Wilson in his blog. (2010).

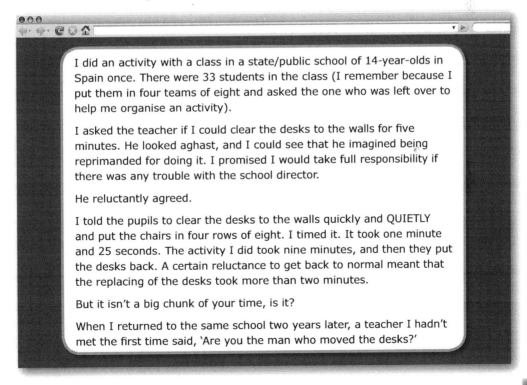

I did an activity with a class in a state/public school of 14-year-olds in Spain once. There were 33 students in the class (I remember because I put them in four teams of eight and asked the one who was left over to help me organise an activity).

I asked the teacher if I could clear the desks to the walls for five minutes. He looked aghast, and I could see that he imagined being reprimanded for doing it. I promised I would take full responsibility if there was any trouble with the school director.

He reluctantly agreed.

I told the pupils to clear the desks to the walls quickly and QUIETLY and put the chairs in four rows of eight. I timed it. It took one minute and 25 seconds. The activity I did took nine minutes, and then they put the desks back. A certain reluctance to get back to normal meant that the replacing of the desks took more than two minutes.

But it isn't a big chunk of your time, is it?

When I returned to the same school two years later, a teacher I hadn't met the first time said, 'Are you the man who moved the desks?'

- How do you feel about the comment, 'It isn't a big chunk of your time, is it'?
- Do other teachers in your department or school ever (or never) rearrange their classes? Have you ever talked to them about why they do or don't, or what problems they have and how they solve them?
- Are you worried about a fellow teacher (or headteacher) looking through a classroom window and seeing your class apparently in chaos?
- Have you ever had a complaint from a classroom next door about the noise your class is making? Was it fair? Did this affect how you viewed noisy moments in class?
- If you frequently reorganise your classes, do you find that students sometimes complain on being asked to stand up and change seats yet again? Do they have a point or not? How do you respond?

4 Effective seating arrangements

> *I always arrange my teenage class in alphabetical order of surnames. I'm starting to wonder if this is the most useful way of doing it.*

Aim

To seat students in ways that are more useful or effective than sequential or random placements.

Introduction

In some schools teachers deliberately ask students to sit in specific seats for whole class work, such as listening to the teacher explaining something. This arrangement may be:

- Alphabetical order of surname or first name.
- Age or height.
- Recent test scores.
- Gender (all the boys on one side, all the girls on the other; or girl/boy, girl/boy).
- Good and naughty (the naughtier you are, the closer you are to the front).

However, very commonly students simply stay wherever they sat down when they came in the room (which, in a multilingual class, might often mean all of one nationality / language group clumped together).

What these ways don't do is creatively match up people for specific reasons, such as those who might work well together or who might support each other. The techniques in this unit suggest some ways that the teacher can arrange people within the whole class. (For making arrangements useful when working in pairs and groups, (see Chapter 5 Unit 8) *Keeping pair work and group work interesting.*)

Of course, if left to choose for themselves, many students will always sit in the same place every lesson. Most of us do it when we enter a classroom. Some seats feel comfortable, safer, more suitable, more like 'ours'. Even experienced teachers who briefly return to the student role on refresher training courses find that they quickly establish their own place in a room.

When we are the teacher with a class of students, we have to decide how much we go with the natural unfolding of things or how much we intervene to reshape the room and events to achieve what we hope will be a better result. Learners might well show reluctance or unhappiness at being asked to change to a different place, but it's worth taking the risk. Part of the job of teaching is helping people discover things that they didn't know they wanted. When students meet and talk with new people, there may be surprising new learning. The extra effort and initial discomfort may be more than counterbalanced by other pleasant and surprising results.

Of course, some seating layouts may prove not to work at all. As a teacher you need to remain alert to genuine unhappiness, people who simply do not get on together and groupings that do not gel.

Techniques: Organising learners in whole-class work

Here are some ideas for organising learners in different ways for different purposes. All of these require the teacher to proactively make the organisation happen. This may be at the beginning of class or at one or more points later in the lesson.

1 Mixed nationalities / language groups

You may decide to deliberately place students from different language groups next to each other – or more importantly, make sure that learners who speak the same language do *not* sit together.

2 Language support

You can sit stronger students next to weaker ones in order that the former can help the latter. This can work well for short periods of time, but may be unfairly demanding on the stronger student if done over a long time and could be embarrassing for the weaker student.

3 Differentiated learning

Contrastingly, you can group learners by language level – sitting stronger students next to each other and weaker students together. This allows you to offer different tasks, or variations on the same task, to different students. Make sure that any differentiated arrangement you make does not visibly separate or pick out the weaker students in any way that could be embarrassing or uncomfortable.

4 Friendships

The 'wherever they sat when they came into the room' arrangement very often reflects friendships, but is also typically quite random – people sit wherever there is a remaining space. You may want to engineer things a little more, deliberately placing people that you know like each other close together.

5 Learner-planned seating

Ask your learners to plan who sits where. This task could be done in groups where each group has a blank plan of the desks and seats. Each group's arrangement could then be used for a lesson (or a week) – and then the next group's plan and so on. You will need to check that there is no deliberate unkindness involved, e.g. placing students who don't like each other together. You may want to allow some time (e.g. after the lesson) when students can feed back to you if they are uncomfortable with any future lesson's seating plan.

Technique: Organising random seating

Sometimes you may decide that you do want an entirely random seating arrangement, perhaps to help energise the class, to break up sitting-together patterns that are getting stale, to help people meet and work with new faces. You could do this, for example, by:

- Asking students to line up in an order, e.g. order of birthdays or alphabetical order of family name or length of hair – then getting them to sit down in the new order.
- Asking students to meet up with someone they haven't worked with in the last three weeks and find a spare desk to sit at.

You will find more ideas for doing this in Chapter 5 Units 7 and 8.

Technique: Getting students quickly into the right places

This is an efficient way of getting students to quickly sit in the place you want them to be in. Draw a plan showing classroom seat positions. Photocopy it a few times for future use and different classes. On one copy, write the names of the students on each desk, indicating where they should sit. Pin this up on the wall outside the room or just inside the door. Train your students to look at this plan as they arrive and go straight to their seat. It will be chaos the first time you try it, but persevere – it gets better when they have done it a few times.

Questions for reflection

- How are students organised in your class? Do you allow them to sit wherever they choose to? If so, is this inertia on your part – or a deliberate decision that this is the best way to do things?
- Which of the ideas for organising your class appeal most to you?

■ 5 Varying teacher positions

> *I seem to get stuck at the front of my classroom throughout most of each lesson.*

Aim

To experiment with various teacher positions in class.

Introduction

In many movies, cartoons and photos of classrooms, the teacher is typically to be found standing centre stage at the front of the room, face-to-face with the students. This is the classic teacher position, for fairly obvious reasons: the teacher can make eye contact with everyone; all students can see him or her clearly; the teacher can make announcements and give instructions with ease. In traditional education, the teacher might well have stayed in this location through whole lessons, days and courses, perhaps even with the addition of a desk as added protection from students.

But then, in the 'old days', there were also very different assumptions about how people learnt, about the importance (or unimportance) of interaction, engagement and active learning, about the unchallengeable hierarchical relationship of teacher to student. In our more active, more interactive, more democratic classrooms, we can usefully challenge the assumption that the front is the default, best or only place for a teacher to be. Why shouldn't instructions be given from anywhere in the room? Why should the teacher be restricted to only one or two places?

There are many reasons why you might want to play around a little with where you stand in class:

- To explore how being in different positions changes the way the class works: Do students understand instructions and tasks any better?
- To experiment with working alongside students rather than watching them from in front.
- To challenge student assumptions about your role in class. By not being at the front, you subtly start to reduce expectations that you are always 'in charge'. You send the message that you are not always about to make an announcement or give an explanation.
- To see how being in different places changes your own feelings about what it means to be a teacher. Do you feel any closer to your students? Do you feel less in charge? More involved? More or less comfortable generally?

→ Try the experiments in this unit alongside Chapter 2 Units 4 and 5, and Chapter 4 Unit 2.

Techniques: Different teacher positions

The ideas listed here are a few simple experiments. Try one or more of the following ideas:

1 If your classroom chairs are arranged in a semicircle, sit mid semicircle, as part of the group, rather than in a separate seat at the front.
2 If your class has fixed desks in rows, make one desk (perhaps towards the back of the room) your *base* for a lesson. Keep coming back to this place rather than to the front of the room. (NB such an arrangement may not be viable in a culture where students would feel they were being rude to have their back to the teacher.)
3 Give instructions from different locations at the side or back of the room.
4 Try clearing a space mid-room, and use this to give instructions. (Yes, you will need to keep turning around to make eye contact with people in different parts of the room!)
5 Have a whole lesson during which you deliberately avoid the front of the room, e.g. never sitting down at the front of the class.

When considering where to stand or sit, bear in mind:

• **Special needs**   Do any of your students have hearing problems? If so, make sure that they can see your lips when you speak to give instructions or explanations. A window or light source behind you can make this much more difficult as you might appear in silhouette.

Techniques: Standing or sitting?

There's no secret rulebook which specifies that teachers have to stand all the way through their lessons – though many teachers do it so much you wonder if they think that sitting down is in some way illegal. But sitting down can have definite uses:

1 **Give yourself a rest**   When students are doing tasks they may not need to be monitored all the time. Take the chance of resting for a few minutes.
2 **Signal changes of tone and pace**   Sitting down suggests a slower pace, a different tone and a less in-your-face teacher mode. Use it to set certain activities apart from the rest. For example, if you are going to read a short story to the class, make a point of sitting down, getting comfortable and opening the book – all classic storytelling preambles. Discussions are another whole-class activity that can benefit from the teacher sitting; they seem to signal *participation* rather than *leadership* in the interaction.
3 **Signal that you are trusting them to work without supervision**   Sitting down sends the signal to students that you are not about to jump in to organise them, stop their task, start suggesting things or offer corrections. This allows students to feel a little more trusted and a little freer. They might relax into the work a bit more.

When considering whether to stand or sit, bear in mind:

• **Cultural issues**   In certain cultures, some postures may be considered inappropriate or offensive (e.g. sitting in such a way that the soles of one's feet are directed at students or sitting on the floor – or asking your students to). If you are teaching outside your own culture, it's important to become aware of and show sensitivity to cultural norms. Locals are very often tolerant and understanding of the foreign teacher's lack of awareness, but all the same, it's much better if you can find out if you are giving offence. Read tourist guidebooks for advice; ones aimed at business people tend to be especially informative. In class, if you notice any odd reactions to a sitting or standing position (e.g. everyone looks away, or perhaps there is an embarrassed giggle), ask students directly about it. Take any comments seriously and try to learn from them.

Questions for reflection

- Do you detect any change of student attitude to you or a change in the quality of teacher-student relations when you change locations?
- Do quieter students talk more with you when you are in their part of the room?
- How does the difference in position affect your own feelings of authority – or perhaps power? Does it feel good or right to deliberately give up some of the power a teacher may be assumed to have?

◼6◼ Using a limited space

> *My classroom is small and cramped. There is just enough space for desks and seats, but nothing left for moving around. Even changing seats is difficult. I'd love to get students moving and interacting, but it seems to be impossible.*

Aim

To create space for moving around, making groups and different classroom arrangements.

Introduction

Thousands of teachers the world over face cramped classrooms. They feel that they have real limitations on what is possible in terms of making pairs and groups or when rearranging the room. Often students end up only ever talking to the person in the desk next to them.

It's one of those problems that seems to impact on everything you do in class, yet can seem insoluble, unaddressable. There is no easy solution, but there may be some things that you can do, whether by addressing constraints within yourself, or perhaps by thinking big and reshaping your whole classroom.

I have seen teachers in quite spacious classrooms who say that they cannot do pair and group work because the room is too cramped. I have also seen teachers working in the most tightly desked rooms imaginable (with hardly space for a mosquito to fly between desks) who get their students to stand up, change places and do exciting group activities – and somehow themselves manage to glide amongst them to monitor. This does make me wonder if the constraint of limited space is at least partly internal (to do with the teacher's confidence, worries, fears or inertia) rather than external (to do with the limited space or fixed desks).

So, one solution to worries about limited space is just to ignore the worries and do it anyway! That might be troublesome, but I'm pretty sure it'll be a lot more enjoyable than having a room full of students doing endless written exercises and who never talk to anyone but the person next to them.

Techniques: Minimum movement variations

- Get students to work not only with the person next to them, but also the person in front of them and behind them.
- Get students to sit *on* their desks to do pair or group work.
- Nominate just a few people (e.g. six) to change places before a task starts. Doing this with different people each time you start a new task will slowly rearrange the whole class over time, giving people new partners to work with.

Technique: Use the front of class

Even in a cramped room, there is usually some space at the front of the room. Make the most of this:

- Get students to come up and do mingle tasks.
- When you do pair or group work, invite some pairs to use this space and do the task while standing. Most students tend to like the chance to get out of their seats when they can – so even giving a few the chance to stretch their legs is good.

Technique: Make the most of other available spaces

For some activities, consider using the corridor. I'm not suggesting moving desks out there – but there must be activities where students need to talk and agree something together, where having some students working outside the room (standing, probably) might be a good option.

Also, consider other spaces around your school. Are there any locations that you could use for all or part of one of your future lessons? Perhaps the hall? A gym? A playing field? The dining area? It's not too hard to think of interesting activities that could take place in most of these. Using a different location might add a new spark to a project, a role play or a communicative activity. Make the move less disruptive by telling students the lesson before that they should go to the other location rather than to their usual room. It may also be worth emphasising that a special change such as this is only workable with the cooperation and discipline of all. Get the class on your side and agreeing to cooperate – so that you are encouraged to do such lessons more often.

Technique: Moving the desks

At the beginning of a lesson, ask students to push all desks/tables to the back or side of the room, arranging them to take as little space as possible. Teach the lesson with students in just their chairs; you'll find it provides a surprising amount of new space to work in.

Technique: The drastic option: getting rid of the desks

Consider the pros and cons of working without desks/tables – moving them all to another classroom or into storage elsewhere in the school. In many cases, the problems caused by the loss of a writing space might be balanced by the new opportunities for rearranging seating. New activities and groupings will suddenly become possible. Here is one teacher's story:

I found that I couldn't do anything that I wanted to with my classes because we were all squashed in like sardines. I asked around the school and found a space where we could store our desks. I had no idea if the experiment would work – so I wanted to be sure that we could get the furniture back when we needed it.

One lesson, I asked one of my classes to help carry most of the desks to the storage area. We left just one row at the back of the room so that there was some writing/ display area if needed.

What happened – well, it was a bit of a miracle. Suddenly the room had space. At first, we arranged seats in familiar rows – then, when we did an activity, students found they could easily move into groups of four or five students – and when we came back into whole class work, we met as a circle. It was amazing – all these new options totally transformed the lessons.

The downside was reading, and writing work, of course. Students didn't like balancing coursebooks or paper on their knees, but most agreed that it was probably a price worth paying. Some students could use the desks at the back of the room – and after a term the school bought some lap trays – they were cheap and really helped, but weren't ever as good as real desks. Anyway, as a result of the change, we do much more speaking work and fewer written exercises. Despite this, I actually think their English is improving faster. The desks are still in storage!

Questions for reflection

- How much do your learners need their desks/tables? Do you consider them essential and indispensable? What would be problematic if they didn't have them?
- If the balance of classes changed from mainly heads-down writing to active speaking and interaction, would this help or hinder the improvement of your students' English?
- Consider whether it really is impossible to change the arrangement of a limited space, or whether your reasons for not rearranging the classroom might have more to do with your concerns about losing control.

■7 Sharing classrooms

> *I'd love to create a special English environment in a classroom, but I don't have one room – I teach all over the school, sharing rooms with other teachers.*

Aim

To create good classroom environments even though you have to move from room to room.

Introduction

For many reasons, it is usually better if you have a specific, dedicated room for your language classes, one you stay in while different classes of learners arrive and leave through the day. It allows you and your students to take ownership of the room and to organise it and decorate it as you wish. Just as much as a physical education teacher needs a gym or field, and a chemistry teacher needs a lab, the language teacher needs a language gym or an activity laboratory of their own: one that allows for lots of moving around, spoken interaction and varied seating arrangements for group tasks.

Sadly, for teachers in many schools, a personalised classroom isn't a possibility. Instead, the students may stay in their room while it is you that move around, carrying heavy loads from location to location. Or you may have to share your room with a number of teachers, possibly all teaching different subjects. In this situation, it often happens that rooms stay dull and unloved; no one does anything to brighten up or give character to the room for fear that it will annoy or upset the other teachers.

This is not an easy problem to solve and only really answered by a change of policy from the school itself. If that doesn't happen, discussion and negotiation with colleagues is your best bet, but worth doing rather than not doing anything.

Techniques: Plan for efficient reorganisation of the room

If you would like a specific layout set up in the room you are going to, avoid wasted time at the lesson start by making sure the moving is completed as quickly as possible.

1 Train students to rearrange the room as soon as they arrive. This could be something done by the first students to arrive, or by those assigned responsibility roles – or by everyone.
2 Prepare a seat plan that they pick up in an agreed place and immediately set to work to create the room layout that they find on it, even if it's before you arrive yourself.

Techniques: Teacher agreements for shared rooms

Try to discuss the issue of sharing a classroom with your teaching colleagues. You may well find that they also wish they could do something to make better use of the rooms, and by negotiation, some workable agreements could be reached.

Here are some ideas for possible agreements:

1 Allocated wall space

Agree that the noticeboard and any usable wall space be fairly divided (either by the teacher or by the different classes that use the room). It may be that some teachers inform you that they don't actually need their part. Even if you end up with a small portion of the room as your own, it allows you to put up at least some content that suits you, and your students' needs, tastes and creativity.

2 Allocated storage space

Divide up the available storage space (drawers, cupboard space, shelf space) so that each teacher has their own area. Use your allocation to store useful boxed materials that you can quickly take out at the start of each lesson to create an instant English classroom without too much fuss. This could include dictionaries, a box of readers that students can borrow, a selection of magazines, your vocabulary box, flashcards, a wall poster or two, a phonemic chart to stick to the board and so on.

3 Separate corners

If you have the luxury of any free space in the room, you could propose that each corner is reserved for a different teacher or subject. Thus, you might have an English corner, a geography corner and so on. Place a table in this space, and even if the area is small, aim to make good use of it, by putting out picture displays, books, magazines and so on.

4 Seat-arrangement rotas

It may be that one teacher really wants the room to be in a certain arrangement (perhaps a traditional one of rows), while you or other language teachers may feel that they want a layout more suitable for interaction and tasks. Sadly, in such situations, it is often the supposed default solution (i.e. rows) that wins, and teachers who want any other shapes end up having to spend time at the beginning and end of each lesson making and unmaking their arrangement of desks and seats.

However, there may be other compromises possible. Discuss and see if teachers might be willing to agree to change the arrangement on a rota basis, either for a week or a fortnight at a time. There is an element of compromise in this, and it may still be too much for some teachers who are wedded to their familiar room shape. This may be one that you need to politely argue: different teachers have different classroom needs.

Questions for reflection

- Quite apart from the ideas in this unit, is there any possibility of changing the school's policy on classroom use? Is it a matter of timetabling necessity or just an unchallenged habit? Could you make the case for having your own room?
- What one aspect of your shared classroom would make the biggest positive change to your work? Can you raise it for discussion with colleagues tomorrow?

8 Improving the classroom environment

> *My classroom is so unwelcoming and dull! Even I feel my spirits sinking when I walk in. Goodness knows how the learners feel.*

Aim

To make the teaching/learning space a more exciting environment to be in.

Introduction

Although a lot of classroom management techniques seem to be focussed on what the teacher does and says, we need to remember that there is only any point to teaching if it leads to learning happening.

I cannot learn for my students. Only they can do that. My main job as a teacher is to create the conditions within which learning is most likely to happen. But what kind of environment is this? Each teacher's concept of it will differ – but it is a vital question to ask yourself, not least because, without reflecting on it, you are likely to uncritically reproduce learning environments that you grew up in yourself as a child, even if you hated them at the time.

You and your students will be spending a lot of time in your classroom. It's worth thinking a little about whether it's possible to make it a better place to be.

I vividly recall the awfulness of some classrooms I have visited or worked in. A few were filthy and unloved. Most were smart, bright and tidy. But so many were deathly dull, lifeless, uninspiring and enthusiasm-killing. I recall the sense of despair I felt when I imagined students having to spend a year or more trapped in such confines. A room full of sterile blank white walls does little to make me feel ready to explore and learn. Almost worse are the rooms which still boast pictures and student work that were all pinned up ten years earlier, slowly curling and fading.

The questions below may help you decide what kind of learning environment you want to create.

1 **Atmosphere**   What atmosphere do I want learners to feel as they re-enter the classroom? What part of this is to do with the physical facts of the room itself? What part is to do with the psychological atmosphere I create? What part to do with what the learners themselves bring to the class?
2 **The learners' view of me**   How do I want the learners to view me? Do I want to be seen as the authority in class? A distant figure? A ringmaster? A manager? A colleague? A friend? Another learner? A resource? A counsellor? A tough boss? A mentor? A prison guard? A work foreman? Is there any tension between who the students expect me to be, who the school expects me to be and who I want to be?

3 **My view of my role as a teacher**   What do I understand by 'teacher'? What do I see as my main roles: To organise? To encourage? To validate? To set tasks? To set goals? To mark? To praise? To know things? To explain things? To answer questions? To control? To discipline?

4 **Rapport**   How will the people in the room relate to each other? Learner to learner? Learner to teacher? Teacher to learner? As 'teacher' and 'students'? As friends? As colleagues? As co-explorers?

5 **Ownership of the room**   How much is it 'my' classroom? How much do I see all learners as owning the space? How does the 'ownership' manifest itself?

6 **Democracy**   In general, who will decide things? Will I set all the ground rules for my classroom, or can this be shared? Who will tell people what to do? Do I expect learners to do what I tell them? If not, how will things be organised and ordered?

7 **Respect**   How will respect show itself? Learner to teacher? Teacher to learner? Learner to learner?

Technique: Putting yourself in the students' shoes

Imagine that you are going to be a student again for a few months, studying a new subject. Forget all that you know about colleges, schools and classrooms. Forget about what the teacher might want.

Start with yourself and your own wishes and needs. Can you imagine the best possible environment within which you would learn most successfully? Think about specific details:

1 Think about physical attributes (e.g. kind of room, furniture, tables, personal space, access to resources and technology and so on).

2 Think about psychological aspects (e.g. how you would hope to feel, what kind of atmosphere you want to work in, how you want to relate to the teacher and other learners).

Now imagine the atmosphere that you'd like to generate in your classroom. Use the following list of classroom metaphors to help you:

Do you want your classroom to be:
• A gymnasium (for mental workouts).
• A garden (where lots is planted and lots grows).
• A reform school (where you have to keep a close eye on misbehaving or dangerous young people).
• A living room (where people just sit and chat and maybe occasionally watch a bit of TV).
• A laboratory (for experimenting with language).
• An exercise-providing machine (with an endless supply of paper).
• A surgery (to diagnose and cure a range of problems).
• A variety show (where the students wait to see the next entertaining activity).
• A multimedia resource centre (providing what people want when they need it).
• A prison (with lots of caged people).
• A zoo (with lots of caged animals).
• A stage (for people to show off their best performances).
• A restaurant (serving up a range of interesting dishes).
• A circus (lots of noise, different activities and performers, a ringmaster controlling it all).
• A counselling service (to provide listening, advice and support).

- A sushi bar (where customers can pick what they want off a conveyor belt).
- A complaints bureau (with a queue of demanding clients waiting).
- A factory (automated production, turning out new users of English).

Once you have a list, look back over it, and consider carefully:
- How different is the list from your current classroom reality?
- Which of your ideas are easily implementable – things that you could immediately do to improve things for your own students?
- In the longer term, how could you move slowly towards some of the more challenging changes on your wish list?
- Are any of the wilder ideas actually possible in any way? Do any provide some inspiration towards something that is doable to some degree?

Techniques: Dealing with physical and environmental factors

1 Light

If the light is not good enough, this is a major problem. Look into getting extra light if it helps, or perhaps moving obstructions such as blinds or furniture. It's certainly worth asking if any students are having problems seeing clearly and taking account of this when making seating plans. Of course, bright sunshine can also be a problem, for example, if it is burning down on a student's head – and, in this case, you may need to ask for blinds for your room.

2 Acoustics

The sound quality of a classroom is a crucial aspect of its usability, but is also a factor that the individual teacher can often do little to affect. Some rooms are very echoey, metallic or hollow-sounding while others absorb sound, and force you to almost shout. If you have students who are hard of hearing, the acoustics (and external noise, below) are an even more pressing concern. Where you can, try experiments to improve the acoustics (e.g. by hanging curtains or rugs on a wall). Carpets can sometimes help!

3 Noise

Some classrooms have thin walls. In hot countries, rooms may be made of bare concrete and constructed without doors or window glass. Such rooms can seem to catch, funnel and amplify every sound from surrounding rooms and corridors. This can be a significant problem and one that is very hard to address without annoying a lot of other teachers (who are probably equally annoyed by your own class's noise). Your best bet may be to raise this issue at a teachers' meeting – not as a complaint, but as a discussion point – in order to see if anyone has a good suggestion as to how to improve things.

Internal classroom noise can also be a problem, e.g. forty desks that all clunk shut. Experiment with solutions, e.g. putting a blob of soft Blu-Tack® inside each desk to dampen the sound as desks close.

4 Ventilation

Teachers (with all their effort at the front of the room) often get hotter than students and may wish to have more ventilation in the room. They often also believe that a room with air flow will help to keep students awake and alert. Students may have different opinions and want windows closed. Some parts of the world have an abiding fear of the danger of draughts. Trying to negotiate whether a window can be opened in a multinational class is one of the trickiest tasks I've faced as a teacher!

5 Temperature

In many countries, the air conditioning is so noisy when switched on that no one can hear anyone else, but switched off the room is unbearably hot and humid. Elegant use of the remote control becomes important! Air conditioning ON for group and pair activities; OFF for whole-class work. If you keep forgetting to turn it on or off at the right moments, try delegating the task to a responsible student.

There is not much you can do about many of these issues, but it is still worth being clear what the issues are (e.g. keeping a notebook of problems) and discussing them with your students and with management. Making non-teaching decision makers aware of problems is important, as they may not understand there is anything amiss until people start (and keep on) saying so. Solutions to issues like noisy air-conditioning are likely to be very expensive or non-existent, but it's still worth regularly raising them as an issue.

Of course, if certain bad conditions can't be changed, you may simply have to abandon some activity types, e.g. if the acoustics are really terrible, don't try and play recorded dialogues in class. Ask the students to listen to them for homework, or read them aloud yourself. Likewise, if the room can't be darkened, don't count on showing them a PowerPoint® presentation!

Techniques: Improving the room

It doesn't take much imagination or effort to improve a classroom. Here are some ideas for giving some extra character to yours. Get your students to make suggestions too.

1 Decorations

A simple way to liven things up is to put lots of pictures and posters on the walls. Many publishers supply posters that combine discreet advertisements for coursebooks alongside interesting educational pictures and text. If you go to a conference, collect as many as you can. Try writing to any local distributors or well-known publishers, and ask for posters. Many magazines provide a good source of posters and images.

Dull-looking noticeboards can look much brighter (and help brighten the whole room) if you cover their surface with large sheets of coloured paper, e.g. a bright yellow.

How about a washing line? Get a long piece of string and stretch it diagonally across a corner of the room, or along a wall, or even across the middle of the room (though you will probably need to use support from a light fitting or something to stop it drooping onto the students). Once you have your washing line, you can use ordinary clothes pegs to hang an ever-changing display of fun stuff on it: students' work, seasonal items, exciting articles, real objects (e.g. leaves, photos, magazines).

If you don't mind spending some money, buy some inexpensive but colourful material that could be used to drape over student desks, like tablecloths. These can really transform the look and appeal of a room.

2 Learners' work

You can also put up posters and writing work prepared by your students.

3 Zones

Take the decoration idea a step further by making distinct zones within your room. Collect together materials and images related to a single topic into one part of the room. As well as using the wall space, add tables for displays of work, interesting items and reading matter. For example, part of the back wall could be focussed on US life and culture; another part could be to do with English as a global language; another could be reserved for learners' work; another could be for resources (see below); another might have lots of word cards and other vocabulary learning aids (see Chapter 7 Unit 6).

If you have a large enough room, create zones for specific activities; e.g. leave the middle of the room clear as a mingle zone, or place a colourful rug and cushions on the floor in a corner as a reading zone for one or two students.

If you can lock your classroom, or a cupboard in it, or if you feel that it will be safe to leave materials unattended, create a resource-rich zone for students to browse in and borrow from. You could let learners access this zone before or after class – and it could be a place that early-finishers go to while waiting for others to complete longer tasks during lessons. Some things that could be in this zone:

- A computer already running a pre-loaded task, game or exercise (that changes every day) or perhaps following a teacher-chosen Twitter® stream.
- Exciting books to borrow, such as graded readers that your students will enjoy. These could be lined up on a shelf or table, or kept in a 'book box' that you remove at the end of each lesson.
- English language films and TV programmes on DVD for borrowing.
- Comics and magazines suitable for your learners' age range.
- Leaflets in English about various local or national attractions and events.
- Word cards, i.e. a set of cards with words that have come up in class, perhaps each having a word on one side and definition on the other. Every lesson a few interesting new items can be added, and learners can check and revise by looking through the pack.
- A selection of laminated, reusable word puzzles, grammar worksheets and discussion questions.
- Commercial word games (e.g. Boggle®).

Questions for reflection

- Is your classroom a place that you feel happy to walk into? How do you think your students feel? Can you see the place through their eyes?
- What small changes could make the biggest improvements?

❚9❚ Design and purchasing decisions

> *My school is refurbishing some rooms, and I'd really like to have a say in what kind of furniture and facilities they buy, but I'm sure no one's going to ask me.*

Aim

To get involved in key purchasing or design decisions about classrooms – and to help make bold, workable, creative decisions.

Introduction

Whiteboards on walls that few students can easily see, chairs that are uncomfortable, tables that are bulky, hard to move and don't easily fit together, storage units that are the wrong size or shape to store the things that need to be stored …

It's amazing how many decisions about classrooms are taken without anyone involved in the decision-making having the slightest idea about how the things are used. When schools refurbish rooms or when they need to buy new furniture or resources, the people who actually use these things (i.e. the teachers or the students) tend not to be asked for an opinion.

This unit is trying to encourage you, as a teacher, to see this as a legitimate and important part of your interest, and to request, cajole, nudge, argue or do whatever you need to do to have your voice heard. You don't need to have big ideas or detailed understanding of budgetary issues. When proposals are made, it would be useful if you can offer one or two comments on what is actually usable (or not usable) in the teaching situation.

It's also worth considering whether the eventual clients or consumers (i.e. the students themselves) might also be able to make a contribution. They sit at the desks. They look at the boards. They feel the heat or cold of the rooms. It seems very likely that they have strong opinions that could also be useful in making such important, long-lasting choices. Even if the school doesn't want to directly bring them into the decision-making process, you may find that you have an important, and very real, topic for class discussions and projects – and that you could pass on what you learn from them to the school management.

Technique: Getting involved

When you hear that decisions are being made, ask the person organising if it would be possible for a teacher to get involved, either as an individual or via any staff forum operating in your school. This will obviously involve some time commitment for discussion, looking through catalogues, walking inspection tours of the school and so on – but it is also very enjoyable.

Here are a few of the key discussion points that may be worth adding into the conversation:

1 Traditional desk/table and chair - or flaps?

Language teaching classrooms are often furnished with flap chairs rather than traditional desks/tables. Flap chairs, or *flaps*, are seats that have either a foldable or a removable flap on one side. This allows students to position the flap in front of them whenever they need to do some writing work, but fold down / remove the flap when speaking is the priority. There is a consequent saving in classroom space (no need for all those large desks) and a lot of new possibilities for groupings and rearrangements. Moving into a new rearrangement is remarkably quick and simple.

Flaps are not problem free. They provide a tiny working space, and students regularly knock things onto the floor – this quite apart from the flap's inherent tendency to collapse occasionally, sending a shower of papers everywhere. Another difficulty is that left-handed flap chairs can be hard to find, and right-handed ones are almost impossible for left-handers to use.

2 Foldable or stackable?

Some chairs stack. Some fold. Foldable tend to be less comfortable, but take up much less space when stored away.

Some tables stack. Some fold. Foldable tend to be troublesome and often involve squashed fingers. They take up less space, but can also be more expensive as they typically require some complex engineering of sliding levers and catches, and they can go wrong.

3 Rectangular tables or shaped?

There are tables and tables. Rectangular tables can take up unnecessary space and be hard to rearrange. Trapezoid-shaped tables (i.e. with two parallel edges and two 45° diagonal edges) can easily fit together to make different shapes.

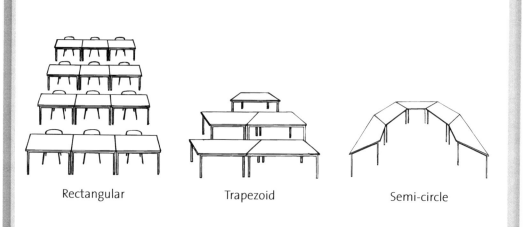

Rectangular   Trapezoid   Semi-circle

This makes it easy to go from rows, to semi-circle, to small groups as needed.

4 Regular furniture or mixed styles?

Should all the desks and tables be the same, or might some variety give the classroom a unique character and the possibility of working in lots of different ways? This could fit in with the idea of 'zones' (see Chapter 1 Unit 8).

Can you imagine a class where some students were sitting at normal desks and seats while others were on a sofa while some were on cushions on a rug or on stools at a 'bar'?

5 Whiteboard on the end wall or the side wall?

Managers tend to place blackboards/whiteboards on the narrower end wall of a classroom. This has an immediate and profound influence over almost everything that will happen in that room. But what would happen if the board was in the middle of a longer side wall instead? For one thing, more people would be closer to the front, and those furthest away from the front would all be less far! This arrangement would immediately encourage a wider front row (if you use rows) or a wider semicircle (if you use that arrangement).

6 Bright colours or muted shades?

Will it cheer up lessons to be in a room that has a lot of yellows or blues, or might it have the opposite effect and be a bit nauseating? Would you rather have orange walls or grey ones? Could the chairs all be different bright colours, or should they all be black or dark blue? Is it better to have less exciting colours on the walls that allow any posters or work put up on them stand out more?

7 Wall space or noticeboards?

Do you think it's a good idea to have lots of noticeboards, or is open wall space better (assuming that you would be permitted to use Blu-Tack® to put up posters, student work and other stuff)?

8 Shelves or cupboards?

Do you want to stock your stuff openly and accessibly, or does it need to be put away out of sight and perhaps under lock and key?

Questions for reflection

- How often have you thought that a classroom's furniture had been badly thought through?
- If you could spend some money on the current room you are in, what would you change?

2 | The teacher

1 Being yourself

> *More experienced colleagues tell me that I should play the role of a confident, knowledgeable teacher. As I walk into my classroom, I feel myself trying to become that teacher, but somehow I'm never comfortable with it and never quite sure how I should be in the classroom.*

Aim

To find an authentic classroom persona.

Introduction

Authenticity means behaving in a way that is appropriately *real*, appropriately *you* – letting the students see something of your genuine reactions to things, your moods and your natural behaviour, rather than covering everything up in a performance.

Carl Rogers, the US educational psychologist suggested that authenticity was the single most important teacher characteristic:

> *The teacher can be a real person in her relationship with her students. She can be enthusiastic, can be bored, can be interested in students, can be angry, can be sensitive and sympathetic ... Thus, she is a person to her students, not a faceless embodiment of a curricular requirement nor a sterile tube through which knowledge is passed from one generation to the next.*

He believed that authenticity created the conditions for good rapport and helped build a real depth of trust and respect, and that this made the difference between a successful classroom and an unsuccessful one.

Rogers claimed that we can subconsciously detect the difference between people who are congruent (i.e. being honestly themselves) and those who are acting – playing a role to a lesser or greater degree, and that we trust the latter much less and we are not able to relate to them as closely. Yet, at the time of Rogers' writing, he felt that he could see 'the tendency of most teachers to show themselves to their pupils simply as roles':

> *It is quite customary for teachers rather consciously to put on the mask, the role, the façade of being a teacher and to wear this façade all day, removing it only when they have left the school at night.*

I wonder how much has changed since he wrote those words back in 1967.

The Rogerian argument for authenticity offered in this unit is, by no means, universally agreed.

Some educational advisors and writers would say the opposite. Here, for example, is Sue Cowley writing on 'Becoming a confident teacher':

Remember that how you feel inside doesn't matter ... Your aim is to develop an air of confidence, self-control and a mastery of everything that happens in your classroom.

She describes teaching as 'putting on a great performance' – one in which you have:

A stage on which to perform ... A show to present ... An audience watching your every move ... A character to step into. ... When you're on that stage, 'being' the teacher, you're not playing yourself.

This view of education leaves me rather depressed. I don't want to spend my life acting the role of a teacher. I want to be able to make contact with learners, human to human.

Many educational cultures will offer a strong force of discouragement to a teacher who wants to be authentic. There may even be legal restrictions on what a teacher can say or do. In a school where all the other staff are adopting the role of distant, formal, dignified authority, it could cause real problems for a teacher to try and buck that trend. A first response from students might be to lose faith in the teacher who is not behaving according to expectations.

In such circumstances, I'd suggest that you don't abandon your intention to behave more authentically, but it would only be sensible to tread carefully, making small changes, chipping away slowly at expectations and, initially perhaps, avoiding too much that might be seen as threatening to other teachers or students.

Techniques: Five steps to authenticity

Here are some small, but important ways that a teacher could work on becoming more authentic:

1 Don't try to be a 'teacher'

Stop yourself whenever you find yourself behaving more as a job title rather than as yourself. Don't speak as if you are some sort of official mouthpiece for the teaching profession or your school. Don't seek out additional ways of differentiating yourself as a teacher. Sit *with* rather than *in front of.* Talk *with* rather than *at.*

2 Have real conversations

When you chat informally with a student, make it a real conversation, where you really listen to what they have to say and respond appropriately. Give your own genuine personal reactions to student comments. If something a student says makes you disagree, say so, instead of 'Hmmm, interesting'.

3 Don't pretend omniscience

If you don't know an answer to a question, say that, rather than pretending that you do know or confusing students with roundabout explanations and avoidances.

4 Be wary of staffroom advice

Colleagues may tell you that being genuinely warm and friendly with students is dangerous, or that it is essential for a teacher to keep up a front – as someone reserved, formal and a little distant. Their comments are probably well-intentioned, but treat such advice cautiously, and make sure you think it through for yourself before you decide to follow it.

5 Be appropriately authoritative

Being authentic doesn't mean abdicating the responsibilities and duties of a teacher. You can still give all the instructions, set all the homework and do all the things that you need to do. You can be appropriately authoritative. The difference is that it is *you* being authoritative, not you using the cloak of teacher superiority and hierarchical authority to do it.

Technique: Dealing with personal doubts

Dörnyei and Murphey suggest two common doubts about being authentic in class:

1 A worry about revealing our own limitations, e.g. a non-native speaker's concern about her own language knowledge, especially within a culture that does not easily accept teachers' admissions of gaps in their knowledge.
2 Questions as to whether we should be completely sincere in situations when we are, for example, mad or very disappointed with certain students. Can we really show that we are tired or depressed or have a hangover?

The authors suggest that although 'these are all valid concerns', the fact that students will be able to see through any pretence means that even though both issues are worrying, it seems likely that more tension and problems will be created by hiding the truth, potentially 'undermining student trust'. On the second point, they also suggest that while self-control is important, 'A teacher's open expression of anger or disappointment with some piece of student behaviour may prove to be more effective in getting through to the student than applying some correct disciplinary procedure and thereby reverting to authoritarian distance'.

Questions for reflection

- Look at this excerpt from Frank McCourt's description of his life as a teacher in the US:

  I often think I should be a tough, disciplined teacher, organised and focused, a John Wayne of pedagogy, another Irish schoolmaster wielding stick, strap, cane ... Sometimes I joke, 'Sit in that seat, kid, and be quiet, or I'll break your bloody head', and they laugh because they know. 'Yeah, isn't he something?' When I act tough, they listen politely till the spasm passes. They know.

  Do you have a similar image of the kind of teacher you feel you should resemble? Do you 'put on' this performance sometimes?
- How do the students react? Do they 'know'?
- Find a quiet minute in class (perhaps while students are working on a task) to reflect on your answers to these questions:
  o How much am I being myself in this class today? Are the learners seeing something like the 'real' me, or am I acting how I think a teacher should be?
  o In what small ways could I be more honestly myself? What might that change in class?
  o Am I worried that students will not respect me if I let down my guard; if I let them see me as *me*, rather than as the teacher, the knower or the figure of authority?
  o How much does the cultural context I work in allow me to be who I want to be?

■ 2 Establishing and maintaining rapport

> *When I observe other teachers, some seem to have a great relationship with their classes while others work in a noticeably cold, unfriendly atmosphere. I can't quite work out what makes the difference. Are there specific techniques, or is this just down to the teacher's personality, or something else?*

Aim
To create a good working relationship in the classroom.

Introduction
The term *rapport* refers to the quality of the relationship in a classroom: teacher–student and student–student. It is not primarily technique-driven, but grows naturally when people like each other and get on together.

Rapport is sometimes characterised as a kind of indefinable magic that some teachers manage to create where others fail, and, certainly, you can often detect when it is present within a few seconds of walking into a room: a sense of lively engagement, a roomful of people who are happy to be together and work together. I recently observed a class where the students were all working on group tasks, and the teacher said nothing at all for more than 15 minutes, yet the quality of rapport was tangible and real.

Despite the appearance of magic, good rapport is all down to a number of distinct, concrete, learnable elements. Any teacher can learn to create better rapport. The crucial foundation block is *authenticity* (see Chapter 2 Unit 1), as without that, any relationship will be a facade rather than genuine. Beyond that, *good listening* (see Chapter 2 Unit 3) and *showing respect and support* (see Chapter 4 Unit 1) are also important, and you can win a lot of students over with *a good sense of humour* (see Chapter 4 Unit 12). Once these are in place, a depth of rapport can grow out of the shared experience of working and learning together. You are primarily their teacher, and to repay their trust, you need to ensure that you provide excellent learning opportunities.

Techniques: Building rapport

1 Be welcoming, be encouraging, be approachable
As far as reasonably possible, build in time and space for learners to talk to you as people. Don't cram lessons full from minute one to the end. Space for unstructured talk is good. Listen carefully when learners tell you things. Respond as a human.

2 Treat each learner as an individual

Don't view the class only as a *class*. As quickly as you can, learn names and start to see and believe in each person as an individual with potential. Let them see that this is how you view them.

3 Remember positive things about your students

Keep a notebook in which you record and remind yourself of positive things individual students do, personal notes about them (hobbies, family, stories they tell, etc.). Let students know that you are interested in their lives beyond the classroom by asking about people or events they have mentioned previously. When a student is feeling down, remind them of their positive achievements.

4 Empathise

Try to see what things look like from the learners' point of view.

5 Be *you* rather than 'the teacher'

Don't feel obliged to be a teacher all the time, jumping in to save or solve. Don't talk from your hierarchical role. Ask genuine personal questions, and listen to the answers (not only the errors).

6 Don't fake happiness or pleasure

This can often come across as 'false'.

7 Be culturally sensitive

Make sure that what you say and what you ask learners to do are not inappropriate for the local context.

8 Avoid sarcasm

It's almost impossible to pitch correctly and upsets people in ways that you cannot always see.

Techniques: Mirroring, leading, pacing

The field of Neuro-Linguistic Programming (NLP) suggests some specific techniques to assist rapport: *mirroring, pacing* and *leading*. I include them here as many teachers have found them helpful, although I retain a nervousness about techniques that may project a surface impression that doesn't necessarily reflect genuine inner feelings and intentions and which, to some extent, seem designed to deliberately manipulate the other person.

1 **Mirroring** means reflecting aspects of the other person, such as their physical position and movements. Thus if I want to establish rapport with you, I note how you are sitting or standing and *discreetly* copy the position myself (posture, arm position, head position, leg position, gaze, etc.). So, if you have your right hand resting on your left arm, I put my own hand on my arm. This mirroring needs to be done in an unobtrusive way that the other person does not notice.
2 **Pacing** means keeping up with the other person's movements as they change – a sort of synchronisation of one person with the other.

3 Leading refers to the way that once I have been pacing you for a while, copying your moves, I can subtly start to initiate moves myself, which you now subconsciously find yourself copying. For example, I could use this to change your body from a closed-up, arms-folded, head-down position to a more open one with arms at your sides, head up and eye contact. Such a physical change may lead to a parallel psychological change, with you more ready to listen to my ideas and suggestions.

These techniques are essentially for one-to-one interaction, but they can be still used as you talk to different people within the whole class.

Technique: Is it OK to be friends with students?

Some teachers would shout 'no' very loudly to that question. Some would answer that they can't imagine teaching without friendship. Others would advise keeping a balance between getting to know your students and maintaining a certain teacher distance. Your own response may partly depend on a number of variables including the context where you teach, the age of your students and the amount of time you have together.

The diagram shows three possible positions on a continuum of beliefs about classroom relationship. Decide where you would place yourself.

Students are workers	Students are students	Students are people
• Who they are outside the class is irrelevant to in-classroom work.	• Who they are outside the class is sometimes relevant to in-classroom work.	• Who they are outside the class is crucial to in-classroom work.
• Interaction in class should be entirely work-focussed.	• Interaction in class should be mainly work-focussed, though there is space for other things.	• Interaction in class should be normal human interaction, person to person.
• The teacher should not ask questions about personal issues.	• The teacher can ask questions about personal issues, if necessary.	• The teacher should take an active interest in the students as whole people.
• Friendship is irrelevant, unnecessary and potentially dangerous.	• A respectful working relationship is more important that friendship.	• Friendship is natural between people who respect each other and work together.

The majority of teachers are likely to place themselves somewhere around the middle of this continuum. It may be worth asking yourself how your classroom might change if you could move, even a small degree, further along the line to the right. Would the atmosphere be warmer? Might students be more or less interested in their work? Would they feel more encouraged and motivated?

Questions for reflection

- How would you characterise the quality of rapport in your own lessons? What factors seem to improve or worsen it?
- How do you feel about those colleagues who deride teachers that have a good relationship with students? Are they right about the inherent dangers, such as loss of discipline or blurring of hierarchical roles?

3 Ways of listening

> *When students have something important or personal to say to me, I find myself still listening in 'teacher' mode, tuning in to the language and errors more than what is being said.*

Aim

To listen in the most appropriate way at different stages of a lesson.

Introduction

Listening is an important skill for teachers as much as for learners. We might assume that how we listen is entirely automatic and that we have no control over it. However, it is possible to move this into the area of conscious choice, to listen with distinct purposes. For example, I could listen primarily in order to notice and draw attention to useful errors, or I could listen with the focussed intention of understanding another person.

I'd like to characterise three distinct varieties of listening:

1 **Conversational listening** Everyday conversational listening is the sort of listening we do when we are in a café and a friend is telling us something that happened to them yesterday. We enjoy their story, but at the same time we allow ourselves to drift in and out a little, maybe thinking of what funny anecdote we can respond with as soon as they have finished. The flow of conversation goes to and fro. It doesn't matter too much if you miss things. And it's always possible to ask a question to help clarify. It's also possible to make a hijack attempt and steal the conversation for yourself. This type of listening is often inappropriate for classrooms.

2 **Analytical listening** When we listen to our friends in everyday life, we don't typically reply by giving them comments about grammar mistakes or their choice of vocabulary, rather than responding to their message. However, this kind of analysing is very common in class. The teacher will often pay attention to the language (and its errors) more than what is actually being said. The teacher analyses what the problems are with the student's communication and gives feedback or initiates reflection that helps the learner convey what they want to say more effectively and more accurately. Analytical listening is listening following the *teacher's* agenda.

3 **Supportive listening** There are also times in class when a learner has something personal to communicate. It's all too easy to find oneself listening in the 'teacherly', analytical way, hearing language problems and not really tuning in to the message. We need to find strategies that allow us to pay full attention to the speaker, do our best to understand, overlook errors and problems, stay with their story (rather than hijacking it with ours) and hear the message they want to convey. Supportive listening is following the *speaker's* agenda.

What distinguishes the last two types of listening from the first one is that both require a large degree of focussed attention. Analytical listening focuses attention on language. Supportive listening focuses attention on the person and the message.

Teacherly analytical listening is the listening skill we are most likely to focus on when we start out as teachers. It takes a lot of work and practice to be able to do it spontaneously and effectively.

But as we become more experienced in teaching, it's important to make sure that this is not the only kind of listening we ever do in class. We also need to work on supportive listening skills.

We can consciously vary the amount of attention we pay to someone speaking. It's like learning to stretch a muscle, and it gets easier with practice. Listening involves the physical act of hearing, together with a mental effort. We may not be able to do much to improve our hearing, but we can learn to pay attention better (partly by stilling the feeling that we need to think of an immediate response), though it requires a conscious effort. The verb *pay* suggests that there is a cost to this, a demand on our energy.

Other skills that can help supportive listening include (1) Being able to empathise with the person you are listening to, and (2) Avoiding judgement.

Technique: Analytical listening

This kind of teacher listening is typically focussed on accuracy – helping students to understand things and get them right. It involves a different kind of processing from what we normally do in conversational listening. Here's an example to show this at work.

Imagine that your student has just said, 'I am be going to make my homeworks this night'.

1 Respond to the message or language?

When a student says something like this in class, you need to run the sentence through a number of checks and tests. First, you need to assess the utterance for acceptability. In this example, you can immediately understand the student's message but there are obviously language errors. Your first decision is whether these things make the message sufficient and acceptable or not. The answer to this will depend on your lesson aims, the aims of the stage, the learner's level, why the learner said it, whether you believe the learner wants a correction and so on. Often it will come down to a simple decision: Am I primarily trying to help them speak more fluently? (= I can ignore the errors in order to encourage them), or more accurately? (= I need to deal with the errors to help them become more correct).

If you decide to accept and ignore the language errors, your response can be based entirely on replying to the message the student conveyed – end of analysis!

If you decide to work on the errors … keep analysing.

2 Analyse the problems

If you decide to respond to the language rather than the message, you now need to take the sentence and put it on the imaginary laboratory bench in your mind:

- Replay the sentence in your head. Look carefully at it.
- Compare it against your own understanding of what makes a good sentence with the same message.
- Cut it up into separate issues.

As a result of these tests, our laboratory examination might pick up a number of separate errors in the sentence:

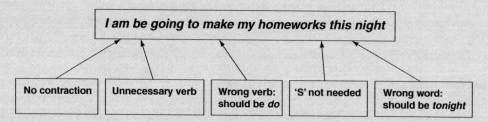

After running the tests you need to decide which are important for the learner or for the class as a whole. Narrow the problems down to possible causes. Guess which reflect things already or partly learnt that have got muddled, and which represent things not yet learnt that the speaker is taking a guess at.

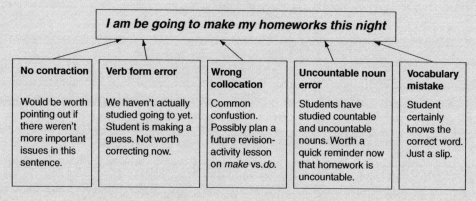

Analysis is difficult and calls on experience of language and learners. It also takes time to do, but the teacher is always under pressure to come up with quick answers, so that time is limited.

3 Decide what to give feedback on and convey it to the speaker

You may have noticed one or many problems. You don't have to give feedback on all of them; that might be overwhelming. Choose what you think is most useful to give feedback on – at that point, on that day, in that context, in front of that class to tell the speaker.

I think language teachers are doing this sort of listening, processing and prioritising a thousand times a day, though it is rarely researched or written about. When we do it well, we have the possibility of being very clear and helpful to learners. If we listen and process poorly, we will pick on the wrong things, miss things or give confusing or misleading feedback.

Technique: Supportive listening

1 Imagine a continuum from zero to ten where the midpoint (five) represents 'normal' conversational listening as we do it every day, i.e. paying partial attention. At the lower extreme (zero) is the kind of listening where the listener is hardly paying more than token attention to the speaker. At the higher end (ten) is the most attentive listening, done with full attention.

0	5	10
Listening in a distracted way; paying attention more to your watch or phone than to the speaker.	Listening as you normally do in an interested, but relatively passive, way.	Consciously trying to clear your head of anything else, and listening with full attention.

2 In class, at various times when you are listening, ask yourself where you are located on the continuum at that moment. Awareness of what you do is the key to improving your listening skills, so simply asking yourself this question is already helping improve things.

3 See if you can consciously move yourself one small step along the continuum towards the right. You can do this by intentionally clearing your mind of other thoughts and placing your attention fully into the listening and with the person you are listening to. Listen with your whole body rather than just with your ears. Don't worry about what you are going to say in reply – put your full attention on listening and trying to understand the other person better. You may find that your response, when it comes, is much easier, because you have heard so much more of the speaker and their concern or problem.

It's useful to practice this technique before you go into class:

1 Work together with a friend or colleague; sit facing each other.

2 Ask your colleague to speak to you in a spontaneous monologue for about three to four minutes on any topic he or she wants. Explain that you will not speak yourself.

3 While your colleague is talking, practise varying *how* you listen to him or her, trying to consciously move to different places on the continuum, each for about 45 seconds.

4 At the end, get feedback from the speaker about on how it felt to be listened to in each of these ways. Did the quality of your listening actively affect the quality of her speaking?

Questions for reflection

• Did you recognise anything that you do in the description of *analytical listening*? Is that the main or only way that you listen in class?

• In day-to-day life, do you 'half listen' a lot? Where is this appropriate and where inappropriate?

• Do you feel that students notice any difference when you use supportive listening? What?

4 Turning the volume up and down

> *I find that I sometimes get locked into talking at 'public-announcement' volume level for everything I do in class and wonder if I can vary this at all.*

Aims

1 Finding a range of possible voice volumes to use in class.
2 Choosing the best volume for a particular moment.
3 Consciously talking more quietly in class where appropriate.

Introduction

Some teachers may feel that they always need to talk loudly in class so that all students can clearly hear them. However, if you permanently remain at 'public-announcement' volume, it can get in the way of creating more intimate or atmospheric activities, and it may actually lead to a decrease in learners' attentions – they just 'turn off'. It is possible to consciously experiment with different volume levels and to vary your own volume to great effect in class.

As with many classroom management techniques, the outcomes may seem counterintuitive. You might expect that speaking loudly would command the most attention from students whereas speaking quietly would lead to a drop of interest and engagement. Many teachers, when they experiment a little, discover that, in fact, the opposite can sometimes be the case.

We face a lot of noise and amplified messages in our daily lives. This means that we have learnt to cope with noise rather well. When someone speaks loudly, one fairly natural human reaction seems to be to completely tune it out and avoid it. Thus, the loud classroom instruction may simply fall on the listener's ears as noise to be ignored, especially if it is simply one part of a general, persistent loud wall of teacher sound. In contrast, the very quiet message or instruction may have greater impact. When we hear someone talking quietly, we are often curious and want to tune in and listen more carefully. To do this, we probably need to stop doing whatever we are doing and especially stop making any distracting or interfering noise ourselves.

Students tend to mirror the teacher's volume. If you have a noisy class, speak quieter rather than louder – and they might too.

Techniques: Experimenting with volume

1 Experiment with using different volumes in class. For different tasks, try varying the volume; for example, using a much quieter than usual voice for one set of instructions, then using a much louder than usual voice for running a game. Notice whether using a range of volumes has any noticeable effect on how stages run. Do students seem to be more active in louder or quieter stages? Does the volume have any effect on their own use of language? Does it provide any sense of extra variety in the lesson?

2 If you often or typically talk quite loudly in class, try out one or more of the following ideas. In each case, you need to find a low volume that will still be audible by all students in the room. If you have students with hearing problems, you will need to also take this into account.

   - Start a lesson very quietly. Rather than kicking off with a big announcement or instruction, simply start talking at a reduced volume. Initially, students may not even notice that you have started. Keep going without raising the volume. Does the class slowly calm down and start tuning in?
   - When you want to start a new task, try giving the instruction extremely quietly. You can repeat it a few times if need be, but don't increase the volume. Do the students listen with as much attention as normal? (Or more? Or less?)
   - Tell an interesting or amusing story or personal anecdote – but do it in an unusually quiet or low voice.

Questions for reflection

- Are you a loud or quiet teacher?
- Do you consciously vary your volume to suit different classroom moments?
- Which are the moments in class when you feel that you really have to be loud?
- For one stage of a lesson, try a lower volume level than you normally use. What differences, if any, did it make to the learners and the activity?

5 Finding the right voice tone

> *I feel that I could use my voice more effectively in class, but I'm not sure what I can experiment with.*

Aim
To extend the teacher's range of voice tones.

Introduction
Your voice tone and how you use it can help create a large part of the atmosphere of your classroom – yet many teachers have never consciously thought much about it or worked on improving their skills.

Tone is distinct from volume. It is possible to project a variety of voice tones at a variety of volumes. For example, an authoritative tone does not require a loud volume, and if you shout, it could diminish the authority and alter into a tone that conveys desperation or dislike. Similarly, an understanding, supportive tone can be projected to a whole room as much as to a single individual.

Technique: Experimenting with voice tone out of class
Choose a short text, for example, picked at random from a book or magazine, or you could use this example text:

> Humpty Dumpty sat on the wall. Humpty Dumpty had a great fall. All the king's horses and all the king's men couldn't put Humpty together again.

Read it aloud a number of times. Each time, aim to project a different tone from this list: excited, bored, angry, in charge, jokey, uncertain, disappointed, overjoyed, impatient.

You do not necessarily need to use these tones in class, but aim to notice the amount of variation that you are able to achieve. Also notice how you change your voice to achieve each of these tones.

Technique: Experimenting with voice tone in class
Within the space of one lesson, set yourself the task of using all the following voice tones:
- An open, warm, friendly tone: for chatting and asking personal questions.
- A factual, information-giving tone: for instructions or short pieces of information.
- A storytelling tone: for a narrative or read-aloud text.

- A personal, supportive, kindly tone: for helping one-to-one when a student has a problem.
- An authoritative tone: for telling someone what they must do, and leaving no space for discussion.
- A humorous tone: for a joke, anecdote or a comment that will make people laugh.
- A hesitant uncertain tone: perhaps when asking for students to correct the teacher's errors, for checking or eliciting.

Try to make each tone distinct. You may want to exaggerate slightly the way that you normally do these in everyday interaction, to help recognise what the distinctive elements are in each tone. Notice how the way you say things affects the impact of what you say.

If you find it hard to make your voice sound different, it may be because you are working at the surface level of voice box, muscles and mouth. Instead, try to start with the *intention* and let this speak. For example, if you want to use an authoritative tone, first firmly establish the belief in your right to be authoritative inside your mind and body – and, only once you feel that in place, say the words.

Questions for reflection

- Is voice tone something you have ever paid attention to?
- Is there one tone you tend to adopt for most of a lesson?
- Are there any tones in the lists that you never use?

■6■ Varying the quantity of your control

> *I'm a very controlling teacher. I tell my students what to do for every moment of the lesson. Not sure it's good, but I can't seem to let go.*

Aim

To find the most appropriate and most effective degree of teacher control for each lesson stage or activity.

Introduction

Micromanagement is detailed, minute-by-minute teacher control of everything that happens in the classroom, for example, telling students exactly what to do, where to do it, how to do it, how to do it better and so on. Some teachers may typically micromanage relatively little or only for short periods of time. Other teachers may do it with a high degree of control or for longer stretches, perhaps throughout a whole lesson.

Here is an example of a teacher who is providing a high quantity of micromanagement for a task in which students have to come up to the board to write their answers to an exercise:

> *OK, Abel, thank you. Sit down again. Now, give the board pen to Luisa. Yes, that's right. So, your turn now, Luisa. Come to the board. Make sure you write your answer right underneath Abel's. No … to your left. Yes. Write a bit bigger. Good. Good. Good. Excellent. Check your spelling of kitchen. Is that right? Magda, can you tell her what she needs to change? Speak louder. Say it again, Magda. Luisa didn't hear you. OK. So now you can change the spelling, Luisa.*

At the other extreme, it is also possible to micromanage far less, giving one initial instruction for a task and then leaving it up to students to provide the necessary organisation themselves.

Does either of these extremes suit you? Do your choices vary depending on the activity, the learners, the time of day, your mood and so on?

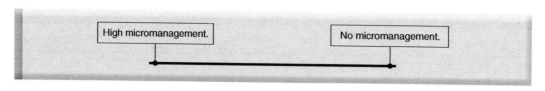

If you wouldn't typically place yourself at either end of this line, where are you most comfortable along the continuum between them? And is that a suitable place from which to best enable successful learning?

Many teachers begin their careers carrying an internal image of how a teacher should behave in class, based mainly on the teaching that they have experienced from the student's seat through years and years of schooling. Typically, this is often a 'high control' image. The teachers they had may have felt the need to keep a constant grip on proceedings, perhaps as a strategy to help keep a large class together or as a way of keeping order. I have found that many people starting out in language teaching think of this the 'obvious' or only sensible way to behave if you want a class to be focussed, disciplined and useful.

However, as with many imagined necessities, it is worth taking a little time to challenge such certainties. Consider these questions:

- Is it possible that over-organising by the teacher takes away or reduces the students' own ability or willingness to take decisions, self-evaluate and organise?
- Would learning be more focussed if students had a larger degree of control over what they did?
- Would activities actually run smoother and more efficiently without the constant interventions (or possibly interference) from the teacher?
- Might it be true that 'nature abhors a vacuum' and that, if you reduce your own talk, participation and control, students will generally fill the gap that your silence creates, even if there's a momentary awkwardness?

Technique: Finding out how changing control changes interaction

Choose three similar simple classroom tasks that students can do together as a whole class, e.g. a grammar exercise with questions numbered one to ten.

On three separate occasions, perhaps with different classes, do the task with:

1 An intentionally high level of micromanagement.
2 An intentionally low level of micromanagement.
3 No during-task micromanagement.

In all three lessons, explain that students should come to the board, one at a time, and write up their answers. Tell them that it is the class's responsibility to try and work together to make sure that, by the end, the answers to all questions are correct.

1 High control

When you first do this in class, deliberately make lots of management decisions yourself, and give lots of micromanagement instructions. For example, decide which student should come up to the board next, tell them which question to write an answer to, ask other students to look at the board and correct any mistakes, point out errors they haven't noticed and ask individuals to suggest corrections, make comments about the students' board writing being too small, too big, too untidy and so on. In other words, remain a very visible and managing presence throughout the stage. Constantly help, direct and interfere. Your voice should be heard through large parts of the task.

2 Low control

At a later date, or possibly with a completely different class, try the same task type (i.e. students writing their answers on the board), but this time after having given the initial instruction and made sure it's understood, deliberately restrain yourself from giving all those micromanagement instructions used the first time. Limit yourself to a small number of really useful and important interventions, e.g. to say that different students should come up and write, rather than the same two or three all the time. (If you make more than ten interventions during the whole stage, count this as a 'high-control' stage, and consider trying the 'low-control' experiment again at another time.)

3 No control

When you try the experiment for the third time, after you have given the initial instruction, make no further interventions of any kind – even if they are doing the task wrongly. Go and sit down somewhere relatively out of their line of sight, and wait. Do not lean forward anxiously. Do not stare impatiently at students. Do not mouth words, drum your fingers, sigh or shake your head. Don't answer any questions (just shrug or point to the board if you do get asked), or decide a very low number of questions you are prepared to answer. Practise looking fairly interested, but in a relaxed and unconcerned way. Continue this until the task has been completed. (If students do nothing at all, wait until at least two minutes have passed, and then simply stand up and restate the initial instruction – then return to your low-visibility role.)

A warning: Students who are used to high levels of micromanagement may well initially respond negatively or unhelpfully to this way of working. This is an experiment to try first with classes that you know well and trust. Once you have discovered the increased engagement that can often come out of such an approach, you may feel more confident trying it with other classes.

Technique : Further experiments with low or no control

If you find that your experiments with lower control make you want to have another go, try some other ways. For example:

1 Write some questions on the board, and then wait for students to start solving them, i.e. without any initial instructions.
2 At the start of a class, sit down and say a sentence about yourself, e.g. 'I had a really strange weekend'. Then shut up and wait. Let the students ask you questions to which you respond. Let their curiosity (rather than your structuring) push the lesson forward.
3 Set a problem for students to discuss and reach an agreement on. Explain that you will not take any further part in the lesson until they have reached their agreement. They need to discuss, negotiate and compromise until they find a satisfactory answer. Stick to your promise and don't join in – even when there is a difficult disagreement, a long silence or they seem to be headed for the wrong answer.
4 When you have a listening lesson, hand over the playback controls to students, explain what they have to do, and then get out and leave them to it until they have completed all the required work.

Questions for reflection

- What concerns do you have about what might happen when you reduce micromanagement control? Do those fears come true or not?
- Is experiment number 3 ('no control') the most difficult for you? Why or why not?
- In the spaces left when there was less or no teacher control, what happened instead? Did the students succeed in taking up the reins themselves? Was the task accomplished with the same, less or a greater degree of success?
- Were students more active or more participatory in the low-control approaches? Was the quality of interaction different? Was it useful interaction? Did any discipline problems occur?
- If the 'no control' task fell apart into chaos, why do you think this was? Can you imagine that any small changes in setting it up (e.g. explaining your rationale to students) might make a difference if you tried it again?
- What other classroom activities might benefit from a lighter control? Which ones do you think would not work well?

7 Gestures and facial expressions

> *I'd like to use more gestures to help make my instructions and explanation better understood, but I can only ever think of one or two.*

Aim

To make use of expressions and gestures to help reduce unhelpful or unclear teacher talk when giving instructions or explanations.

Introduction

With low-level classes, gestures and expressions add a crucial element to instructions and explanations. They provide visual support that helps learners to understand what is being said. They also allow the teacher to say less, which by itself may help to make the instruction or explanation clearer.

When you start to use gestures, learners will learn to associate the gesture with an instruction. After you have used a gesture a number of times, you will find that you can actually reduce the words you need to say – or even say nothing. For example, the gesture for 'get into pairs' along with the word 'pairs' may well be sufficient to get the class organised.

A word of warning though! Gestures and movements do not always mean the same things internationally. If you are working outside your own culture, or with students from other countries, try to learn which gestures have inappropriate or rude meanings. You can't take anything for granted; in Bulgaria and some other countries, nodding left/right means 'yes' and up/down means 'no'!

Techniques: Gestures

The following gestures and expressions are widely used in language teaching:

1 Classroom organisation and instructions

Hands apart, with palms facing in, as if to 'fold' around the individual.

Meaning Work on your own.

Hands wide, shaping a pair.

Meaning Get into pairs.

Hands dividing class down middle.

Meaning Get into two teams.

Hands held out in front, palms up, pushing upwards.

Meaning Stand up.

Hands held out in front, palms down, waggling downwards.

Meaning Sit down.

Hand at lips, making imaginary mouth, flapping in a 'talking' manner.

Meaning Speak your answers.

1   Classroom organisation and instructions

Hand holding imaginary pen midair, wiggling.

Meaning Write your answers.

Hands held out wide in front as if to 'fold' round the class, moved upwards.

Meaning Everybody say together.

'Rodin' fist to top of head.

Meaning Think.

Hiding paper gesture.

Meaning Keep your piece of paper secret.

Finger held up.

Meaning First, you must …

Two fingers held up.

Meaning Secondly, you must …

1 Classroom organisation and instructions

Three fingers held up.

Meaning Thirdly, you must … (etc.)

2 Classroom interaction

Finger at lips.

Meaning Shhh!

Finger zipping lips.

Meaning Stop talking.

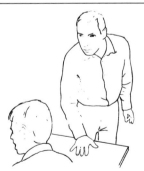

Place a hand firmly and decisively on the desk in front of a student (and make eye contact).

Meaning Everyone else has stopped talking – I want YOU to as well!

Hands flat in front of body palms down. Sliding/cutting gesture side to side.

Meaning Stop work now.

2 Classroom interaction

Cupped hand at ears.

Meaning Listen to me.

Cupped hand at ears and hand indicating a student.

Meaning Listen to her.

Hand, palm up, held out to indicate a student.

Meaning Inviting a student to answer.

Both hands held out and wide, palms up. Quizzical look, eyebrows raised.

Meaning Does *anyone* have an answer?

Traffic cop hand out, palm facing student or facing down.

Meaning I don't want to hear from you now.

3 Feedback on language and errors

Hand stretched out, waist height.

Meaning Not quite right.

Hands held in front of body, waist height, palms facing each other.

Meaning Make a longer sentence.

Hand doing rolling gesture.

Meaning Say it again.

Thumbs up. (NB may not be appropriate in all cultures.)

Meaning Good sentence.

Thumbs down.

Meaning Bad sentence.

Thumb sideways, wiggling.

Meaning Problematic answer – could be improved.

3 Feedback on language and errors

(1) Mouthing 'OOO',
(2) Mouthing 'EEE',
(3) Mouthing 'TH'.

Meaning Showing mouth shapes for correcting a sound.

Two fingers – other hand squashes them together.

Meaning Use a contraction.

Finger pinching in midair gesture.

Meaning It's a little word.

Finger in the air drawing 's'.

Meaning You forgot the third person 's' in the Present Simple.

Two hands palm down, held high, index and middle fingers meeting.

Meaning These two words mean the same.

Make a circle with pointing fingers on each hand. Turn them 180° round the circle.

Meaning Change the order of the words.

4 Indicating time

Hand/finger pointing back over shoulder.

Meaning Past.

Hand/finger pointing straight down.

Meaning 'Now'.

Hand/finger pointing ahead.

Meaning Future.

Techniques: General guidance for using gestures and expressions

1 Be sure your gestures are clear. Make them confidently. Don't half do them because of embarrassment.
2 Go for bigger, wider gestures, rather than cramped-in, closed-up ones.
3 Remember that your gestures are seen from the opposite viewpoint from the one you have. Visualise what the students can see from their angle, and adapt if necessary.
4 Allow enough time for your gestures to be seen before you stop them. For some key gestures, this may mean at least four or five seconds, rather than just putting your hand out and immediately withdrawing it.
5 Think of making gestures in three moves: (1) Making the gesture, (2) Holding it, as if 'on pause', (3) Stopping the gesture. It is Stage 2 (holding it) that is often the crucial one that goes wrong because it is done too quickly.
6 Eyebrows are very helpful for conveying reactions, especially for showing interest and encouraging further speaking. Exaggerate your normal eyebrow movements in class. And please don't use raised eyebrows only to convey 'That was bad behaviour'!
7 Don't forget to encourage students to also use gestures and expressions. So much classroom practice is 'armless'! Yet even dull repetition drills and exercises come alive with the added use of gestures. When you want students to repeat a sentence, check out your own way of saying it, and see what gestures and expressions you naturally use (such as a widening of arms). In class, model saying the words with the gestures, and get students to repeat words and movement. For example, imagine that you want to teach 'I can't stand … '. If you get students to repeat sentences without feeling, expression or gesture, it is very forgettable. But if you yourself model saying, 'I can't stand broccoli' with a face that reflects your negative reaction and perhaps an appropriate, 'Keep it away from me' hand movement, this is much more enjoyable for students to copy and say to each other – and also far more memorable.

Techniques: Eye contact

One of the most important tools at your disposal is eye contact – and it's definitely one to work on improving if you find it hard. The key techniques are to:

1 Make eye contact with students (rather than avoiding it). Don't use pieces of paper or books as a way of hiding. Try to keep in regular eye contact with people in the class, even when doing focussed tasks such as writing on the board.
2 Allow your eye contact to remain relaxed, warm and unthreatening (rather than cold or staring).
3 Express how you feel, showing the person behind the eyes, your warmth, your changing reactions, sense of interest and enjoyment (rather than just mechanically moving the eyes).

A few suggestions:

• You cannot make eye contact with a whole class at once, but you can make eye contact with a number of individuals in it. When you teach the whole class from the front, don't speak to 'the room in general' or 'a space slightly above everyone's heads' or 'the back wall of the room'. Similarly, don't lock your gaze onto one or two individuals and stay with them all the time you talk. Try making eye contact with one student, holding it for five to ten seconds, then gently bouncing your gaze round the room to a random different person ... and so on through the time you are speaking. Make sure you catch the eye of people in different parts of the room: back, middle and front, left centre and right.

- When you talk with students working in pairs or groups, try the same technique, looking at one for a while and then undramatically shifting your focus to another.
- When you talk with an individual, use your eye contact to show that you are 'with them' – listening and interested.
- Use eye contact to indicate who you want to talk to. Sometimes this can do away with the need for a verbal instruction.

Gower, Phillips and Walters suggest another important technique. You can use eye contact:

> To keep in touch with other students in the class or group when you are dealing with an individual, perhaps when correcting. Your eyes can say to them: 'You're involved too'.

The same authors also point out that a teacher needs to be aware about when eye contact is potentially unhelpful: 'During any activity that doesn't demand teacher-centred control, avoid eye contact unless you are specifically asked for help or choose to join in ... As soon as you establish eye contact, you are brought into the activity.'

An example of this would be when students are making front-of-class presentations to their peers. They will have a natural inclination to focus on telling you and watching for your reaction, rather than speaking to the other students. Help them direct their attention to the whole class by deliberately not making eye contact with them. Instead, keep your eyes in a relaxed way on the people they are presenting to.

Questions for reflection

- Do you often use gestures? Which ones do you tend to use most?
- Are your gestures clear?
- Which of the gestures from the lists that you do not currently use would you like to add to your repertoire?
- Do you find it natural and easy to make eye contact with students in class?

8 The teacher's language

> *Sometimes when I give instructions or explanations, I notice them staring at me as if I was speaking Ancient Norse. I really want to use real English when I speak to them, but I also need them to understand what I'm saying.*

Aim

To become more aware of the complexity of language I use and messages I give in class, and to make informed choices as to appropriate teacher classroom language.

Introduction

There are good reasons to grade language in class, for example, to make sure that all students follow some important instructions. When a teacher decides to grade his or her own language, it is important that he or she still uses a recognisably accurate, acceptable version of English. There is no value in exposing your students to a false, impoverished model of English. Graded language is still real English.

Another important question connected with the teacher's language is to do with whether he or she can use the learners' first language for explanations or instructions in class – and if so, how much is appropriate.

This unit focuses on the teacher's language. For specific ideas on instructions, see Chapter 4 Unit 3.

Techniques: What can be graded?

There are a number of aspects of language that the teacher can grade when speaking to the class. You might choose to grade none, one, some or all of these:

1 Grammar and lexis

Restrict language to those items below a certain perceived level of difficulty, for example, by avoiding any grammatical or lexical items that have not yet been covered in the learners' coursebook.

2 Sounds

Avoid listening difficulties that might be caused by pronunciation features, for example, by avoiding elision and assimilation (e.g. saying, 'What do you want?' with each word pronounced separately, rather than running them together as, for example, /wɒdʒu:wɒnt/).

3 Stress

Simplify what is said by stressing important words more strongly. Leave short pauses before and after the stress to aid understanding, for example, 'I want you to answer only the ... *third* ... question'. This is known as *punching* key words.

4 Sequencing of content

State information in a logical order, perhaps mirroring the order that students will have to do things.

5 Speed of delivery

Regardless of the language items used, slow down (or speed up). Introduce longer – or shorter – pauses between clauses or sentences.

6 Discourse features and noise

The clarity of what is said can be affected by language used that is not central to the core message. Any *noise* or unnecessary wrapping around the key message may add comprehension difficulties and lead to confusion. Noise may be words or expressions (e.g. 'you know', 'Well, what I want you to do is ... '), entire sentences that add nothing to the message or distracting pieces of information or commands about other things, such as discipline issues. Repetitions of information in slightly different wording can also cause problems.

7 Complexity of message

Quite apart from the language used, there is also, of course, the issue of how complex the ideas conveyed by the language are. Break difficult concepts down into smaller, more easily understood pieces.

8 Quantity of message

Aim to say very brief things and avoid much longer ones.

Here is an example of different degrees of grading in terms of some of the issues mentioned above. The teacher wants the class to work in pairs and write answers to a grammar exercise. Notice that the shorter graded instructions actually contain more of the useful information.

1 **Ungraded** 'So, could you please – what I wanted you to do was to talk together to do the exercise in pairs ... so get together with a partner, could you ... and it's on page 22 ... so, OK, when you've sorted out your pair, make a start on what you've got to do, and jot down the answers.'
2 **Graded** 'OK Everyone. I want you to get into pairs, please. Turn to page 22, and do exercise B. Talk together to agree the answers.'
3 **Highly graded** 'Get into pairs.' (Waits for students to do it.) 'Page 22.' (Waits for students to do it.) 'Exercise B. Work together.' (Uses a gesture to indicate 'pairs'.)

Techniques: What level of grading is appropriate?

At what level should the teacher pitch the classroom language he or she uses? There are a number of options. The grading of language can be:

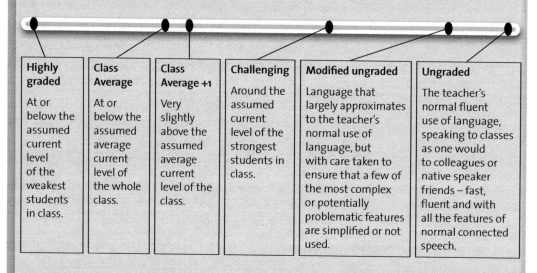

Highly graded	Class Average	Class Average +1	Challenging	Modified ungraded	Ungraded
At or below the assumed current level of the weakest students in class.	At or below the assumed average current level of the whole class.	Very slightly above the assumed average current level of the class.	Around the assumed current level of the strongest students in class.	Language that largely approximates to the teacher's normal use of language, but with care taken to ensure that a few of the most complex or potentially problematic features are simplified or not used.	The teacher's normal fluent use of language, speaking to classes as one would to colleagues or native speaker friends – fast, fluent and with all the features of normal connected speech.

My choice will depend partly on the overall language level of the class. Generally speaking, the lower the level of the class, the more graded my own language. With an advanced class, it may well be appropriate and useful if I use ungraded language at least part of the time.

Some teachers do not grade their language to students at all, perhaps because they believe that students will learn best by being exposed to realistic (if complex) language use. This is, however, rare – and, in most language classrooms, you would find that the teacher is grading his or her language to at least some degree. Other teachers adopt a level very slightly higher than the perceived general level of the class; this is influenced by Professor Stephen Krashen's theory of Comprehensible Input: the idea that learners are most likely to take in new language if it is both understandable and a little above their current level, so that they have to think and try to work out the form, meaning and use of any items they don't know.

Techniques: Bilingual instructions

If you speak the L1 (first language) of the students you teach, you have a number of other useful options for speaking to students (e.g. when giving instructions or explanations).

1 Sandwiching L1 and L2

Give an instruction in English, and then immediately repeat the instruction in the learners' L1; then once more in English; thus, making a sandwich: L2‖L1‖L2. This is particularly useful at lower levels. It allows you to speak in much less graded English than you might otherwise need to, while, at the same time, familiarising students with how instructions are worded in the new language. After using the same instruction a number of times, you may find that you no longer need to use the translated version; students will understand the L2 instruction.

2 Code switching

Make use of both languages, but within the same flow of speech. For example, you might give most of the instruction in English (possibly miming to help) – but when there is a phrase or word that the class may have difficulty understanding, you offer a translation instead of (or as well as) the English words. For example, 'Now, please open your books ... page *cent vingt-deux** ... do Exercise 7 ... please work in pairs ... *travaillez à deux*' (*page 122).

Techniques: Good reasons to use the learners' first language

Teachers of monolingual classes have sometimes felt a little guilty that they do not always follow the received wisdom that suggests they should use English as much as possible. Clearly, the more English that is used in class, the better for language-learning purposes. However, there are many occasions when it is faster, simpler or more efficient to use the learners' L1; but we do need to make sure that we do not use these shortcuts too often or when they are not really justified. It's all too easy to relax until suddenly the whole class is being delivered in L1 – because students seem to want it, and teachers find it easier. David Atkinson suggests a check question that teachers can ask themselves about using L1, 'Will it help the students' learning more than using English would?'

Here are a number of example instances when use of L1 might well be appropriate and tick a 'yes' to Atkinson's question:

1 One vocabulary item is seriously getting in the way of the lesson proceeding. You have tried explaining and demonstrating using English – but they still look blank. Just saying one word in L1 could unfurrow brows and solve all problems.
2 You want to do a quick check to find out if they can see how the meaning of a new grammar item compares with a similar-sounding construction in L1. You say, 'Can you translate that into ... ?'
3 You have spent some time teaching a grammar point, and towards the end of the lesson there are two issues that students can't seem to get their heads around. You switch to L1 to talk with them about them.

4 A student seems upset and wants to talk with you, but is struggling to say what the problem is. You respond in L1 and say that he or she can use L1 to talk to you.

5 You want to get some honest feedback on how a certain part of the course went to help you decide whether you should ever do it again. The students' language level was up to doing the activity, but not good enough for them to explain their reactions.

6 You want to do some in-depth tutorials with low-level students about their progress.

Techniques: Varying grading by task and aim

Teachers may deliberately choose to vary the amount of grading they use at different stages of a lesson, or from lesson to lesson. For example, here is one teacher's language use:

1 **Instructions and key explanations**   Use the simplest and clearest graded language I can.
2 **Discussing reading texts**   Use language just slightly above the average level of the class.
3 **Informal chats with students**   Use much less graded language, possibly a few steps above the learners' supposed current level.

The reason for varying this may be that the teacher feels that ...

- It is essential that task instructions and explanations are fully understood (as misunderstanding could cause much greater difficulties).
- It is helpful to use language just slightly above students' current level when discussing texts, as this may challenge them and help learners to subconsciously notice and acquire some new language items.
- It is also important for students to be exposed to something more closely approximating real, everyday use of language, and that informal chats with students may be a good opportunity to provide such exposure.

Questions for reflection

- Do you vary the grading of language according to levels you teach and stages of a lesson?
- Which elements do you grade most carefully?

9 Using intuition

> On our training course, they said that I should plan everything in advance and know what I am going to do all the way through a lesson. But I find that, in class, I keep thinking, 'I could do this instead', or 'This might work now', but I feel unsure whether I should trust this inner voice or my plan.

Aim

For the teacher to learn to place more trust in their own intuition.

Introduction

Using intuition intelligently is an essential teacher skill, yet one that is largely unacknowledged or undervalued on training courses or in professional development.

Trainers, conferences and books like this can give you a certain amount of insight into teaching, but the real job of teaching is live, on-the-spot, at the board, where the teacher has to make instant decisions second by second. You can't go back and check the literature for each problem, and, anyway, the instruction book doesn't work because every teaching event is significantly different. The handed-down guidelines break down in the face of real people with real, unpredictable responses.

Instead, you rely on your intuition – deciding to do this not that, taking risks, trying things out, varying pacing or voice tone, reading people's faces and so on. You do this not on the basis of known, certain knowledge, but on the basis of some spontaneous feeling, insight or understanding that does not seem to be based on study, logic or experience.

Yet, despite this seemingly magical appearance, intuition is actually drawn from our depth of experience; it derives directly from our growing stock of processed (or partially processed or unprocessed) previous experience and understandings. Insights from these bubble up to the surface as and when we need them.

There is a danger that incorrect intuitions may get set in concrete as 'correct' solutions. One needs to constantly challenge and consciously upgrade one's intuition, and I suspect that much of the process of learning to be a better teacher is a process of collecting feedback and information (about learners, language, teaching ideas, etc.), in order to become more spontaneously and accurately intuitive, on-the-spot, in class.

Technique: Observing my intuition at work

1 Turn up and tune in

When teaching a class, try to notice and tune into that small quiet voice inside you – the one that is offering sudden unexpected insights and making suggestions the whole time you are teaching. Try turning its volume up a little and asking yourself these questions: What is it saying? Is it something that feels odd or unexpected? Is it hinting at what one of your learners is thinking? Suggesting ideas about what might work well in the next few minutes of the lesson? Telling you something about the pace you are working at? Hinting at a problem you've been overlooking? Wording a surprising response to a learner?

2 Decide who to trust

Compare what your intuition says with what the voice of your training, or your school or your colleagues is saying. Are they the same message? Which one sounds more sure and reliable? Which one sounds more risky and potentially exciting?

3 Be bold!

See what happens if you go with your intuitive response rather than the other way. Afterwards, reflect on whether it was good or not. Learning from what you did will help to fine-tune your intuition to inform your future teaching.

Technique: Prepare but don't plan

Some teachers only feel confident if they have every stage of their lesson planned out in advance. It feels professional. The problem is that the more one plans, the more one can feel tied into a predetermined series of actions, with limited flexibility for changing or responding to what happens in the room. Yet good teaching is responsive and flexible, working moment by moment with the people in the room. By weaning ourselves off this total planning, we can slowly learn to trust our spontaneous intuitive teaching more. One way to do this is to experiment with working without a plan for small sections of lessons. For example:

1 Select a reading or listening text from a website, newspaper or book to use in a future lesson. Photocopy or print the text, but don't choose any tasks, exercises or activities to go with it. Read the text through to familiarise yourself with it. Notice interesting or problematic language. Let your mind flit around the topic. But don't plan to do anything specific in class.
2 In class, hand out the text to students, and then use your experience and intuition to spontaneously create the lesson as you go. Watch yourself as you do this, and notice the intuitive decisions you take along the way: why you asked this question rather than that one, why you focused on the vocabulary items you did, how you dealt with a student question and so on.
3 Continue the experiment in further lessons, with different kinds of teaching, varying the amount of preparation you do. Explore what it is like teach 'live' and in the moment, without a safety net. Seek to find the best balance between intuitive spontaneity and good preparation.

Technique: The cat in the classroom

Read this text. Does it ring any bells with you? Does it inspire you to change anything in your own practice?

> I like to think a thing part way through and feel the rest of the way.
>
> I have a jumbled mind that only achieves clarification at times and then under pressure, as in a classroom. Then the material provides the unity, the random insights.
>
> By suggestion, by insinuation, by intuition, let the material speak for itself – elucidate quietly. There's a shorthand in teaching, just as there is in poetry.
>
> To teach by suggestion or 'intuitively' takes more time than teaching by precept or lecturing. For you carry the students in your mind and, in reading, think, 'There's a swell example to show Flossie …'. To teach very fast, by associational jumps – to teach a class as a *poem* – is dangerous, but very exciting.
>
> In the classroom, as instinctive as a cat and as restless.

Theodore Roethke (1909 – 1963) US poet and teacher.

Questions for reflection

- How much do you trust your intuition? Does it provide helpful insights and solutions, or does it lead you into trouble?
- Do you over plan lessons? To what extent do you distrust yourself in those moments when you move away from your plan?

10 The teacher as researcher

> *I would like to find out more about myself as teacher, in the hope that this can help me develop. But research sounds like a rather big thing to do. I've no idea where to start or how to go about this.*

Aim

To begin some everyday research into a teacher's own work in the classroom.

Introduction

The most useful things you learn about teaching will be the things you learn about yourself, what you do and how you do it. A book like this can give you ideas that have worked for other people at other times, but I, the writer, can never know who you are, what your teaching situation is like or who your students are. The aim of research is to help you see these things more clearly for yourself.

The structure described below is a sort of classic classroom research model, but feel free to redesign it to suit your needs.

Technique: Classroom research

1 Start with either ...
   - A problem or a question related to your class *or*
   - Something that happens in class that you wish to learn about: maybe something that you do or something that your students do.

Choose small, specific, discrete areas of behaviour or classroom practice, rather than big, generalised things. For example, 'How much do I shout at students in a lesson?' is hugely more researchable than 'Is my teaching effective?'

Here are some ideas for possible research:
- Are my instructions clear?
- What kind of attention and support do I give to particular students?
- Do I talk too much?
- Do I have any mannerisms, verbal or gestural, such as saying 'OK' all the time?
- Why do the faster students seem to get bored as the lesson goes on?
- How efficiently is the room reorganised?
- What do students do when I'm not monitoring them in group work?
- Why do only half the class do the homework?
- Do students understand how I mark their work?
- How much do I help students with new vocabulary during the lesson?
- What does it feel like to be a student in a room with me as their teacher?

- Write a clear statement about whatever you have chosen, making sure that you define exactly what you hope to explore.

2 Think about how you could investigate this in your lessons. What could you use to help you find out some useful insights? Look for methods that will (a) provide you with solid factual quantitative information, and (b) give you more reflective, qualitative insights. Consider these possibilities:
   - Ask another teacher to come in and observe part of a lesson.
   - Ask a senior teacher, head of department, head teacher or trainer to observe.
   - Design an observation form with specific questions or tasks for an observer to use.
   - Record your lesson (audio or video).
   - Give your students a questionnaire to fill in.
   - Train your students to observe critically and give feedback on specific aspects of the lesson.
   - Reflect on what happened as soon as a lesson is over.
   - Keep a regular diary or blog.
   - Observe other teachers as a comparison to what you do / what happens in your class.
   - Look at students' assignments, notebooks, workbooks.
   - Keep notes through a lesson, e.g. a tally of how many times something occurs.
   - Interview students about their lessons and course.
   - Look with a critical eye at materials you use: handouts, board design, etc.

3 Decide organisational basics such as: How long will the research last? When will I know that I have enough information? What will I do with the information once collected?

4 When you have gathered the information, you can analyse it and make decisions. You may want to implement some changes in class and then undertake a second round of the same research.

5 Plan what you will do to make bigger or more long-lasting changes to your practice. Action research (looking at what you do now) feeds naturally into action planning (deciding what you can do in the immediate future), and the two build into a cycle that is the engine of development.

However, if you are researching aspects of your own behaviour, you may find that doing the research is in itself enough. By noticing things, typically, we already start to think about them, and even without implementing action plans, we find ourselves altering how we behave. The noticing is already the change.

Questions for reflection

- What are the things that would be useful to know about your teaching, but which you do not know currently about your teaching?
- There are 'known unknowns' (e.g. that you think, but are not certain, that you may talk too much in class), which you can choose to research. There are also 'unknown unknowns' (e.g. You sometimes give a lot more questions and classroom speaking time to male students, rather than female ones, but you have no idea that you are doing this). You'd have to find out what these are before you could plan to research them. How could you do that?

3 | The learners

1 Learning names

> *I suddenly realised this morning that I didn't know the name of about four or five children in class ... and I wasn't completely sure about some of the others.*

Aim
To learn and remember the names of all students in your class as quickly as possible.

Introduction
Some teachers do not learn students' names and do not see this as important. 'Too many students' is a common complaint, or 'It takes too long to learn so many names'. I'm not sure that either of these excuses stands up well. Even if your memory isn't good, it really isn't very hard to do, and it makes an important difference.

If you don't know their names, students are just anonymous members of class. Knowing and using a name acknowledges each person as an individual, someone you pay attention to and are interested in.

Similarly, it's important for class members to know each other's names so that they can get on better together and work better together. If you teach in a secondary school where students have been together in the same class for some time, this isn't a problem, but in other teaching situations, perhaps with short-term classes and a lot of turnover in student numbers, this becomes very important.

The techniques in this unit will help you learn and remember the students' names. If your class also needs to learn names, many of these techniques will also be useful for them.

Technique: Preparing to meet your class
Before you meet a new class, study the list of student names. Ask advice from other teachers on pronunciations you're not sure of. Learn the names if at all possible. Doing all of this will make it easier to connect name to person when you do meet your new students.

Technique: Name cards or labels

Ask students to take pieces of paper and fold them in half to make stand-up name cards and to place these at the front of their desks. Alternatively, get students to write names on sticky labels and wear them.

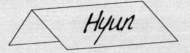

Technique: Individualised cards/labels

Instead of having students write their names, ask them to prepare a card with a picture or diagram that characterises themselves in some way, e.g. a favourite hobby, an item they possess, a food they like, a sport they play, a personal characteristic, etc. The students then introduce themselves, explaining why they drew the picture they did. You can make notes listing names and pictures (which can be referred to later on whenever you forget a name). Having only a picture on the students' cards forces you to do a little bit more work to recall their names, but this may help you remember the names better in the long-term.

Technique: Turning the cards around

Rather than being embarrassed at the fact that you haven't yet got everyone's names, make the fact that you are trying to learn names open and transparent. This allows you and the class to laugh at times when you get names wrong, rather than it being awkward. One way of doing this is a variation on the name-card idea (above). When you think you know someone's name, ask that student to turn their card around so that you can't see the name from the front of the room. The class will enjoy watching you make progress and seeing if you can remember all the names they have turned away from you.

Technique: Room map

Draw a simple sketch plan of the room and the seats, desks or tables. Write the names of each student at the place they are sitting in the room. Use this as a handheld reference when you talk with students. Also use it to help you to learn the names (see *Testing yourself* below).

Technique: Noting memorable characteristics

When you meet students and first hear their names (e.g. when you go through a register), keep a note of something that will help you to recognise that person again (e.g. has brown glasses, fair hair, has a large green bag, etc.).

Technique: Photo poster or booklet

Ask each student to bring in a photo of themselves or email you a digital copy. Stick these down on a large sheet of paper to make a poster, or make them into a digital collage or booklet. Add names to each picture. The resulting poster or booklet can be put up on the classroom wall, or a copy given to each class member.

Technique: Put a photo with a commentary on the Internet

If your class has a web site, ask each student to upload a photo and a short recording (e.g. made on a phone) of them introducing themselves. Alternatively, use public websites that are set up for such exchanges, or get students to send emails or messages to each other. (This idea was suggested by Russell Stannard in *Modern English Teacher* magazine.)

Technique: Class photo

If school guidelines (e.g. signed permission from parents) allow you to, take one or more photos of the class on the first day. After you have printed out a copy, annotate it with students' names, and keep it with your class documentation ready for quick reference. As with the previous idea, the picture could be displayed.

Technique: Testing yourself

Whatever method of collecting name information you choose, it's vital that you take some time going over your list/plan and testing yourself, e.g. covering up names, looking at the class and seeing if you can name each person, referring back to the list/plan only when necessary.

Technique: New English names

If you work with students within your own culture, the following point is not likely to be an issue. However, if you are a teacher with a multicultural class, or if you are working in a country other than your own, then there will probably be a number of names that are difficult for you to say or which you are completely unfamiliar with. Perhaps some of them will look deceptively familiar to you, but may be pronounced very differently to the equivalent English name.

I wonder how you feel about this exchange from a teacher who is just starting to work in China:

Teacher: And what's your name?

Student: Xiao Lee.

Teacher: Phew ... that's a weird name (makes a garbled effort to say the name), a bit too difficult for me I'm afraid! Sounds a bit like Sheila! Is it OK if I call you Sheila?

Arguably the solution of giving an English name is better than the teacher repeatedly mangling the pronunciation of the student's Chinese name – and certainly, there are many classes around the world where students all adopt English names. In China, students often do this as a long-term practice, taking a new name from class to class through their language learning (and possibly on into their career). I'm never entirely comfortable with this, as I feel that someone's given name is personal, important and not to be lightly given up.

If you adopt the idea of students taking on new English names, you can either assign these names yourself or let students choose them. If you let students choose, you may need to offer some guidance, perhaps by:

- Offering an initial list of good, possible names that students can choose from.
- Indicating which names are male and which female, and which are typically surnames rather than first names.
- Suggesting names that sound similar to their own name, or which have similar meanings or connotations.
- Helping students choose names, perhaps based on writers, musicians or film stars they like.
- Advising as to what might be considered odd or unsuitable names (e.g. adjectives like 'lovely' or names from fantasy games on their consoles).

Technique: Learning the right names

If a student's name sounds complex to you and near impossible to pronounce, don't immediately give up. The default position for some teachers seems to be 'hear the student say their name twice, repeat it as best you can (perhaps wrongly), despair, continue using the wrongly pronounced version for as long as the student is in your class'.

But it's worth the extra effort to get closer to a good pronunciation of someone's name. Showing that you are interested in trying to get it right also demonstrates that you are interested in the person. It also shows that you too are a language learner and one who, like them, doesn't necessarily get things right on the first attempt.

To get better at saying a name:

1 Ask the student to say their name again. Listen carefully.
2 Ask detail questions about the pronunciation, e.g. What is the first sound? How many syllables are there? Could you say the second syllable again? Where is the main stress?
3 Talk a bit about the name, e.g. Does it mean anything in the student's mother tongue? Is it a name that other family members have? Is there a short version?
4 Try saying the whole name or parts of it, but get feedback, e.g. Did I say the first sound right? What did I get wrong? Help me to say it better and so on.
5 If you can't get it within a reasonable time, apologise, but make it clear that you will come back to it. In future lessons, or after class, go on working on the name until you feel that the student is really happy with how you are saying it.
6 You may find it helpful to record student pronunciation of names (many phones now have easily accessible voice-recording facilities) so that you can replay them later for practice at home.

Technique: Anagrams

After showing an example anagram or two using your name or some famous people's names, e.g. MIJ (Jim), RPICEN RAHRY (Prince Harry), invite each student to make an anagram of their name and write it on a slip of paper. Collect these slips together at the front of the room. When ready, invite a student to come to the board, choose a random slip and write the name up. The class should try to guess which student's name it is. When it has been correctly guessed, the student whose name it was comes out and picks the next slip ... and so on.

Technique: Mnemonics

Ask students to think of something true and memorable about themselves that includes the first letter of their name, e.g. 'I'm Jim, and I'm quite jolly!'; 'I'm Fatimah, and I hate people talking about football!'

The class should mingle – including you as teacher – meeting up and introducing each other (e.g. 'This is Untidy Ursula, and here's Chandra who likes chocolate'). Everyone has the task of collecting a list of the whole class's memorable sentences. Afterwards, in the same lesson, and in future ones, have fun seeing if people can recall the phrases for each person.

Technique: Bingo names

Get students to call out their names one by one, and write them all on the board. Then ask them to each draw a three-by-three grid (i.e. like tic-tac-toe):

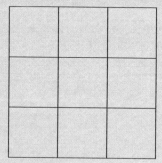

Students (and you) should select nine different names from the list on the board and write one name in each square. Having done this, you now have a choice of doing one or more of these activities:

1 Students stand up, mingle and chat with other students. They have a brief chat with each person they meet ('Hello! What's your name?' etc.), trying to find the people they have on their grid.
2 Ask all students to stand up. You call out names randomly. When students hear a name, they have to all indicate the correct student (who can then sit down). Students cross out any names they hear if they are on their own grid.

3 Get students into groups of three. In each group, one student shows their grid to one of the others, who has to identify which people in the room have those nine names. That student gets a score for the number they get correct. He or she then passes their grid to the next person in the group to test them in the same way (and so on).

Questions for reflection

- Would any of the techniques here work better than your current way of learning names?
- How well do your students know each other's names?

2 Helping the group to work together

> *My class just isn't gelling. When I try to get them to work together, they just look sullen, and then they hardly talk to each other.*

Aim

To help a class to become a group and work together.

Introduction

Within a lesson, you may form a number of short-lived groups for specific tasks, but the one big group, the class itself, goes on from day to day, month to month.

A class can have an identity, life and energy that are more than the sum of its component parts. Many teachers will have experienced the sense that a class has a distinct character quite apart from that of the individuals in it: that it may live and have moods just as humans do, that it can focus or lose focus, get excited or lose interest, love or dislike things, be friendly and helpful or sour and unfriendly. Beyond the obvious central job of teaching language, part of the teacher's job is to help create the feeling that everyone is working together in a coherent group.

Techniques: Getting to know you

Getting To Know You (GTKY) activities, sometimes referred to as *icebreakers*, tend to work well if they follow these guidelines:

1 Make sure students learn each other's names and feel comfortable using them (see Chapter 3 Unit 1).
2 Get students standing up, mingling and talking with as many others as possible. Use tasks that combine speaking practice with finding out not-too-intrusive pieces of personal information (e.g. the classic 'Find someone who': a list of cues that get students to mingle, talk and find people in the room who '... have seen a kangaroo', '... can play the guitar ...', 'would never go bungee jumping', etc.).

It's also important to get students to feel comfortable and a part of both small groups and the class as a whole. Do this by setting tasks that:

1 Are more discussion based than language focussed (but still have tangible 'take-away' value, i.e. learners feel that they have learnt something useful).
2 Require groups to work together to come to compromise or fully discussed solutions.
3 Are likely to be enjoyable and provoke laughter and creative responses.
4 Encourage learners to work together for a combined goal (e.g. team quizzes and competitions) – though be wary of activities that might pick out individual students as either strong or weak.

5 Include personal elements that encourage learners to reveal some aspects of their life, interests and tastes.
6 Get students thinking and comparing ideas about the course to come, what they hope for, how they want to work and what they would like to achieve.

Try to engineer opportunities for each student to work with a wide variety of other students, mixing groups up on different tasks. And, most importantly, include some facilitated whole-class discussion that allows a wide range of different voices to be heard.

Techniques: Creating a sense of community and purpose

A group becomes a group when it gels, which comes when a sense of collective identity and purpose starts to appear. It comes when learners really listen to and show tangible support for each other. It comes when, as well as working to get wherever they want individually, people also work together to achieve things. Some of these ideas may help a group to gel:

1 As well as the more normal work on language and skills, also keep mixing in work that doesn't have overt language goals, but, instead, aims to build the group and the quality of relationship and interaction.
2 Take the risk of adding in occasional activities that invite (but do not require) a greater level of personal revelation (e.g. drawing a 'road of my life' with key events marked, which can then be introduced to a partner and discussed).
3 Start an ongoing group project that runs through a period of the course – for a month, a term or longer. The project should be one that is only achievable when the class work together, one where everyone has a role, or a number of responsibilities, but they build together to make a single group achievement. This might be:
   • A school news and discussion magazine (or website or blog) that could be distributed or sold to the school as a whole.
   • A class play or film, written and acted by all the students, performed for another class or maybe for the whole school.
   • A fund-raising project, selecting a charity, collecting information, planning and running one or more fund-raising events.

When the project is worked on in lessons, take time to help reinforce the group-building goals.

Technique: Creating synergy

The term *synergy* refers to the energy and achievement that comes when people combine their abilities and efforts to work together, seemingly achieving more than the sum of what all the individuals could achieve on their own. Here is an example: Student A (who is good at spelling, but poor at grammar) is working together with Student B (who is good at grammar, but poor at spelling) on a written practice exercise. It is likely that this will produce a better result than either of them working on their own. While they could in theory agree together on wrong spellings and grammar and, therefore, achieve a worse exercise than either would do on their own, it is more probable that each individual student's confidence in what they consider to be correct would influence their final consensus answers.

For a whole group to achieve synergy, it seems likely that the following conditions are met:

1 Participants listen to and respect each other; they do not ignore, dismiss or ridicule what others say.
2 Because members feel valued, trusted and safe within the group, they are more willing to state their own opinions, make their case robustly, argue positions, take risks, make odd suggestions, offer to take on difficult duties, rethink their views, change tack when things don't work, etc.
3 They are task-focussed, working towards achieving the goal that has been set or agreed.
4 They are process-focussed, showing awareness as to how the work affects individual group members and aiming to make sure that all are involved and that things are done fairly.
5 Their teacher believes and trusts that they can achieve more than they think they can.

To achieve synergy doesn't necessarily mean that no one in a group should disagree with others or that all will be sweetness and light. Part of the success of effective groups comes from working through different ideas, arguments and challenges to discover complementary skills, insights and ways forward to solutions and task achievements.

Here is an example of a whole-class activity that encourages synergy: *dictogloss* – a one-time, one-sentence dictation.

- The teacher chooses a text to read. It should be interesting, easy to understand and use language that the students are familiar with.
- In class, the teacher explains that students will hear a short dictation and that he or she will read it only once. The teacher tells them that he or she expects the class will be able to write the whole text correctly, despite only hearing it once! He or she also tells them how many words it will be (e.g. 20 words) and ignores their protests about the impossibility of the task!
- The teacher warns them to listen carefully (without writing anything) while he or she is reading the dictation. As soon as the teacher has finished reading, each individual starts writing everything they can recall (without discussing with others). Of course, the students will not believe that it is possible for any of them to recall a whole text that they have only heard once – and, unless they have exceptional memories, it's very unlikely that any student would be able to do it.
- After each student has written whatever they can recall (maybe just six or seven words – or a chunk or two), the teacher invites them to pair up and compare. They are likely to find that each of the two students in a pair have remembered different bits and that, by putting them together, they end with a slightly longer text.
- When the teacher now invites pairs to meet up with other pairs, the same effect happens. Eventually, he or she asks the whole class to try and work together to reconstruct the entire original text on the board.

Amazingly, classes can often do this, getting a complete (or very nearly complete) version of the text. The ability of the whole group was significantly greater than what individuals could achieve. A seemingly impossible task was achieved through collaborative effort.

Techniques: Quick fixes to change the class mood

Classes have moods. Teachers sometimes come into the staff room talking about how the group came across. Often this is positive:

- 'They all seemed really interested. I've never seen the class so quiet and focussed.'
- 'They're full of beans this morning, almost bouncing off the light fittings!'

But sometimes their descriptions are more negative: Do any of the following ring a bell?

- 'It's like stirring mud in there today.'
- 'They just didn't seem on my side in that lesson.'

When your class seems temporarily sluggish, tired, uninterested or downright hostile (perhaps when you have no idea as to the cause), what can you do to brighten them up, get them enthused and working happily? I'm not thinking of long-term attitude or behaviour issues, which is a different kind of problem, but that unexpected change of mood that appears suddenly, gets in the way of everything you want to do and sends you back into the staff room saying, 'I've no idea what's got into them today. I thought they'd love this activity ...'.

The ideas below are not long-lasting solutions; they are quick fixes. They are also pretty hit and miss.

If your class mood is really wrong, try one of these. If it doesn't work, try another!

1 Pause the current activity. Say in a humorous way what you have noticed about how they are, as clearly and unambiguously as you can. Ask them if your interpretation is correct. (Don't immediately ask, 'What's wrong?' as this can lead to students clamming up and saying nothing. Start with checking whether they agree that they have a mood.)
2 Stop the current activity. Whatever it is. Do something different. Watch their amazement as you abandon something half way through. Don't explain until or unless they ask. Then you can say, 'You didn't seem to be enjoying it'.
3 Start an activity that creates a sudden, dramatic change of pace. The obvious way to go is *faster* – getting students to take part in a task that is time-pressured.
4 Start an activity that gets students moving. Standing up and moving around is often a quick cure to students who have got tired of sitting down and listening for too long.

Technique: Recognising stages in a group's life

Here are two different writers' descriptions of the stages a group moves through from first meeting to saying goodbye. They most obviously apply to a relatively short-lived group (say over an intensive two-week course), or one which has a limited number of focussed tasks to do, but, even so, the descriptions are useful for helping us to think about the longer life of a class, say, over a year.

1 The rhyming stages

Bruce Tuckman suggested the following typical stages of group development:

- **Forming**   People come together as a group. Individuals arrive with many personal worries about their own likely successes or contributions. They tentatively check out other members and start to find how they fit into the group as a whole, probably seeking not to get involved in conflict at this point.
- **Storming**   Once the immediate initial personal worries are calming down, the group can start to attack the task(s) they have. A lot of ideas and attitudes will fill the air. There may be a lot of energy, and perhaps disagreements and uncertainties, as working relationships are established. Leadership and other roles will establish themselves, and there may be arguments about what to do and how to do it.
- **Norming**   Things begin to settle down. Arguments and disagreements subside. People start to agree what it is they need to do and how to do it. They start engaging with their own responsibilities for the task at hand, collaborating and supporting others where necessary.
- **Performing**   This is the stage (which may last a long time) when the group is functioning at its peak, doing the task well, moving towards its goal. Engagement and achievement is high. Everyone is working to their best ability.

Different writers and speakers have suggested variations on what comes next. I think the following two are helpful additions:

- **Informing**   (Lawrence, quoted in Jaques and Salmon): 'The group starts to give voice to the outside world, communicating …' This is the passing on of whatever has been achieved – telling others what you have done.
- **Mourning**   (Tuckman and Jensen, quoted in Petty) 'As the group's lifespan comes to an end, and breakup is imminent, a strong sense of sadness and loss colours the remaining work. People find their own ways to say goodbye and to leave the work and relationships behind, before moving on.'

In terms of a school class's existence over a term or a year, these stages may still be recognisable. However, we may need to imagine the storming–norming–performing stages as a sub-cycle, repeated many times over the life of the class, as different people assert themselves, different attitudes rise and wane, and different needs and new aims become important. The class has to take a step back, renew and reinvigorate itself at various points:

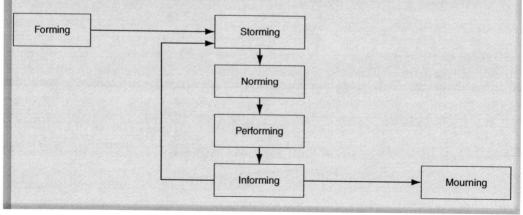

2 The four seasons

An attractive alternative description from John Heron uses a metaphor of the four seasons:

- **Winter** 'The ground may be frozen and the weather stormy.' As a new group begins, there are various tensions and a lot of defensiveness.
- **Spring** 'New life starts to break through the surface crust.' People start to trust each other and feel less anxious. Protective defensive attitudes start to relax.
- **Summer** 'There is an abundance of growth, and the sun is high.' People are much more trusting and open, working together to fulfil their goals.
- **Autumn** 'The fruit is harvested and stored; the harvesters give thanks and go their way.' The achievements are made and reviewed. People prepare to leave the group to go back to their outside lives.

This description has the added bonus of allowing us to also see the students and teacher's role in a metaphorical way. If the teacher is a farmer and the students farm workers, we can see that he or she has the job of preparing the ground, welcoming the workers and making them feel comfortable, initially inducting and training them in the tasks they need to do, showing them how to plant and nurture the crops and encouraging them to work together to achieve tasks. As time goes on, he or she will need to be able to let them do their work without a lot of monitoring and supervision, and as they become more autonomous and capable, perhaps he or she will even consider passing the whole farm over to them.

Questions for reflection

- Have you ever noticed synergy in class activities? Which activities do you use that seem to foster synergy? Which new activities could you try to encourage it?
- How aware have you been of the life cycle of classes you have worked with? Were there noticeable changes in class character over time?
- Which of the two descriptions of a group's life cycle appeals most to you?

3 Mixed-level classes

> *I'd enjoy teaching a class where the students all had similar levels, but my class has such mixed levels, it seems almost impossible to teach them together.*

Aim

To offer work at different levels within the same class.

Introduction

One of the most common complaints from teachers is that their class has too wide a range of levels in it. If the teacher goes at the speed of the faster students, she loses the weaker ones; if she goes at the speed of the weaker ones, then the stronger students get bored.

Although there are no easy solutions, this unit offers a number of ideas to try.

Many of the possible solutions involve variations on two options: either dividing the class (i.e. separating the different levels out) or offering *differentiated* work (i.e. different work to different people).

Techniques: Some ways of dividing the class

1 Make short-term pairs or threes (e.g. for a single task), deliberately mixing stronger and weaker students together.
2 Make long-term pairs, threes or groups (maybe for a month or half term), each including one stronger student who is openly given the task of guiding and supporting the other students.
3 Divide the class into two halves (or more subdivisions if useful) for some parts of each lesson. Prepare tasks at two (or more) different levels. While one part is working independently on a task, you can work with the other half. Later, you can swap over, giving a task to students in that group while moving over to teach and work with the other.

In deciding whether to divide your class or keep it together, there are a number of pros and cons to consider:

	May be good because …	May be problematic because …
Separating weaker and stronger students into halves/pairs/ groups:	Students can work together with peers of a similar level. Stronger students can go ahead at their own pace, not being held up by slower ones. Weaker students can contribute more and work at their own level, without being discouraged or outshone by faster peers.	Some students might start to feel that they are 'better' than the others. They might behave rudely or unkindly to other groups. There may be some loss of class identity. Students may feel themselves a part of their subgroup more than a member of a single class.

	May be good because …	May be problematic because …
Keeping the class as a single mixed-level group:	Stronger students can support the weaker ones. They improve their own skills and gain a better understanding of lesson content through trying to help others understand it. Weaker students benefit from hearing stronger students using English. A class identity is maintained and grows. An atmosphere of mutual respect and support can be encouraged.	Stronger students may find the class slow. They could get bored waiting for weaker ones to answer questions, say or write things. Stronger students get frustrated at frequent wrong answers and teaching that is directed to issues they feel they already understand. Stronger students talk over or ignore the weaker ones. Weaker students can't keep up and 'switch off' or misbehave. Maybe it isn't fair on the strong students to be required to support and teach the weaker ones?

Technique: Split-and-combine workflows

A split-and-combine workflow is one where the whole class starts work on something together, but, later in the lesson, different subsections of the class separate off to do different work (maybe the same tasks at a different pace, or tasks that have a similar focus, but with different challenge levels). These groups then later come back together … and so on. For example:

Stage	Subgroup 1 (stronger)	Subgroup 2 (weaker)
1	Lead-in discussion.	
2	Teacher input on grammar point.	
3	Students work without supervision on Practice Exercise 1.	Teacher sits with subgroup to review and reinforce the input, answering questions and checking understanding.
4	Class does a restricted speaking exercise together (e.g. drill).	
5	Teacher sits with subgroup and offers more challenging speaking practice.	Students work on Practice Exercise 1.
6	Students work on Practice Exercise 2.	
7	Teacher checks answers to Exercise 1 with the whole class.	
8	Students from Subgroup 1 act as teachers to Subgroup 2 while they try to answer Practice Exercise 2.	

Techniques: Differentiated worksheets

Prepare separate tasks, exercises and worksheets for different levels:

1 Make unified worksheets that include a range of question types – easier and harder, perhaps divided by a horizontal line on the page. Ask weaker students to complete only questions above the line and stronger students to do the whole page. Alternatively, you could have a core set of questions that everyone has to do, but add on follow-ups after each question for those who want to go deeper, as in this example from a reading comprehension worksheet:

	Everyone must do these questions.	Do these questions if you have time.
1	Where did Imelda go after swimming?	Why didn't she go to the café with her friends?
2	What time did she get home?	Why were her parents angry?

2 Set the same task in a choice of versions. For example, offer an open writing task for stronger students (Worksheet A) and a similar task for weaker students, but with added support, e.g. guiding questions, a partially-written text or a list of ready-made phrases (Worksheet B).

A

You are going to make a short business trip to Sydney, Australia. Write an email to the Royal Swan hotel, asking if they have any vacancies. Explain when you want to stay, and ask about the prices. Think of one special request you have for your stay, and enquire about that too.

B

You are going to make a short business trip to Sydney, Australia. Write an email to the Royal Swan hotel. Use the notes below to help you.

Dear Sir or Madam,

Ask if they have any vacancies for three nights beginning 7th January.

Do you ...

Say that you need a single room with Internet access.

I need ...

Ask how much it will cost.

How much ...

Make a special request. (Think what you want to ask for!)

I would like ...

Thank them. Say that you look forward to hearing from them.

Thank ...

3 Set the same worksheet for everyone, but have add-on tasks ready for students who finish early or need a greater challenge.

Techniques: Multilevel tasks

Offer multilevel tasks, i.e. tasks which are the same for everyone, but which have different outcomes, depending on what students can do. These include tasks that do not just have single correct answers, but instead offer a variety of more open-ended outcomes. Here are some more examples of multilevel tasks:

1 Making sentences   A task that asks students to make as many sentences as they can from a selection of words, prefixes and suffixes. Stronger students will push themselves to find longer, more challenging sentences while weaker students should still be able to make a reasonable number.

2 Making stories   All students can be asked to prepare a story on a particular topic or title. Students will naturally work at their own current level, and you can give feedback and guidance suitable for what they are able to do. You can offer different resources if it's helpful, e.g. lists of useful vocabulary, phrases or structures – and these too could be graded.

3 Poster-based tasks   Place posters around the room with different tasks or questions on them. Your class can wander around, adding comments, ideas and answers in any places they want to. When everyone has finished, you can review the work together, perhaps gathering the class round each poster to discuss it.

Techniques: Letting students choose what to do

1 Let students choose their own tasks, work speeds, outcomes, etc. Rather than imposing your own plans and expectations, allow students to make these decisions. This could be via discussion and planning, or by a simple, on-the-spot choice, such as by using a marketplace: Place tables with chairs in key locations around the room. Prepare a number of different activities (speaking, writing, listening, reading), and place copies on the tables so that each table has multiple copies of one task. Label the tables clearly with a table name (e.g. 'A'), a task name, a short description of the task, difficulty level and an approximate range of times for completing it (e.g. 10 to 20 minutes) – or prepare a 'menu' handout with the same information. In class, let students browse around and then do whichever tasks they want to for as long as they want to. Set individual goals if you wish (e.g. by the end of the lesson, you must hand in at least one completed writing task and one listening task).

2 Organise 'pass-it-on' tasks (suitable for individual, pair or group work); for example, students start doing an exercise. When the teacher rings a bell or taps the desk, they pass their exercise on and receive a new paper from the student to their immediate left or right, which they now continue working with (correcting, amending, adding as appropriate). In this way, a weaker student may start a task, but then pass it on to a stronger one who can edit and correct things, while the weaker student might receive a stronger student's answers to the questions he was just trying to do, and learn from them.

Techniques: General suggestions for mixed-level classes

1 Ask for in-class learning support. Some schools appoint assistant teachers or invite parents or trainees in to help. An assistant teacher is supervised by the main teacher, but is able to work directly with students who need particular help in class.

2 Set different time requirements for different groups. Expect stronger students to work faster and do more tasks in the same time that it takes a slower group to do one or two.

3 Discuss and agree personal learning plans with each student. This would include discussing goals, materials, tasks and the kind of support they will need. Once done, this means that, for at least part of each course, every individual in your class can work on their own priorities at their own speed.

4 Use techniques in whole-class teaching that ensure that it is not only the louder, faster students who answer. techniques such as *not putting up hands, nominating students, not rubberstamping* in Chapter 5 Units 4 and 6.

5 Create a self-study area in the classroom. This might be a table along one wall or a corner. Place useful work materials and resources there, for example, photocopied exercises and worksheets, language games on a computer, digital film clips to watch with viewing tasks. When students have finished tasks set in class, they are encouraged to go over to the self-study area and choose something to explore on their own or with others.

6 Target questions creatively in whole-class work – asking more difficult questions to stronger students and less challenging ones to weaker students.

7 Differentiate homework. For weaker students, set work that repeats and consolidates work done in class, but offer stronger students tasks that extend and apply that work to challenge and move them forward. You could let students self-select their level, e.g. prepare three different homework worksheets and place them in piles on a table by the door labelled 'Easy', 'Medium', 'Hard' – and ask each student to choose one to take home.

8 Try teaching a lesson where, instead of overtly teaching language, you teach them how to do a real-world activity, either using real items (e.g. how to play the game mahjong) or using pictures, diagrams, mime, etc. (e.g. how to scuba dive). Your hope will be that language is learnt through the process of trying to understand the content. For example, you could do a lesson in which you aim to introduce your class to something that really interests you – maybe the joys of orienteering, or why *2001* is a great film, or how to repair a watch or how to enjoy Gilbert and Sullivan or … whatever! Focus on helping them understand the content. Don't do any teaching of grammar or vocabulary, other than what is immediately needed for understanding the subject. You could ask learners to prepare a similar lesson themselves for future lessons.

The paradox of content teaching is that taking the focus off the language and putting it onto the subject still allows the language to be understood and learnt, and perhaps even more deeply. For a mixed-level class, the change of focus away from linguistic work may allow students who do not respond to a language-focussed lesson to shine in a new way.

9 Make sure that tests are fair to all. If not everyone has done all the work, you may either need separate tests or tests that are general proficiency tests and not directly linked to what has been studied. Design progress tests to let students demonstrate what they can do as opposed to what they don't know.

10 Don't panic about 'covering the book' (see Chapter 7 Unit 3).

11 Instead of trying to solve the apparent problem, might it be possible to 'dis-solve' it? Can you turn your own perception around so that you can start seeing these differences between individuals as a source of strength, as a resource, as a positive benefit, rather than as a deficit or weakness or a 'problem'?

Techniques: Early and late finishers

You probably want to avoid having students who have finished early sitting around twiddling their thumbs for minutes while the slower ones finish their work. This means that it helps to spot the nearly-finished as early as possible – as this gives you time to vary or add to their task. Just because you gave a task instruction before they began doesn't mean that you can't alter the task while they are doing it.

1 Early finishers: adding to tasks

A good tactic with early finishers is to give an extra task in addition to what they were originally asked to do. Often this can be asking them to combine previous answers into some compromise or summary viewpoint: 'Well done. I see you've nearly finished the task. So, now see if you can write one extra answer summarising the key things the expedition leader must remember.'

2 Early finishers: preparing a report or presentation

If there is quite a lot of remaining time for an early finishing pair/group to fill, it can be very useful to ask them to prepare a public report back, e.g. a presentation of their ideas or answers.

3 Early finishers: joining other groups

Send students to go and work with groups that are still working. You could instruct them to help or just observe. If they help, you may want to brief them on 'helping like a teacher', i.e. not just saying all the right answers straight away, but rather giving hints or suggestions to help the new group to find their own way.

4 Slow finishers: easing tasks

Just as you can add to some groups' work, similarly, you can ease the load on those who are struggling; for example, 'Just do questions one to six. Leave the last four' or 'Don't discuss the second question. I only want you to agree what you will do about the first'.

Technique: Reducing teacher workload for differentiation

If you decide that you want to increase differentiation in class, perhaps by using one or more of the techniques in this unit, you'll find that this probably gives you an increased workload. For example, instead of preparing one worksheet for your entire class, you might decide to include more tasks or questions, or even make two different worksheets. As the classroom teacher's day is already tiring enough, it's important that one doesn't accumulate too much extra work.

1 Find ways to offer differentiation without needing lots of extra material from you. Use digital texts where possible so that you can quickly edit texts, copy and paste questions and so on. Store all materials carefully so that you can access them again in future.
2 Exploit your coursebook. Don't assume that everyone has to do every task or exercise, or even every section or page or unit. Review your book, and decide which work is essential for all to do and which elements could be given to only some of the class. When making such decisions, don't sacrifice skills work, such as listening and speaking, for the sake of grammar input. Everyone needs a range of work on systems and skills, but they don't necessarily need to do all the work. If you think that reading or listening tasks in your coursebook are too difficult for your students, try keeping the same text, but offering different tasks to precede the coursebook tasks, easing students into the text more gently.

Technique: Understanding levels

The level names we use for classes and students are a shorthand, a simplification, an average. When we learn that a student is A2, or 'elementary' or 'intermediate', it's important to remember that this doesn't tell us much about the individual. Each learner has a number of levels rather than one level – varying degrees of knowledge and skills over a range of systems or skills. For example, one student might be very good at listening and speaking while another might have a totally contrasting profile, being strong at writing and reading, but very poor at speaking and listening. Yet both are labelled intermediate and study in the same class.

We can't assume that all students in a class resemble one another in levels, beyond the fact that they average out somewhere in the same area. If the students have studied within the same school in the same culture, there is more chance of similarity – but if you are teaching a multilingual class with students from different places, then the mixed levels will really make themselves apparent. Whatever the name of your students' coursebook, remember that it doesn't give you any depth of insight into the real levels of learners in your class. They are all at different places on their own road of learning, each at a different 'somewhere-in-the-middle' point.

1 Get a better insight into levels by assessing your students in separate areas: speaking, listening, reading, writing, grammar, vocabulary, and pronunciation.
2 Help learners to understand their varied level profiles by plotting their data as a simple graph (e.g. marking different levels for grammar, listening, pronunciation, etc). The resulting graph may well show a 'spiky profile', i.e. some distinct peaks and valleys.

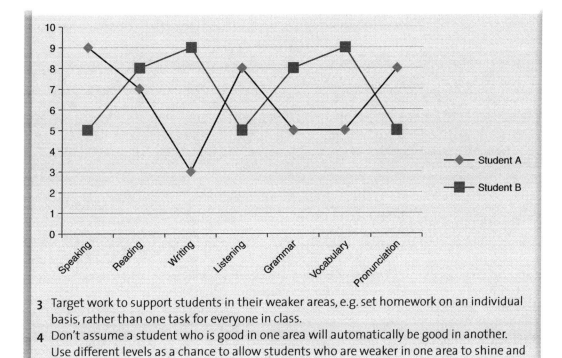

3 Target work to support students in their weaker areas, e.g. set homework on an individual basis, rather than one task for everyone in class.

4 Don't assume a student who is good in one area will automatically be good in another. Use different levels as a chance to allow students who are weaker in one area to shine and show off a little in areas where they are strong.

Technique: Coping with extreme mixed-level classes

Schools sometimes allocate what seems to be an impossibly wide range of levels to a class, e.g. beginners in the same room as post-intermediate. This may happen because students are placed in classes by age group or achievement in subjects other than English language level, or because of some necessity such as not having enough teachers or rooms. If you face this problem, consider making a permanent division within the class so that you have two (or maybe three) classes running independently and separately in different parts of the room, perhaps only bringing all the students together for certain games or movement activities that all can do. Share your time as fairly as you can between these sub-classes, though you are likely to find the lower level students needing more.

Questions for reflection

• Is the mix of levels in your classes a significant problem for you? What strategies do you have for dealing with it?

• How do your students react to the range of levels? Is it something that they notice and comment on? Does it lead to any participation or behaviour issues?

• How do teachers of other subjects in your school deal with mixed-level classes? Do some teachers have well-worked-out differentiation strategies? Do some mainly teach at the speed of the fastest students?

▋4 Large classes

> *My biggest teaching problem? There are just too many students in class.*

Aim

To teach large classes more effectively.

Introduction

There is no law that says that the larger a class, the poorer the learning must be, though many parents, teachers and students would argue that this must be the case. Similarly, there is no guarantee that small classes must lead to more learning. Of course, the better the ratio of teacher (and assistants) to students, then the more chance there is to give personal support and guidance; so in this respect, smaller is better. But learning is something that can only be done by the individual. It is always done privately, one student at a time. And that means that there is no reason why a student cannot learn (or fail to learn) equally well in a class of one as in a class of one hundred.

What is a large class depends a lot on what you are familiar with. Mentally, I find myself drawing a distinction between roughly these ranges:

- One-to-one teaching.
- A very small class (2 to 6 students).
- A small class (7 to 13).
- A standard class (14 to 25).
- A large class (26 to 45).
- A very large class (45+).

Many school classes fall into the large category, though, in some countries, it may be normal to have even bigger groups; a teacher may have to teach 70, 90 or 120 in a single class. Each size calls for slightly different teaching approaches, though, for all of them, the same basic teaching skills will be more important than any changes caused by the group size. What applies to a group of 12 often equally applies to 70. You always need to find ways that get all the students engaged and working, and these are essentially the same ways whether you are teaching one or a hundred.

Techniques: Working with large classes

1 Don't feel that you can only do teacher-led, whole-class teaching

Some teachers feel that, because they have such large numbers, they can only use up-front teaching approaches. In fact, it's really the opposite that is true. Large classes are likely to benefit from lots of pair and group work if learners are to get any chances to really use or practise the language themselves.

2 Make sure they know that you know them all

One thing often missing in a large class is the sense that the teacher really knows you and is interested in you. Help this by learning names quickly (see Chapter 3 Unit 1) and using names when you ask questions or talk with people. Keep notes of some personal information (family, home, interests, etc.) about each individual, and ask them about it when you have a chat. It's important that students have no doubt that you know who they are.

3 Create systems for managing materials efficiently

The larger your class, the more likely it is that materials will become a problem. Maybe you don't have enough coursebooks, so students have to share. If you use handouts, you have to prepare huge quantities. Just to distribute them around the room can seem like a major operation. Collecting in and sorting tasks, tests and homework can get very complicated. If students see you as the stationery supplier for pens, paper, erasers and so on, you will spend the whole lesson running around sorting out their needs. Deal with this by making robust systems for managing materials. Maybe use responsibility roles (see below), or train students to do specific tasks in regular ways (e.g. always giving handouts to the back row, whose job is to take one and pass forward down their row). Set up clearly labelled areas for storing books and materials so that students can easily collect things from there. Similarly, set up areas for students to hand in tasks and homework.

4 Take a long hard look at the room

Don't assume that the class has to look uniform and dull. Can you improve the use of space to make it feel more welcoming and less crowded? Would it help to get rid of the traditional rows? Is it possible to create some open space in the room – for meeting up, movement, mingling, sitting on the floor and so on? Make sure that students who have difficulties with hearing or seeing are placed so that they don't have problems. Consider grouping weaker students where you can easily get to them to help. Get students to suggest their own ideas for improving the room. (See Chapter 1 Units 1 and 2 for more ideas.)

5 Train students in how to be organised

Devote some class time to training students to be more organised and in 'learning to learn', showing them ways to become more autonomous and less dependent on the teacher telling them everything. Get routines in place for starting lessons and for tidying up at the end.

6 Don't get stuck at the front

Even more than with a small class, it's vital that you make use of the whole room. Move about a lot. Do input, instructions and explanations from lots of different places. Have lots of conversations with various individuals (but remember that if you come up close to the individual and talk quietly, it can quickly exclude the rest of the class). Circulate: move round the room following different paths between rows, rather than always patrolling the same columns. (See Chapter 1 Unit 5.)

7 Try mini classes within the class

How about creating four or five very different 'classrooms within the classroom' – clumping groups of seats together in different ways to make separate islands for working subgroups? Teach them independently for parts of the lesson.

8 Don't spend all your time getting tied up in discipline issues

Sometimes there is so much going on in a large class that the teacher seems to have to spend all his or her time dealing with micromanagement of discipline problems. Find a simple catch-all solution that minimises wasted time for such issues. (See Chapter 6 Unit 2 for ideas.)

9 Offer private contact time

In a large class, students can feel that they never get the chance to talk privately with the teacher. Compensate for this by offering specific times when any student who wants to can talk with you. This could be for half an hour after school once a week or even within lesson time – perhaps an in-lesson slot every week when you set a quiet task for students to do while anyone who wants to talk with you can book a five-minute slot.

Techniques: Use in-classroom support

If your school already operates systems to give you in-class support, make the best use of it you can. If this doesn't exist, argue the case for appointing assistants – or see if you can get permission for using volunteer assistants in your class even if it isn't a general school policy.

1 Teaching assistants

An assistant is someone who can help you in any aspect of classroom life. They may be parents, trainee teachers, volunteers, retired teachers or anyone who would like to be involved. Show them ways that they can help you in basic classroom management (e.g. distributing handouts, organising seating changes) and close-up help (e.g. supporting students who have a problem and/or need clarification, etc.). Trainee or trained teachers can help you in delivering the up-front teaching content as well. You may decide that the best use of some assistants is in supporting specific members of class, e.g. weaker students, or those who have specific problems.

2 Student deputies

Appoint students to help you in a similar way, taking wide-ranging responsibilities to help you in both administrative and academic ways. These could be long-term appointments (e.g. a half-term) or short-term (on a rota, changing lesson by lesson). These posts could be awarded to students who show particular progress or make an individually significant achievement in a previous lesson. Alternatively, they could be given on a rota basis, or voted for by students themselves.

3 Student monitors

Allocate students specific roles to help get your class organised and running efficiently. They should be able to take over a lot of the nitty-gritty organisational stuff and free you up to help where it is really needed. For example:

- Hand a seating plan to the seating monitors who ensure that people sit in the correct places for this lesson as soon as they come into the room.
- Materials Monitors then distribute books, handouts, worksheets, etc.
- Group makers help to form groups according to your instruction.
- Task Monitors have a copy of task instructions that they go over with a group, once you have read them out ... and so on.

Using monitors and student deputies has the added advantage that a large number of students are actively involved in making the lesson work and have a stake in things being done well. This may well reduce discipline and nuisance problems.

For these roles (and perhaps for the student deputy roles discussed above), don't assume that only the 'good' students can do them. You may find that giving a 'troublemaker' a responsibility to carry out might just turn everything around, and the previously impossible student becomes the new advocate of good behaviour and order.

Questions for reflection

- Imagine that you have volunteered to work for a month as an English teacher in a developing country. You have just learnt that the size of each class will be around 70 to 80 students. There will be very limited materials and facilities. Which techniques or ideas from this unit would be of most use to you? What other possibilities come to mind?

5 Individuals

> *Well, of course, learners are different, but I have a whole large class to teach – so what can I do about it?*

Aim
To recognise and work with all the different individuals in my classroom.

Introduction
→ Chapter 5 Unit 3 looked at different learner levels. This unit explores other differences between individuals.

When I was a pupil in secondary school, the teachers taught the class as if it was a homogenous group of people. I can only recall one or two teachers who ever really acknowledged me as an individual or who showed any interest in a student tentatively asking if it was possible to do things differently. We all got one lesson and made the best of it we could. The students who understood things quickly were the clever ones. Those of us who struggled or got lost were the lazy or stupid ones. Expressions of individualism were typically seen as symptoms of naughtiness. The idea of offering different work to different students, or of making sure that lessons addressed their subject matter in different ways to reflect the different abilities or personal styles of learners, had probably never occurred to most of those teachers.

However, if I were to revisit my old school nowadays, I'd bet that differentiation has become a key feature of what the teachers are asked to do. Geoff Petty expresses this very neatly: 'We used to teach subjects and classes – now we teach students.'

Differentiation involves offering different content, levels of content, teaching methods, student tasks and working methods to different students in order to most effectively help each individual achieve the most and the best that they are capable of.

Students can be individual and different in many ways, including:

• Level of English.
• General ability at academic subjects.
• Preferences for ways of studying (i.e. their learning style).
• Disabilities.
• Subjects and topics they find interesting and motivating.
• Personal and social skills.

This is just the start of a long list. There are many contrasting analyses of learner differences and learner styles. In this unit, we will look at three analyses that are widely used and referred to.

Technique: Using sensory preferences – Visual, Auditory, Kinaesthetic (VAK)

Some descriptions of individual differences have shown themselves to have remarkable intuitive appeal and staying power in staffrooms. One of the most successful comes out of the field of Neuro-Linguistic Programming (NLP) and concerns sensory preferences.

The idea is that everyone has a primary or preferred way of taking in new information: whether by seeing it (visual), by listening to it (auditory) or by learning it through physical means – touch or movement (kinaesthetic). The two other input channels of taste (gustatory) and smell (olfactory) are less obviously relevant to language teaching.

Visual, Auditory, Kinaesthetic (VAK) preferences would suggest, for example, that a learner who is primarily a visual learner would have more difficulty with a course that was presented through lectures (i.e. auditory). The conclusion would be for the teacher to make sure that his or her input matches the student's preferred sensory channel. And this is what many teachers around the world now do, planning carefully to make sure that they include activities that appeal to V, A and/or K senses as appropriate.

Of course, *any* sensible teaching has to allow students to study, respond and record learning in varied ways over time. Despite the popularity of VAK, there is no hard evidence that playing to a particular sensory preference is the right thing to do. It's possible that schools which credit VAK with tangible improvements in student work are only noticing that using a wider range of engaging working methods makes a difference, especially for classes where the teacher previously mainly talked at students.

English Language Teaching has always been fairly adventurous in methodology. A large number of ELT teachers offer varied, active, engaging, interactive lessons by default. They often make use of visual, auditory and kinaesthetic activities. I would suggest that these teachers really do not need to worry too much about sensory preferences.

If you would like to experiment with using VAK in your teaching, you could:

- Do a VAK audit of your students (see Audits below).
- Devise teaching approaches that involve a mix of visual, auditory and kinaesthetic work.
- Observe how students respond to different sensory channels in your teaching.

Technique: Multiple Intelligences (MI)

Intelligence has traditionally been seen as an uncountable noun, something connected to academic and cognitive skills that you have more or less of, and which is indivisible. As a contrast to this, Howard Gardner has proposed that it is more useful to think of humans as each having a number of distinct intelligences, present in varying degrees. His proposed list comprises:

1 Linguistic
Being good with words and language, reading and writing.

2 Logical/mathematical

Being good with numbers, maths, logical processes, patterns, relationships between things and abstract concepts.

3 Spatial

Being good with pictures, diagrams, maps and visual representations.

4 Bodily-kinaesthetic

Being good with physical skills, sports, activities with tangible objects, dance, mime and acting.

5 Musical

Being good with music, noticing sounds and recognising tunes.

6 Interpersonal

Being good with other people; being good at communication and social skills.

7 Intrapersonal

Being reflective and insightful about one's own psychology and internal life; being intuitive and self-confident.

8 Naturalistic

Being good at recognising and understanding aspects of the natural world around us, e.g. animals, birds, plants, looking after animals and pets, etc.

Gardner's proposed list is not intended to be complete or definitive.

As with VAK (see section above), MI has been widely picked up and applied in school environments. Many teachers feel an intuitive truth here and find that thinking about students' different intelligences helps them plan and teach. As with VAK, you can prepare lessons that deliberately set out to appeal to a wider range of intelligences.

However, as John White points out, the fact that MI is popular and widely used doesn't necessarily mean it is true or that it is validated. He suggests that it is not hard to see why MI has been so popular in schools. 'It is liberating – because now everyone is intelligent in different ways. It allows teachers to value all pupils – not just those traditionally seen as bright. Kids can escape from labels like "thick" or "dim".'

Ginnis comments that the 'upgrading of ordinary household abilities into "intelligence" suddenly gives everyone a place in the world'. No one is written off anymore.

Technique: Gregorc's 'mind-style' differences

A third way of looking at differences is proposed by Anthony Gregorc. I learnt about this through Paul Ginnis. It is an analysis of the different ways that our minds perceive and categorise information. It starts with these two continuums:

1 Perception: concrete – abstract

People perceive along a continuum from concrete to abstract. At one extreme, concrete perceivers take in the objective, tangible, physical reality. Abstract perceivers, in contrast, quickly generalise, extrapolate, connect, find subjective meanings, notice patterns and hypothesise theories.

2 Storing: sequential – random

People store information in their minds along a continuum from sequential (i.e. sequenced, logical, linear, ordered) to (apparently) random (seemingly chaotic, yet creative and intuitive, ordered in personal or idiosyncratic ways).

Combining these two continuums into a single diagram gives us four places to be: Concrete sequential, abstract sequential, abstract random and concrete random.

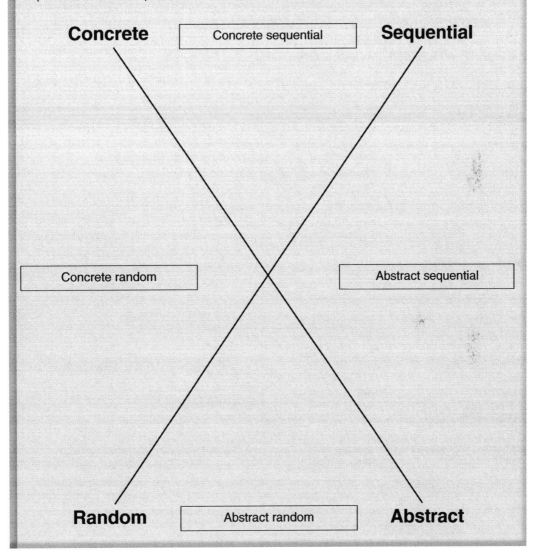

These generalise some useful differences between learner styles:

1 A *concrete sequential* learner likes organised, step-by-step work. They appreciate fixed clear-cut tasks with logical rules and instructions.

2 An *abstract sequential* learner also enjoys structured guidance in their work (e.g. worksheets, exercises, input), but likes unearthing conclusions, connections and meanings for themselves.

3 An *abstract random* learner finds unstructured work helpful, e.g. activities that allow them to explore, discuss, make intuitive leaps and respond creatively.

4 A *concrete random* learner enjoys planning their own work and its structure, rejecting other people's rules and guidelines. They are happy experimenting, but also want to reach definite goals that they can be satisfied with.

As with VAK and MI, a teacher might decide that they want to check their lesson preparation to see whether they have catered for this range of learner styles over time. The following checklist from Ginnis is a useful lesson-planning tool for reviewing the variety of activities and working modes offered.

Checklist from Ginnis

Abstract sequential		Concrete sequential	
Reading	Analysis	Hands on	Maps
Ideas	Evaluation	Concrete examples	Diagrams
Reasoning	Sit down and work	Doing things	Short explanations
Theories	Lectures	Clear-cut objectives	Lists
Debate	Libraries	Structured	Follow rules and
Note taking	Academic work	Step-by-step	conventions
Content	Research	Data and figures	Tried-and-tested
Logical	Intellectual	Checklists	methods
Knowledge	Essays	Clear instructions	Specific answers
Thinking	Quiet	Attention to detail	Tangible outcomes
Individual study	Comprehension	Computers	Methodical
Tests	Philosophy	Charts	Honesty
Structured	Documentation	Outlines	Field trips
Mental exercises	Objectivity	Deadlines	Consistency
Hypothesising	Comparisons	Manuals	Plans
Vicarious experiences		Real experiences	

Concrete random		Abstract random	
Problem solving	Creating models	Group work	Intuition
Investigation	Own timetable	Humour	Self-expression
Ingenuity	Up and doing	Games	Own timetable
Finished products	Practical	Movies	Imagination
Choice	Broad guidelines	Non-linear	Peer teaching
Independence	Tangible outcomes	Relationships	Open-ended tasks
Experimental	Connected to real	Own ideas	Art
Risks	world	Belonging	Discussion
Exploration	Experiments	Music	Drama
Open-ended	Creativity	Human angle	Media
Questions and tasks	Trial and error	Emotions	Creativity
Big picture, not	Options	Colour	Fantasy
details	Challenge	Spontaneity	Personalised work
Curiosity	Mini-inputs	Flexibility	Poetry
Originality	Games	Stories	Time for reflection
Exploration	Flexibility	Cooperation	Subjectivity
Invention	Lots of resources	Visualisation	
Few restrictions		Movement	

Technique: Audits

The audit is the key tool for finding out about your students' learner styles. It's a means of gaining useful concrete data about the area you are researching. Typically, it will involve students answering a set of written (or oral) questions. With low-level students, these might be done in their first language.

Here are some sample audit questions for determining VAK preferences:

- Do you prefer to listen to the teacher explaining grammar or to read about it in a book? (i.e. auditory versus visual)
- When you want to learn vocabulary, do you prefer to say the word again and again in your head or imagine the word written down on a page? (i.e. auditory versus visual)
- When you listen to different syllable patterns in words, would you prefer to pick out the correct diagram of the pattern from a printed selection or arrange coloured bricks of different sizes on the table to show the pattern? (i.e. visual versus kinaesthetic)
- Do you prefer to stand up and role play / act a new dialogue or listen to someone else reading it aloud? (i.e. kinaesthetic versus auditory)

Here are some sample yes / no audit questions for recognising multiple intelligences:

- Do you like to do word puzzles and word games?
- Do you enjoy singing?
- Do you fairly regularly write a diary, journal or blog?
- Are you good at doing simple maths problems in your head?

Do an Internet search to find ready-made audits in the areas you want to investigate. Do double check them to make sure that the questions are relevant and intelligible to your own students.

Bear in mind that the answers to individual questions may not reveal very much – and if you only use a few questions, they may give contradictory information. It is *en masse* that the answers may start to give you some clear overall picture.

Technique: Taking learner styles with a pinch of salt

Much of differentiation makes a great deal of sense and should form a core part of any definition of what good teaching is. However, differentiation can involve a lot of extra work for the teacher. We need to ensure that this extra effort bears real fruit and is not mainly aimed at pleasing our observers and inspectors. Crucially, the real demand of differentiation is in asking for an attitudinal change in the teacher more than just adding in a token extra task or two for the slow students. Differentiation means that the teacher has to see him- or herself as someone who is genuinely teaching all the people in the room – not just the stronger, faster ones – and this attitude has to affect every aspect of his or her planning, material selection, task choices and moment-by-moment work in class.

There are also areas where we need to bear in mind that the theories underpinning VAK and MI may be wrong. When I read in a lesson plan that an activity is designed to appeal to olfactory learners, I lose heart a little. In an editorial in 2010, the UK's *New Scientist* magazine characterised Multiple Intelligences (MI) as a 'neuromyth' that used 'neurojargon to make half-baked ideas seductive'.

The descriptions and analyses of how people differ are all suppositions (i.e. believed, but not proved) and, at best, only a glimpse at a wider truth. Perhaps their main value is in offering us thought experiments along the lines of 'what if this were true?' – making us think about the ideas and, in doing so, reflecting on our own default teaching styles and our own current understanding of learner differences and responses to them.

So … experiment with learning styles in order to understand your students and your own teaching approaches better, but hold back a small grain of scepticism before you sell your soul.

Technique: Working with the clown and the scapegoat

These two interesting classroom stereotypes are described by Zoltán Dörnyei and Tim Murphey. Many teachers will recognise them.

1 The clown

The clown is a self-appointed role, found in just about every class: the joker who makes everyone laugh and injects a necessary jab of humour into proceedings. In pricking the bubble of seriousness, they can paradoxically help make students feel more serious and focussed. They may help to bring a touch of realism and sanity to tasks that might otherwise prove overwhelming or too serious. The teacher can often happily support and permit the clown if the humour helps the class atmosphere, and so long as the humour is not cruel or directed inappropriately at individuals. However, clowns may sometimes require some management: 'The problem with clowning is that it very easily gets out of hand – clowns often find it difficult to stop, and the group can get caught up in the clowning, even if they regret it later.'

Deal with this kindly, humorously, yet firmly. Where possible, keep the stopping of clowning as lighthearted as the clowning itself. A clear, whispered request may be more appropriate than an upfront command. Take care not to destroy the clown's self-confidence or put him or her off further humour in the future.

2 The scapegoat

In many groups, one person can come to be the focus of blame, resentment, abuse or ridicule: It is so convenient to settle issues by claiming, 'If only that person were not here, things would go well'.

As the teacher, you need to watch out for students who seem to be being placed in this role. Take care not to go along blindly with student prejudices or to tacitly accept them by not challenging them. Respond to blame, accusations and claims with questions that focus students back on their own responsibility and achievements within the group.

Questions for reflection

- Have you or your school been influenced by VAK or MI? What impact does it have on your classes and teaching?
- Are you able to recognise and describe your own learning style? How neatly does it fit into any of the categories discussed in this unit? Might it have helped your own education if your teachers had been more aware of your preferences?

6 A learner-centred approach

> *I find it so hard to motivate my class. I try to be bouncy and do jolly activities that I think they'll like, but although they smile and seem to think I'm quite funny, the lessons never really take off.*

Aim

To find ways of making classes that are more genuinely focussed on learner needs and wishes.

Introduction

Many teachers nowadays would say that they want their classes to be student-centred (or learner-centred or learning-centred), but what exactly does it mean? It's one of those widely used, contemporary buzz phrases. Teachers often seem to use it to mean, 'I included some pair work in the lesson', or 'They were all talking and doing things' or 'I, the teacher, didn't talk as much as I usually do'. I get an impression of active involvement: group and pair work, students doing things, talking, asking questions – all in the expectation that being involved will lead to more learning; that if a student is actively taking part, he or she will take in more than if he or she is simply absorbing messages from a teacher transmitting.

However, there's something missing here. As a student, I can be working in a group or a pair – I can be talking and doing things – and yet find that the subject matter is of no interest or relevance to me, and I find myself doing things simply because I have been told to do them. It doesn't matter whether I'm listening to my teacher talk about making a pot, watching my teacher make a pot, or trying to make a pot myself; if I don't want to make a pot and have no interest or wish to have a pot, I'm very unlikely to learn much from the experience. It doesn't feel like the class is centred on my interests, needs, wishes or skills.

The phrase *learner-centred* suggests that the learning is not just directed at the learner, but in some way focussed on them, drawing its sense of direction from them, maybe drawing its energy and power from them. And this requires not just a methodological shift in how you organise activities or a rearrangement of the chairs. Putting you into a small group and telling you to discuss a problem doesn't mean that you want to do it. It may well be more enjoyable than just listening to the teacher explaining things. It may well be easier to take on ideas and learn from them. But it doesn't make it relevant to you. It doesn't make you want to learn it if you don't want to learn it.

Learner-centred teaching is about having trust in your students' abilities to learn and in their abilities to make decisions about what and how to learn. It is about a greater degree of empathy with each individual. It is about creating a political climate in which students can be more autonomous within a class. This is all quite separate from the physical description of what goes on in a class. I can be student-centred standing in front of the class and lecturing them. Because the only thing that needs to change is my attitude.

But how much is leaner-centredness desirable or possible anyway? Maybe the teacher and the school and the educational system have the right and the responsibility to make intelligent decisions on behalf of those who they believe are not ready or informed enough to make them. This is a decision you will need to make for yourself, but it's important to remember that there is a direct trade-off against motivation. The more a person makes decisions for themselves, the more motivated he or she is likely to feel. The more a person is told what to do, and the less say he or she has in what, how and when, the less the person is likely to feel interested or committed to the task. I am reminded of Carl Rogers' warning, 'When I try to teach, as I do sometimes, I am appalled by the results … It seems to cause the individual to distrust his own experience and to stifle significant learning'. If you ever find yourself saying, 'My class is so unmotivated', then this learner-centredness is an important issue for you to consider. You may find that even very tiny steps towards giving students more ownership of their learning can make significant changes in their engagement and motivation.

Technique: Recognising the political shape of your classroom

Much of traditional education happened on the far right of the diagram below: the teachers mainly working on topics that the learners had not chosen or had any say in, using methods and approaches that they had no influence over.

A lot of contemporary English Language Teaching happens somewhere in the centre and to the right; there is a certain amount of negotiation and discussion about work and working methods, but the teacher/school/government agenda usually carries most weight.

A more radical, fully learner-centred, learner-led approach would mostly be in the centre left. Learners make their own autonomous decisions about what to work on, how to study and so on, perhaps taking account of guidance, advice or information from the teacher. This can be done within any existing constraints; for example, if there is a syllabus and coursebook set by the school, the learners can still make decisions about how to work with those things.

For teachers whose experience is in traditional schools where most or all key decisions are taken without reference to student opinions or wishes, such a strong learner-centred approach can sound unworkable or naïve.

However, whole schools have been organised on this principle. If you believe that students are more likely to be engaged, learn and succeed if they feel that they are studying something that they have chosen to do, in ways that they want to work, then this left-hand section is important. The fact that it is almost entirely unfamiliar to most teachers is also worth thinking about.

In the left section of the diagram, the teacher's role is not to abdicate all responsibility and sit back reading a newspaper. There is a real need for expert facilitation skills, i.e. to do those things that help people learn to work autonomously, work together, listen better to each other and discuss and negotiate successfully.

If, on reading this, you feel that you would like your class to be further to the left side of the diagram, go slowly. Use some of the ideas later in this chapter, but don't suddenly shift your whole way of teaching overnight; that will probably only provoke confusion and resentment. Try a step-by-step approach. Even one small movement along the path from right to left may make a significant change to how your classes work.

Students decide.	Students and teacher decide together.	Students have no choice.

Traditional education

Much of modern classroom ELT

Self-study

Learner-centred education

Techniques: Making your class more learner-centred

A teacher who feels that they want to make their classes more learner-centred may find many worrying questions in their way:

- How can you get a group of separate individuals to state what they want when, as far as they are concerned, they haven't got any idea what they want and don't want to think about it anyway?
- How can you get them to listen to each other, at least to notice that different people have very different views about what they want?
- How can you help them to agree what to do? How does the negotiation not descend into argument and chaos? How do we avoid wasting time with endless discussions?
- How do you ensure that learners do not simply take the easy option and avoid choosing tough or challenging choices?

Moving students from their familiar, obedient, non-decision-making role to one where they are consulted and their opinions are taken into account (and may actually change what is done or how it's done) doesn't necessarily come quickly or easily. They may feel nervous or uneasy if the teacher suddenly asks them to start thinking about questions that have never been asked before. If not approached carefully, they may feel that the teacher is lazy, or unskilled or abandoning them. The teacher has to train the class to start reclaiming the power that their previous experience has trained them to relinquish. Many teachers choose to do this in a gentle, unthreatening way, gradually introducing more and more chances for students to behave autonomously – small bursts of democracy that build slowly to a changed climate.

The following ideas are arranged (approximately) from straightforward to more demanding. You may want to begin by trying out some of the low-risk suggestions that come earlier in the list, and then, as you and the students become more confident, move on further through the ideas.

1 Start small

Don't jump in the deep end, offering huge decisions for students to make. Start by offering very small choices in discrete points. For example, 'Would you like me to explain that again?' or 'Shall I write that on the board?' The crucial point is that you go with what they decide (rather than what you think best for them).

2 Offer binary choices

Give limited A or B options to offer some decision-making power, but to constrain the choices, e.g. 'Would you like to work in pairs or groups of three?' 'Would you like to have five minutes or ten minutes to do this task?' 'Would you like to write a story or do a grammar exercise for homework?'

3 Allow divided outcomes

There doesn't always need to be agreement on decisions. If half the class chooses one option and others choose something different, where possible, allow each student to do what they chose.

4 If you offer a choice, make it genuine

Don't offer a choice if you are not able to go along with the outcome. If students make a decision that you don't agree with, swallow hard, make your views known if you wish, and then go along with their decision.

5 Make any constraints absolutely clear

If there are some things that are not discussable (e.g. the school requires you to use a certain coursebook or do a certain exam), then make sure that students understand that this is not negotiable. The interesting thing is to take creative decisions within those constraints (e.g. we have to use this book … but *how* shall we use it?).

6 Don't make a big deal about choices

Initially, don't announce that you are trying an experiment or that you want to make students more autonomous. Just start doing it. Just let students get used to the fact that you are giving them chances to say what they want a little more.

7 Get students to notice that not everyone has the same viewpoint

When you start offering choices, differences of opinion will quickly appear. Don't simply go with the first to shout out. Allow a number of students to give their view. Actively encourage quieter students and weaker ones to state what they think. Encourage everyone to get involved. It also helps that everyone takes responsibility and is accountable. In cases where a majority verdict is appropriate or when it is important for everyone to see that the outcome is fair, you could have a vote (e.g. by a show of hands).

8 Avoid wordings that imply that the teacher is someone who needs to be pleased

Students need to work for themselves and start to be able to evaluate their own successes or problems. Watch out for habitual instructions, such as 'What I'd like you to do for me now ...' that imply that students are working for the teacher rather than for themselves.

9 Get students discussing some decisions

When you have time, and the decision seems worth discussing, get students to state why they think their decision is the best one, and try to persuade others to change their minds.

10 Demonstrate that you are listening, but also have an opinion

You are also a member of the class and an important one. Feel free to join in any discussion about what to do, suggest what you think is the best path, but don't browbeat or sledgehammer them into following your suggestion. The class will be very impressed if you make your case strongly, they decide another route and then you are seen to follow their choice without argument. This will send a powerful message about how you trust them and are willing to genuinely share your power.

11 Don't always go with the majority

You may feel that there is not time to discuss every decision, and it may well not feel like time well-spent if you did so. So when you offer a decision to students, the simpler option is usually to go with the majority answer, 'Most students said that they wanted to do this ... so let's do that'. However, the minority may need to have their voice heard, especially if they seem to be frequently overruled. Reserve the right to go with their choices at times, maybe by saying something like, 'Well, we always do it that way ... so how about doing it this other way, for a change?'

12 Ask different people to make each decision

As an alternative to whole-class decision making, for some decisions, ask an individual to decide. For example, 'For the next task we could do the speaking exercise on page 96 or listen to a song I've brought in. Karl? What shall we do?' Make sure that you ask a range of people over time.

13 Don't let decision-making get boring

Get decision-making crisp and to the point. You need to find a balance between offering students a real decision and taking too long to reach the conclusion. Students will soon get bored if they find that they spend too long bumbling around, making decisions that drag on too long. Once the class has been trained in making decisions, avoid offering basic or pointless choices. Don't string things out too long. Don't waste time on fruitless fine points. Take appropriate teacher authority to decide inconsequential or humdrum classroom-management decisions.

14 Restrain yourself from being the power, the authority, the decider

Look for opportunities where students could do something themselves that until now you have habitually done on automatic pilot. Slowly, over time, train yourself not to automatically jump in to make decisions, to order, to select, to organise. Build up your portfolio of things that you can really trust the class to do. This is a significant shift for a teacher who is used to doing these things, so give yourself time. Notice your urge to 'be a teacher'. Smile kindly at yourself, as you restrain yourself from actions that you don't need to take.

15 Offer choices more often as days go by

Over time, slowly increase the number of choices offered.

16 Offer more open decisions as time goes on

Move on from binary decisions to more open ones that allow a range of ideas and possibilities.

17 Offer more important decisions

Start to offer decisions that are about more crucial or longer-term issues (e.g. whether to start a big project). These will almost certainly require discussion.

18 Train your learners in listening and negotiating skills

Point out when students don't listen to or talk over each other. Encourage them to state their cases more clearly. Discourage any angry or dismissive comments. Teach students to summarise all points and arguments and to look for balance and compromise. (See Chapter 5 Unit 5 for more ideas on these areas.)

19 Train students to evaluate themselves

Get students used to reflecting on their own progress and assessing their achievement and level clearly and honestly against criteria. *Can-do* statements or a learner portfolio are a good starting point. With time, learners will become more demanding on themselves and start to set more challenging goals.

20 Hand over a big decision and a strategy for deciding

When you feel that your class is ready, give them a big decision (e.g. what project to do, which coursebook to choose) to make on their own, but also lay down the method by which they will reach that decision. Write out a timed plan for them to follow, e.g. brainstorming possible projects, appointing advocates to consider plus and minus points for each one, selecting the decision-making method (e.g. majority vote); and then plan a discussion meeting at which proposals are introduced by advocates, discussed and eventually a decision is made.

21 Ask big questions

When you feel that you and your class are ready, start opening up the biggest questions for discussion: 'What's the point of learning English?' 'Is this the best way to study it?' 'What other ways could we learn the language?' etc. Argue your beliefs, but don't feel that you need to push or guide them to correct or school-approved answers.

Technique: In at the deep end

The techniques listed above represent a softly-softly approach, gradually introducing elements of learner autonomy over time. However, some educators would argue that this is wrong – that learners need to be aware of key issues right from the start of a course and that the best way to do this is to start the way you mean to go on, with what you believe is right.

An in-the-deep-end approach would look shocking to many teachers in most schools. But don't dismiss it as impossible or crazy. When done effectively, it is potentially the most powerful way of getting real learning going. However, the perceived high risk factor is going to make this more likely as an approach in adult classes than in secondary schools, and with smaller classes rather than large ones.

The following is a description of one teacher at work, rather than a general route map to follow:

> On the first day of the intermediate adult course, Carolina forms the chairs into a circle before the 12 students arrive. At this stage, the students don't know each other. They come in and sit down, a little shy, hardly talking, waiting for the lesson to begin. They look at the teacher, waiting for her to start the lesson. She simply chats with the students near her. After a while, she introduces herself briefly and then asks, 'OK! What shall we do?' One student quietly suggests that she is the teacher, so it's up to her. Carolina says, 'No, I don't know what is best! What do you think we should do now?' A second student says, 'Please decide. We don't know! You are the teacher!' A third mutters, 'We paid you to be our teacher!' Carolina smiles in a kindly, relaxed way and waits for almost a minute. The pause might feel very long or awkward, but doesn't seem to worry the teacher. After this silence, another student suggests that it would be good to learn everyone's names. Rather than saying 'That's a good idea', Carolina passes the idea back to the class, 'What do you think? Should we do that?' and when many of them say 'yes', she asks, 'OK, how can we learn names in an interesting way?' Two students suggest a game. Carolina gets the class to decide which one to do and then asks the student who suggested it to organise it and run it. The class play the game.

Notice how, right from the start, Carolina is putting onto the students the onus of making the course what they need it to be and is showing them that she will not organise or save them. This is a different way of being a teacher than we are generally used to. The teacher is not riding in on a white horse to save everyone, but is quietly creating the conditions for the learners to take ownership of their course. One can imagine this course continuing with the teacher explaining any constraints (e.g. what book they have to use) and then getting students to decide what kind of lessons they want, how they want to work and so on.

It won't be easy. It takes a big leap of confidence on the teacher's part. It requires experience to know how long to wait, how far to push. Some students will get frustrated and feel cheated. There will be arguments and anger. Learner expectations – that it is *your* job to decide everything – may need to be addressed (before a deputation is queuing outside the Head's office to complain about you). The storming phase (see Chapter 3 Unit 2) will be a real storm. But after working through these, the net outcome may be astonishing: an energised, focussed, fully-engaged class – one that the teacher never has to say 'they are so unmotivated' about – because they are entirely in charge of their own learning (and it isn't her problem anyway).

Techniques: Small bursts of democracy

Even if you don't go for a fully learner-centred classroom, you can still make occasional use of many of the techniques listed above, or try one of these ideas for introducing learners' ideas and opinions into your lessons.

1 Menus

Offer students lists of things (perhaps a choice of special off-the-coursebook extras) that could be done in class, and allow them to select their favourites. This could be done once a month or once a half term, with you promising to do the most popular choices.

2 Speaker's Corner

Set up a corner of the room with a special rug or defined area of some sort (alternatively, a small raised platform, perhaps in the centre of room!). Agree a rule that anyone who goes there, at any point in a lesson, will be listened to for at least a minute. This could be a student, or the teacher.

3 Encourage questions

Encourage questions, especially the difficult, very confused, challenging, uncomfortable ones. These are all OK so long as you don't feel obliged to answer them all yourself, maintaining a 'teacher knows all' or 'teacher knows best' attitude. Say 'I don't know' or 'I'll get back to you' where appropriate, or get others to answer or research answers. And remember …

4 It's not either/or

You don't have to plump 100% for teacher-centred or learner-centred for a whole course. There is no reason why, if you wish to, you can't do both, on different days, in different lessons, as appropriate. But try not to confuse your class by giving mixed or unclear messages.

Technique: Making the case to students

Do the learners want learner-centredness? The common answer is often 'no', at least initially. Because of other current or previous experiences of education, learners may not expect to make any important decisions about their course or class. They may be used to being relatively passive and 'obedient' – being told what to do, having the teacher take little account of their wishes or preferences and respecting teacher decisions without much questioning. This can lead to deep-seated assumptions that teachers always know best about what to do and how to do it. Once we start to challenge this assumption, students may slowly realise that they are capable of making valid choices and decisions and that, if they do this, it is likely to lead to much greater engagement in the course and better results – because they are doing what they want to do in ways that they want to work.

1 Don't shy away from explaining why you believe in learner-centred work. Students won't necessarily understand the important reasons unless you point them out.
2 Ask questions that get students thinking about their own learning and discussing it. For example, 'Can I learn for you?' (To which the answer is obviously 'no'), 'How much does my teaching help you to learn?' (A little, I hope), 'Who has to do the hard work that helps you learn something?' (Only the student can do this).
3 Try some of the magic-dispelling strategies in the section below.

Technique: Casting off the wizard's cloak

Students often come to class with an extraordinary belief in the magical abilities of the teacher. They trust that he or she will know, as if by telepathy, exactly what they think, what they want and how they want to do it. But, of course, the teacher doesn't. All the teacher has is whatever information he or she can glean from written information, by observing, asking, talking and testing. It's important that students understand that the teacher is not a wizard and does not have mind-reading powers.

1 When students say, 'You know best, teacher' or similar comments, point out that you don't.
2 When students ask you a question you don't know the answer to, say 'I don't know'.
3 When students ask for advice, don't jump in with advice before you are fully aware of the problem and know if you can really help or not. (See Chapter 4 Unit 8 on *catalytic listening*.)
4 When students give up or can't find ideas, don't save them by offering instant solutions and ways out. These will be your solutions and ideas rather than theirs. Ask questions instead. Help them to save themselves.

Technique: You can't motivate anyone

You can't motivate anyone. This may sound a provocative statement, and certainly it's not what the majority of ELT teachers believe, but I think it's true and important.

A lot of teachers believe that they have the task of motivating their students and that this is one of the most important parts of their work. Teachers may moan that their classes are unmotivated and feel a desperate need to find ways to get them interested and engaged, so they try to be funnier, more amusing, more interesting or more entertaining at the front of class. They think that, without this, students will sit glumly and without engagement. Sometimes this becomes a real drain on the teacher's energy as they feel that they have to make each lesson more dramatic and exciting than the one before. It's one of the reasons that teaching can feel so exhausting.

The trouble is that when one tries to be fun and 'motivate' learners, the learners tend to sit back and expect a performance. If the performance is good, the learners are pleased (and perhaps think it was a 'good' lesson). If the performance is poor, they get bored and complain.

When a teacher sets out to motivate, the focus is on the teacher. The teacher finds him- or herself in an impossible situation: he or she expects to have to motivate the students, and students expect to have the teacher motivate them. This is not sustainable. It ends with disappointed students and worn-out teachers wondering, 'What more can I possibly give them?'

Humans are naturally motivated to learn. We have this from childhood. The problem is not finding ways to motivate people – it's finding a way of not closing this natural motivation down. Rewards, prizes, entertainment, enthusiasm, 'Do this for me', 'Do it to please me' may lead to superficial success, but they don't lead to long-term motivation. Schools, by their rules and lockstep teaching and the way they operate their systems to process large numbers of people in a way that is as untroublesome as possible, tend to close down natural motivation. They cannot generally cope well with individuals working at their own speed, enquiring in their own ways into whatever it is that is interesting to them at the moment.

However, the dangerous truth is that the best answer to 'my class is so unmotivated' is not to sing and dance and perform more at the front to class, but to find ways of letting students' natural motivation to start emerging again by allowing them to make decisions about their study, to redirect the work in small ways towards what interests them – in short, by making the class more learner-centred. This would mean, even to a very small degree, allowing students to make choices about what they study, what methods they use, what speed they work at. The more say we have in what we do, the more control we feel, the more engaged we are likely to be. Self-appropriated learning is motivating. In the average classroom, it may not seem possible to achieve this fully with 45 teenagers, but even small crumbs of democracy make a difference.

Technique: Learner-centred work in low-level classes

It can be more difficult to introduce elements of learner-centredness into classes where the learners' language level prevents any depth of discussion in English. In addition, many beginners may feel at sea with the new subject and expect a lot of direction and structuring from the teacher. However, the working habits you set up in these lessons will play a key role in setting expectations for many years of English learning to come, so issues of autonomy, democracy and motivation are worth addressing right from the start.

1 Discuss in their L1 if you can

If you can speak the same first language as the students, this means that you can raise and discuss many learner autonomy questions and issues from an early stage in the course. Just do it in L1 rather than in English.

2 Don't underestimate them

It's surprising how easy it is to equate low language level with limited ability to make autonomous decisions. Of course, the truth is that the students you are teaching are fully functioning humans of whatever age they are. Find ways to treat them just as you would advanced students of the same age and background.

3 Don't train them into over-dependency on the teacher

Just because students ask for help, don't assume that you have to do everything they ask for. Look for opportunities for students to do things themselves (e.g. checking answers against an answer sheet, finding the meaning of a word in the dictionary, etc.).

4 Train students to start making decisions about what to do

It's never too early to start students making choices (e.g., 'Which story shall we read tomorrow?' or 'Would you like to do grammar or speaking?'). So long as you can convey what needs to be decided, they can decide.

5 Get them to make tests for themselves

Even very low-level students can create little exercises for themselves (e.g. simple gap-fills), and of course, the creation of questions also helps to teach about what is being tested. Ask students to make three questions at the end of one lesson. Next lesson, let them do their own questions. Use this as a small step into getting them used to preparing more things for themselves.

Questions for reflection

- Where would you place your own classroom in the diagram on page 110? Is that where you would wish it to be?
- Has reading this unit changed your ideas about learner-centredness and motivation at all? In what ways?
- 'You can't motivate anyone.' Would you agree or argue this one?

4 | Key teacher interventions

The teacher affects the learning process by being him- or herself with a group of people and by doing things or saying things that lead (directly or indirectly) to some change in how that learning happens. The things the teacher does or says are *interventions*.

Some interventions may be very small (for example, a teacher might say, 'We'll do that tomorrow' or raise an eyebrow or press *play* on a CD player). Some may be large (for example, an explanation on the Present Perfect). Individually and cumulatively, they are central to the creation of the learning environment.

Interventions, whether pre-planned or spontaneous, need to be purposeful and effective. They are more than a formula of words or a set of actions. They are intentions made visible. The more aware we are of why we are intervening and what we hope to achieve by doing so, the more fine-tuned our interventions can be.

The following units gather together fourteen key types of intervention a teacher can make.

1 Being supportive

> I want the learners in my class to realise that I value them and care about them – which I really do. It's just that I'm not sure how to show it, or how appropriate it is to show it.

Aim

To show support to your students by affirming them and their worth.

Introduction

By creating an overtly supportive environment, you help your students to feel valued and in doing so, you help them to value themselves.

Being supportive is perhaps the crucial foundation stone to everything you do in class. If students feel valued and respected, this will result in good rapport. A positive classroom atmosphere will inevitably affect students' attitude towards the work they do in class and their level of engagement with the language.

Techniques: Showing support

Humans often feel great support for others, but can be reticent in showing it or stating it. But it's very powerful to say something supportive and can do a great deal to enhance the other person's self-esteem.

1 Paying attention

Attention is one of the most powerful gifts a person can give someone else. Make eye contact. Clear your head of your own concerns, your worries, random thoughts and distractions. Feel that all your energy is available for paying attention to the other person in a relaxed, unthreatening, supportive way. You can do this even if the other person is not speaking. You can show that you are *with* them, just in a look or a stance. On the receiving end, people blossom in the warm glow of this attention. It is very powerful, yet rather underestimated as a factor in classroom life. Just one warning: you have to feel it, not role play what you think it should look like. Beware of overdoing it, overacting.

2 Affirm and validate

Give a simple, clear, affirming comment to someone in your class. For example, tell a student something that you really like about the way that they behave in class. Say it as simply and clearly as you can. Be very concise rather than rambling at length; one short sentence is best. You could start, 'I really like the way ... '.

3 Be specific

Respond to a student's work, not with general bland praise, but stating specific things you have noticed about the work they put in or the scale of their achievement – such as how much time you observed them spend on the task or the number of new expressions they used. You could start 'I noticed that you … '.

4 Support not flattery

Be careful that what you offer is genuine support and not simply unrealistic flattery or vague praise.

Techniques: Being supportive in different ways

Being supportive doesn't only mean saying positive things. You can show support in everything you do and say, even the smallest, most apparently insignificant actions, passing comments and reactions. Rather than just saying things automatically, decide that you want to convey them with an added element of support.

1 Use people's names

Add names to comments and questions when appropriate, e.g. 'What do you think, Heidi?' feels more personal than 'What do you think?' Avoid overdoing it, as it can quickly sound false, e.g. 'Well, Marcel, I thought this was interesting. What do you think, Marcel?'

2 Good morning!

Imbue everyday greetings with genuine warmth. When students arrive at your class, say 'Hello' or 'Welcome' in a way that lets them know that you really mean it. Ask how they are. Engage in chat. Let them know that you do care about them.

3 Everyday interaction

Similarly, add a depth of support into all of your regular interactions. Try experimenting with how much support you can add into everyday words or phrases like 'yes' or 'Start now'.

4 Make eye contact

Don't avoid people's eyes. If you are low in confidence, it can be tempting to look at and talk to the room in general. On the receiving end, this will feel increasingly cold and distant. Get into regular, positive, warm, encouraging eye contact (as opposed to threatening or 'I'm watching you' eye contact) with as many students as possible.

5 Smile at people (lots)

As well as general, aimed-at-the-whole-class smiling, regularly direct warm smiles to individuals (and not just the good ones who cause you least bother). The act of smiling releases endorphins that actually make you feel like smiling!

6 Demonstrate that you enjoy being with them

Be someone who visibly enjoys what you do, what they do, what they say, things that go wrong. Do what you might do in the company of friends. Laugh at your own silliness. Sigh comically when you drop your pen. Use any gestures or expressions that come naturally to you.

7 Show support when the news is bad
If you have to convey negative results or bad news, make sure that the hearer knows that you fully support them and continue to believe in them.

8 Look outside the classroom
Show consideration for problems learners might have external to the class. Trust rather than be suspicious.

Technique: Support at specific moments

There will be many moments in your teaching day when you can show support to individual students, for example:

1 If you notice a student putting a lot of energy and attention into their work, comment on it.
2 If a student takes an active role in a group task, notice it and tell them that you have noticed it.
3 If a student does a good piece of work, put it in the noticeboard or washing line (see Chapter 1 Unit 8), or read it out.
4 If something is good, put positive reactions on written work; don't get locked into only commenting on negatives and errors.
5 If you spot a learner who is switched off and isn't doing anything, try genuinely asking if they are OK. Find out whether you can help, rather than automatically telling them off for laziness.

Questions for reflection

- Do you explicitly tell students what you like about how they work, or are your comments reserved only for the work they produce?
- How much do you make a point of picking out factual positive things to draw attention to and convey to students?
- When you add a stronger element of support, is there a point at which you start to sound insincere? Experiment, and find the best amount you can add to remain natural and without it sounding false or overdone.

■2 Asserting authority

> *When I ask students to be quiet, few students seem to listen. Half the class are chatting. Others are finishing the previous task. Two are arguing (discreetly). One or two are lost in thought, gazing out of the window.*

Aim

To discover and use your own natural authority, rather than relying on the power that comes from the job title and your position in the school hierarchy.

Introduction

Geoff Petty argues that rapport passes through two stages:

> *In the first phase, you achieve a position of power by virtue of your role as a teacher. If your students are never likely to challenge your authority, offer a brief prayer of thanks ... Phase two ... is a gradual shift from this formal teacher authority towards the teacher's personal authority ... The source of the teacher's power becomes the desire of the students to please the teacher and to build their own self-image through the teacher's approval.*

He quotes David Hargreaves who says that:

> *A teacher starting out with a new class must insist that the students accept his or her 'formal authority'. Teachers must convey that their authority is legitimate, that it exists to maximise learning; and they must show confidence in their ability to enforce their authority.*

These quotes present a fairly widely agreed on contemporary view of power, authority and relationships in the classroom: establish authority first, and only become a human later. When I first started as a secondary school teacher, my experienced trainer gave me (quite seriously) the classic advice, 'Don't even smile at them until Christmas'. (Petty quotes the even more cautious version, 'Never smile before Easter!') He suggests that you should:

> *Stride about the room as if you are absolutely confident of your ability to control the group. Appear to be self-confident, relaxed and in control – especially when you are not.*

Clearly a classroom without respect and authority is going to be troublesome. This is especially the case with secondary-age students. If you feel that you are likely to have discipline problems or you feel that your own confidence levels are a bit wobbly, then you might do well to listen to Petty and Hargreaves. There is a depth of common sense and experience in their advice.

For myself, I have never been comfortable with, or able to use, this approach. I find that I can only teach if I am me, and behave as me and discover ways to be authoritative as me. I am also convinced that most students will easily see through the 'striding' solution, should I try to put it on.

What I need to do is find the natural authority in me and believe in it myself. Rather than acting more authoritatively than I actually feel (which will be seen through), I need to find a way to live and breathe an appropriate authority that is honest to my life and attitudes. I need to find ways that allow us to discuss and agree things without always relying on the hierarchical power residing in my job title. All my natural instincts lean towards democratic solutions to any life problem; I fail to see why this is not equally possible in a room full of interesting, interested, questioning teenagers or adults, as much as it is in any other human meeting place.

Technique: Attracting attention

There are some simple, effective ways to attract attention to yourself, for example, when you need to make an announcement:

- Say, 'Listen'.
- Tap the table three times loudly and clearly.
- Ring a little bell (e.g. a hotel reception bell).
- Turn a rainstick upside down (making the noise of falling rain!).
- Use any other noise-making device that you like.

Interestingly, the most effective attention-getters often seem to be the quieter, gentler, less obtrusive methods. If you use a loud alarm or speak through a loudhailer, don't be surprised if everyone ignores you!

Many teachers train their students in the following technique:

- When a student sees the teacher holding up their hand, they should stop working or talking and also raise their hand. As people notice others putting up their hands, the room quickly fills with hands, and the room quietens and focuses on the teacher.

Technique: Gathering authority

In a classroom where students do a lot of different tasks, making sure that they understand what to do is crucial. Obviously, the delivery of the actual instructions is a big part of this (see Chapter 4 Unit 3), but even when the teacher's language is well-graded and the instructions well-structured and easily comprehensible, it can still all go wrong because the students were not focussed and listening with attention. This then leads to requests for repetition of the instructions or muddled doing of the task itself. How much better to make sure that students are really tuned in and ready for the instruction before you even start to speak!

What teachers need to do, before they even open their mouths, is to gather authority to themselves, asserting themselves as people that students should listen and pay attention to. In becoming the still, central focus of the classroom, the teacher pulls the unfocussed students' attention from the hundred things they are doing to a narrow focus on him- or herself.

The following technique is for well-intentioned, noisy, chatty or over-excited classes, rather than for badly behaved or ill-disciplined ones. When you want to say something important to a class (such as an instruction or an announcement):

1   Stand in a location where you can see everybody. This does not have to be the front of the room. At this point, it doesn't matter if you can't make eye contact or if their backs are turned.
2   Just wait a little. Feel a sense of 'gathering authority' to yourself:
    • Breathe slowly, deeply, confidently.
    • Stand a little straighter.
    • Let a sense of feeling unworried seep through you.
    • Look and feel like someone who is about to say something important.
    • Believe in your authority as it grows inside you. You are not misusing or abusing your authority. You are their teacher telling them something that they need to know.
3   When you are ready, say quietly, firmly, clearly and confidently, 'Listen'. Place a cupped hand to your ear and keep it there. Do not shout. Do not use a teacher 'public-announcement' volume. It should be loud enough to be only just audible, heard above the background chatter. Say it once only.
4   Return to your calm waiting. Don't look anxious, angry or impatient. Keep your hand to your ear. Move your head around to make direct eye contact with every student who looks at you. Look like someone who is confidently expecting quiet.
5   It may be that students are already starting to quieten down. If so, let the room manage itself as much as possible. Some students may wonder what is happening and turn around. Catch and hold their gaze for a second or two. If students start *shushing* other students, let them.
6   It's wonderful when a whole class quietens down from just the one 'Listen', but don't worry if it doesn't. Gather authority to yourself and say 'Listen' again. You can do this more times if you need to, but do allow a little space between each go. If possible, avoid getting into the standard louder and louder repetition of so many classroom instructions.

You might guess that the louder a class, the louder you'd need to give your instructions. But it's one of the paradoxes of classroom management that the obvious everyday solution doesn't always work so well, and it may actually be the polar opposite that succeeds; in this case, being very calm, assured and quiet.

→ For another classroom paradox, see *Walking away* in Chapter 5 Unit 5.

Technique: Using L1

It makes sense to mainly use English for classroom instructions and orders, as this will provide a lot of incidental exposure to the language for students. However, there may be occasions when it's useful to say something in their first language (L1) – even if it is just the first word or two, e.g. *Hoert zu* ('Listen'). The surprise of hearing something in their own tongue might have the effect of helping to attract attention or emphasising that what you are about to say is special or important. Of course, if you start to use L1 a lot in class, it will soon lose its impact, and students might start to expect more and more in their own language.

Technique: Associate a specific place with orders or instructions

Choose a place in the room that would be suitable for giving orders or instructions from, but which, otherwise, is not a spot you might typically stand at. Whenever you need to make an authoritative intervention, go to the same place in the room. Students will soon learn to associate your moving towards that place as a cue for heightened attention.

Technique: Giving successful orders

A task instruction (see Chapter 4 Unit 3) is, of course, a kind of order, one that the listener can if they wish respond to, question, discuss and conceivably choose not to follow. In this section, we are looking at orders that the speaker expects the listener to obey, usually without much discussion. They are a use of hierarchical power to require someone else to do something and can be located on a continuum as illustrated below.

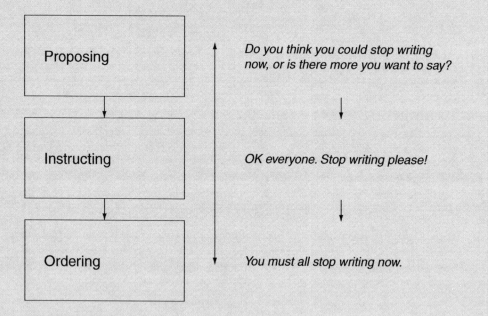

Proposing — *Do you think you could stop writing now, or is there more you want to say?*

Instructing — *OK everyone. Stop writing please!*

Ordering — *You must all stop writing now.*

In most (though not all) educational establishments, it is assumed that a teacher has the right to give commands, to tell someone that they should do something. The students, school and maybe parents or fee payers generally expect teachers to take responsibility for ensuring that time is used well, that learning takes place and that disruptions are kept to a minimum.

In traditional classrooms, this power has at times been overused or misused, but that doesn't mean that it can't be well used.

For example, picture two teenage students who are chatting and laughing, having their own conversation in the middle of the classroom while you are trying to explain a piece of grammar, ignoring requests to be quiet. This is proving a disruption and an impediment to the rest of the class hearing you or concentrating. What can you do?

This seems an appropriate moment for the valid use of your authority. Assuming that polite requests have failed, there will come a point at which you need to tell them what to do. Depending on the age of the students, the place where you are teaching and your hierarchical relationship to them, there may be various options in terms of what you require them to do, for example, telling them to go outside the room to talk (for adults) or to stop talking (for teenage school students).

To give successful orders:

1 Don't speak when angry or irritated. As far as possible, remove any negative emotion from yourself before speaking, even if this means that you delay some seconds before speaking.
2 You need to get attention. Say 'Listen', or the names of the people you want to give the order to.
3 Make steady, relaxed eye contact with the person, or people, you want to talk to. If you cannot immediately catch their eyes, try again, for example, by repeating their names.
4 Don't shout, unless it's absolutely necessary to be heard. Shouting tends to add to the temperature of events and increase tensions. Above all, avoid getting into a shouting match, where you and the person you are speaking to each come back with a louder and louder response.
5 The first time you speak, speak slightly quieter than normal. While this runs the risk of being completely ignored, it might also help to start calming things down.
6 Find a firm, matter-of-fact, down-to-earth voice tone.
7 Speak slowly, rather than quickly. Let each word have its own weight.
8 Keep what you say brief and to the point. Let the facts speak wherever possible.
9 Add 'please' if you are able to say it honestly.
10 Avoid ridicule and sarcasm.
11 If useful, point out factually how their behaviour is causing a problem for others.
12 Keep to the current event, avoiding generalisations or statements about other occasions when similar things happened. If you need to address these, do it later, after the current situation has been resolved.
13 A basic order uses an imperative, e.g. 'Do this!' 'Stop talking!' 'Come over here!'
14 To strengthen an order or make it sound more formal, use modal verbs, e.g. 'You must stop talking now', 'You have to come over here right now'.

Questions for reflection

- Do you sometimes find yourself speaking – then shouting – louder and louder for attention? Does the increased volume usually work or not? How do you feel when you have to call very loudly before learners even start to listen?
- What is your initial reaction to the 'paradox' mentioned at the end of the Technique *Gathering authority?* Why might this work differently from everyday life?
- What are the most difficult classroom orders you have to give?
- Think of a lesson (or course) in which you didn't manage to assert your authority appropriately. What caused the problems and what could you have done differently?

3 Giving instructions

> When I give an instruction, I sometimes seem to confuse students. They don't know what to do in the task, and I have to spend five minutes going round everyone, checking and telling them again what to do.

Aim
To give clear, effective instructions.

Introduction
Even though they may sometimes only last as little as five or ten seconds, the times when you give instructions are critical moments in any lesson. Get them wrong, and they will cause problems that ripple through the following activity and on into the rest of the lesson. In many classes that I've observed, a whole activity has failed because of student misunderstanding about what it is they were expected to do. Sadly, it's very often the learners who get blamed for doing things wrongly, when the real problem was actually the original instruction.

This unit looks at the instructions themselves. Remember that for an instruction to be heard and understood, you will first need to make sure that students are listening to you and paying attention. (See Chapter 4 Unit 2.)

Techniques: Giving instructions to lower-level classes
The reason that some instructions are unclear or misunderstood is often because they are too long, too complex or delivered too fast. Try some of these techniques:

1 Use grammar and vocabulary that is at or below the learners' current level.
2 Use short sentences. Don't put more than one instruction in one sentence. Chunk your instructions: one piece of information at a time.
3 'The least that is enough.' Don't ramble. Keep instructions simple, concise and to the point. Avoid digressions.
4 Speak a little more slowly and clearly than you would normally do.
5 Pause after each instruction to allow understanding: processing time.
6 Sequence the instructions. Deliver them in the order that you want students to follow them.
7 Use signposting language, e.g. 'First ...', 'Then ...', 'Finally ...'.
8 Where practical, get students to immediately do each separate part of the instruction, step by step, rather than waiting until they have heard the whole sequence.
9 If students can see your lips as you speak, this can aid comprehension.

10   Write a few key words on the board as you speak to help listening, understanding and memory of the instructions. Alternatively, use little sketched icons (for example, a pen and paper) to help students.

11   Use gestures and facial expressions to support your instructions.

12   'Punch' the keywords, i.e. say the essential words in a sentence with a little more stress and separation from other words than you might typically give it. For example, 'Write your answers on the … *other* … side of the paper'.

13   It's often worth checking if an instruction has been understood. Rather than asking 'Do you understand?' ask a question that checks if they caught specific points, for example, 'How many questions are you going to answer?'

14   Choose the best moment to give out any materials, or tell students to open books, exercises, etc. Once they are staring at a text, they will lose concentration on what you are saying. It's often best to keep books closed and materials undistributed until after the key instructions have been delivered. Having said that, with some activities, students will need to have materials to hand, in order to clearly follow the detail of an instruction.

15   Don't let students start doing the task before you have finished giving and checking instructions with the whole class. Having some people rushing into the work distracts others and adds to the noise level. And, of course, they may well not have fully understood what to do anyway. Say, 'Wait – don't start yet', and make sure everyone really knows what to do before you say, 'OK – start now'.

16   Until you are comfortable with giving good clear instructions, plan them before the lesson.

Technique: Recognising elements of an instruction

Scott Thornbury categorises a number of possible features of an instruction in his A-Z of ELT. You could use this framework to put together some good instructions when you are planning a lesson. Any single instruction could contain all – or more likely, some – of these elements:

1   **A frame,** i.e. a way of indicating that the last activity has finished and a new activity is about to begin. Typically this takes a verbal form, such as 'Right … ', 'OK now … '.

2   **A brief summary of the task and its purpose,** such as 'We're going to play a game to practise asking questions … '.

3   **The organisation,** i.e. whether the task is to be done in pairs, groups or individually.

4   **The procedure,** i.e. what it is that the learners actually will be doing – such as filling in a questionnaire, or rehearsing a dialogue, etc.

5   **The mode,** i.e. whether it is a speaking or a writing task, for example.

6   **The outcome,** i.e. what they will be required to do as a result of the task, e.g. report their results to the class, perform the dialogue, etc.

7   **A strategy** to adopt in order to facilitate the task, as when the teacher tells learners just to skim a text initially, before reading it intensively.

8   **The timing,** i.e. how long the learners have to complete the task (roughly).

9   **A cue,** such as 'OK, you can start' so that learners know when to begin the task.

Technique: Being very clear about concrete details

Students often get lost because while they understand the general task (e.g. do an exercise), they are unclear about the specific details of what they have to do (e.g. 'Think about the answers, but don't write anything', 'Write full answers in your exercise book', 'Do only questions one to eight', 'Don't write whole sentences – just the correction', 'Write whole sentences', 'You need to think of three suggestions or more' and so on).

It's a good idea to emphasise these very clearly when you speak, perhaps repeating the details and checking them back with students. You don't usually need to write a whole instruction on the board (though it sometimes helps), but it's often a good idea to write up the key details in shorthand, e.g:

- Qs 1 to 8 ONLY
- Write whole sentences.

Techniques: Showing materials, doing worked examples and giving demonstrations

The clearest way to help learners understand what they have to do is usually to show them.

1 Indicate the tasks

Hold up any documents or books they need to work with. Point clearly at the exercise or text. Don't take your hand away too quickly.

2 Show materials

If learners will need to use any materials in a task (e.g. word cards), hold these up, and read out what is on one or two examples. If you have an interactive whiteboard, you could show a zoomed-in version on it. Otherwise, you could make an enlarged photocopy.

3 Do worked examples

When you set an exercise, do one or two worked examples on the board before students start to work on it themselves. When you show example questions, allow a little thinking time for the whole class to work out possible answers and suggest them to you. It may be useful to write up a wrong suggestion and elicit reactions and reasons why it is incorrect – all before filling in the correct answer.

4 Demonstrate the task yourself

You can deliver a monologue of yourself doing the task, making your actions and thought process explicit. For example, 'So, now I'm looking at the photographs of different notices. I want to find any words that are wrong. Ah ... "Do not walk in the grass" – That sounds wrong. I'm crossing out "in" and writing "on".'

5 Role play the task with a student

For pair work or group tasks, get a volunteer student or students up front with you to do a live role-play demonstration of the task. You do not need to do the whole thing. Usually, it's sufficient to show how to start the activity.

Techniques: Reducing the level of detail in your instructions

Part of the act of teaching involves training your class into ways of working that you use. A class that is doing a pair-work information gap for the first time will need careful step-by-step explanations (about how to form pairs, what the task involves, what to ask, etc.) and demonstrations (to show how to sit, how to hold the pieces of paper, how to take turns, etc.). However, after they have done this kind of activity a few times, full-blown detailed instructions should be less and less necessary. It may be possible to reduce the instruction giving to 'Get into pairs' (pausing while they do), 'Keep your picture secret' (while handing out the pictures) and 'Find what is different in your partner's picture'. You might even want to reduce some of these even more, perhaps to single keywords or gestures: 'OK ... Pairs!' If the activity is a type that you regularly do with the class (e.g. back-to-back telephone information gap), it may be sufficient to say the name of the activity, and students will immediately move into the right positions.

Techniques: Making up for bad instructions

While your aim is, obviously, to give good instructions first time, they won't always work. You need to find out quickly if there is a problem and then retrieve the situation.

1 Monitor for potential problems

As soon as you have finished giving an instruction and learners have started on their new task, you will usually need to check to find out if they really know what to do and are doing it. Wander around, unobtrusively listening in to speaking tasks or reading what they are writing. If you see a lot of hesitant or puzzled students, you may have a problem!

2 Avoid multiple repetitions

If you find that a number of students keep asking you for help because they didn't understand the instructions, it's usually better to cut your losses and re-give the instruction to the whole class, rather than repeating it one-to-one forty times. Find a suitable location, say, 'Listen' and get the whole class's attention; then give the original instruction again, allowing space for checking and questions.

Techniques: Giving instructions to higher-level classes

At lower levels, teachers need to pay careful attention to their choice of language, speed of delivery and complexity of ideas in instructions. These remain important at higher levels – after all, the priority is that students successfully understand what they have to do – but it is also valid to exploit instruction-giving to help tune learners into listening to more natural speech. You might want to deliberately introduce some elements of everyday discourse into your instructions:

1 Sentence headers: 'What I want you to do is ... ', 'So what I'm going to ask you to do is ... '.
2 Normal pronunciation features of fluent connected speech: weak forms, assimilation and elision.
3 Hesitations and filler chunks: *um, er, I dunno, I suppose.*
4 Vague language: *sort of, things, thingamajig, about.*
5 Oral sentences that flow rather than have discernible beginnings and endings: '... and put all your answers in this box, and then you're gonna need to get together with ... '.
6 Talk around the task – for example, suggesting strategies for doing an exercise or telling learners the *why* as well as the *how.* So, for example, not just, 'Write answers to Exercise 3', but adding, 'This is designed to help you choose the correct particle for the phrasal verb. A good way to approach it would be to ... '. Alternatively, you could ask the learners what they think the aim of an activity might be.

Techniques: Learners give instructions

1 Learners read from the book

In lower-level classes, learners can read the instructions aloud from their coursebook, and you can then show an example or check if they were understood or not. While individual learners' pronunciation will perhaps be hard to understand, doing this will usefully slow the instruction down and encourage students to read it in their own books.

2 Learners read from cards

Split up the instructions you need to give into separate small parts and put each one on a separate card. Number them in order, e.g. (1) 'Stand up', (2) 'Find a partner', (3) 'Ask your partner your first question. Write their answer on your paper', (4) 'Find a new partner', etc.

In class, hand out the cards, each to a different student. Ask the first student to read card number one out, and students do what they are asked to do. When ready, indicate that the second student can read their card. The students follow that instruction, and then the third student reads theirs ... and so on.

Using a technique like this involves extra preparation from the teacher and may be quite time-consuming in class. It is only worth doing if you consider the benefits to outweigh these issues – for example, it might get more students involved in the lesson, may give a chance for quieter students to speak when they read the cards and could prepare students for a greater step towards autonomy (e.g. running a whole task themselves) later on in the course.

3 Learners correct the teacher

A good way to build learner confidence and start training your class in taking a little more responsibility is by deliberately giving wrong instructions yourself, and getting them to correct you. You don't need to explain what you are doing, but make the first one or two mistakes so obvious that they will catch on quickly. They may be hesitant to correct you at first, but if you maintain a happy, 'silly me' atmosphere, they will soon get into it. For example:

Teacher:	Turn to page 82. Look at the text about turtles.
Students:	Uh? 82? No text! ... Teacher! It's on page 79!
Teacher:	Oh ... sorry. Yes, you're right. So the text about spaceships on page 79 –
Students:	Turtles.
Teacher:	Turtles. Yes, OK. Look at the ten pictures.
Students:	There are six pictures.
Teacher:	Yes ... six ... of course! And there are ten sentences.
Students:	SIX!
Teacher:	Six ... thank you. Six sentences above the pictures. ...
Students:	Underneath! (And so on ...)

In deliberately subverting your own authority and omniscience a little, you actually help to create a more cohesive, cooperative, democratic classroom. Because you are seen to have made mistakes deliberately and with preparation rather than because of carelessness or ignorance, it may even have the effect of increasing their respect for you. Paradoxically, because the learners were listening so carefully and with such engagement to what you said (trying to catch you out), there is likely to be a much greater understanding of what to do in the subsequent task than if you had given 100% correct instructions.

4 Learners prepare instructions

In classes that have sufficient English, individual learners (e.g. early finishers of the previous task) can be briefed to prepare to give instructions to others for the next task. This might be to a group of students rather than to the whole class. Where possible, allow time for them to practise with you and get feedback before they do it for real. Getting learners to take on 'teacher' roles can be very confidence-building and motivating.

5 Learners plan and organise

In a fully democratic classroom where learners have taken an active role in deciding what to do and how to do it, the need for teacher instructions naturally diminishes. The learners will be much more in charge of what is done, when and how and can take responsibility for organising work themselves.

Questions for reflection

• Do students ever get confused by your instructions? Which element seems to cause the biggest problems (and could most usefully be improved on): language level, complexity of the thing being explained or speed of delivery?

4 Telling

> *I find doing an 'input' rather embarrassing. I get the feeling that students think I'm boring to listen to. And then I always end up talking too much.*

Aim

To convey facts, information or procedural guidelines that will be useful for students to know – in a way that is clear, comprehensible and memorable.

Introduction

Teachers need to tell students things for two main reasons: (1) to explain what to do and how to do it, i.e. organisation, procedures, activity rules and so on (see Chapter 4 Unit 3), and (2) to convey facts and information that form part of the teaching content of the lesson (this unit).

Geoff Petty offers an interesting thought experiment:

> *Imagine going to an evening class to study GCSE biology and finding that the teacher simply read from a textbook, or sounded as if he or she was doing so. Why would this be unsatisfactory?*

He suggests a number of problems:

> *Our short-term memory would soon be swamped and with no time to process the new information, it would never become structured enough to pass into the long-term memory, and so it would quickly be forgotten. Nor would we have any chance to practise using the ideas that we were learning. There is more to teaching than telling.*

Curious then that telling students things still plays such a significant role in so much teaching, even in language teaching.

Telling things to students was for many years seen as the core central job of the teacher, almost even a definition of teaching itself. The stereotypical teacher at the front of class talking at his or her students was conveying (or attempting to convey) facts and information. Whether the students managed to receive and learn those things would be open to speculation.

Nowadays we often call this kind of teaching 'input'. While many input stages in lessons will include elements of *Eliciting* and *Guided discovery* (see Chapter 4 Unit 5), there is still also a valid role for a straightforward teacher explanation. However, because of the limited language abilities of classes, we need to be careful that this is comprehensible and useful. Teachers who give long explanations may not realise how little of what they say actually gets through.

Technique: Preparing good explanations

It's appropriate to give teacher explanations to convey facts or information if you can honestly agree with these two statements:

- 'I think there are some things my class need to know and the most effective and efficient way for them to find out about them is for me simply to tell them.'
- 'In this case, I don't feel that it might be more helpful to make use of more interactive ways of helping students to construct knowledge' (e.g. eliciting, guided discovery).

Some considerations:

1 What is the clearest way that I can convey this information?
2 How long do I expect it to take? How long is the absolute longest I should take?
3 Can I support my explanation with written examples, diagrams, PowerPoint slides, visual aids and notes on the board?
4 Can I convey this information in a short statement, or does it need a longer 'lecture' type of method?
5 Is the learners' role simply to listen? What else must they do?
6 Is there scope for a listening task to help focus listeners?
7 Is there scope for interaction within the telling?
8 When can listeners give feedback, respond or ask questions?
9 What is the balance of *me* talking to *others* talking during the telling?
10 How will I know if the learners have understood?
11 What kind of record will the learners have? Their own notes? A handout from me?
12 If learners take their own notes, how can I ensure that these are accurate and useful?
13 Can anyone else give all or part of the explanation? What preparation would they need? How could I support them?

Techniques: Structuring and delivering an explanation well

1 Signpost well

Explicitly indicate where parts of what you are saying start and stop. Announce what you are going to talk about before each new stage. For example, 'First, I'm going to tell you how to make passive sentences about the past …', 'OK, so now we're going to look at the verb forms …'

2 Start with things they know

Revisit and remind students about them. Move on, small step by small step towards things that are new for them. Build new understanding on the foundations of what is already understood.

3 Speak to people, not to the room or to the board

Keep making eye contact with different people. Talk for a short time (e.g. a sentence or two) directly to one person, then to another. This may feel odd at first, but try it! Tell what you have to say to humans, rather than as a speech to the ceiling or the back wall.

4 Use your voice

Making small alterations to how you say things greatly increases the clarity of explanations:

- Use pauses, changes of volume, changes of pitch, hesitation noises and repetitions.
- Change pace occasionally. Speak very slowly or do a few words very fast.
- *Punch*[1] key words (i.e. say them with slightly more stress and a pause before and after). For example, 'The verb we need here is the ... *infinitive* ... not the past form'[1].

5 Use yourself

Use gestures, facial expressions, your hands, e.g.:

- Make a puzzled expression when you outline a problem.
- Hold your hands out, palms up, to make a rhetorical question (i.e. one that you are not really expecting any student to answer, but which you will go on to answer yourself as part of your explanation).
- Count on your fingers to indicate first point, second point, third point – or first, second, third word in a sentence, etc.
- Raise eyebrows when you state important points.
- Bang an imaginary table, or thump your fists together to emphasise a point.

- Make a 'karate chop' movement for sudden or dramatic points.
- Find personal gestures for important words and expressions (e.g. a rolling hand movement for 'a long time' e.g a sweeping, side-to-side hand movement for 'never').
- Move around rather than staying rooted to one spot. Change place when you start a new part of the talk, e.g. walk from the side of the room to the board.

6 Include visual support

Giving people something to look at helps support what you say. Use diagrams (pre-prepared or drawn as you go). Use tables. Use flow charts. Add to a list of key words on the board. Use flashcards and pictures.

---

[1] NB Take care if you want to *punch* a weak form word. By stressing it, you change it into a strong form and are now offering an incorrect and actually misleading pronunciation model, e.g. 'We say ... *AN* ... egg, not a egg'. Students being students, you can be sure that '*AN* egg' is the one thing they will remember from that day's lesson and will copy your wrong pronunciation, learn it and repeat it back to you forever after!

7 Beware 'Death by PowerPoint'

In the connected 21st century classroom, it has become very tempting to put every word of an input presentation onto PowerPoint slides and then have a lesson that involves showing the students the slides while the teacher reads all the words on the slides aloud. This is a guaranteed recipe to turn the whole room off. Use PowerPoint to support your teaching (e.g. diagrams, key words, images), not to script it.

Technique: Instant playback

If you need to give long input explanations, it's important to devise ways to help the learners listen, understand, make notes and remember. This is one way of doing that:

1 Put students into groups of three to five.
2 Explain what is going to happen, i.e. stages three to five below.
3 Give a small section of your input, not more than about one to three minutes. The students should listen carefully without taking notes.
4 As soon as you stop, the groups can get together, discuss and see if they can agree on what was said. If your group is monolingual or has groups of students with shared languages, you could let them discuss in their first language.
5 When they have agreed, each person can then take notes of the important message. You might want to ask for a brief summary from one or two groups (just to check that they are on the right lines) before you move on. Alternatively, allow students to go and have a quick look at another group's notes to see if they have got the same sort of understanding.
6 You continue with the next part of the input, and then groups meet up again, and so on.
7 At the end, ask each group to make a summary poster covering the most important points.

Technique: Bite-sized input

There are many mid-lesson occasions when a little piece of bite-sized input is just what is needed, for example:

1 **The correct word,** e.g. 'This is a *bench*.'
2 **Short grammar rules,** e.g. 'We say, "If I go to London … ", not "*If I will go to London…*". After *if*, we don't use *will*.'
3 **Giving correct answers to exercises,** e.g. 'The family bought the new caravan in December.'
4 **Confirming students' correct answers,** e.g. 'Roberta's right. It's *walked* not *walking*.'
5 **Correction of a spelling error,** e.g. 'You spell it with double t – *fit > fitted*.'
6 **Correct pronunciation,** e.g. 'Listen. This word is pronounced *mountains*.'

The key to doing such bite-sized inputs successfully is to keep them concise and clear. If working with lower-levels, grade your language to make sure that you use grammar and vocabulary that is wholly or mostly within their current level. Don't embed the short, clear piece of information in lots of unnecessary surrounding wrapping.

Questions for reflection

- What sorts of things are best told? What sorts of things are best discovered? What sorts of things are best learnt through doing/practice?
- How much telling do you typically do? How efficient is it? Does it feel useful, or is this something that could be reduced?

5 Eliciting

> 'I think I probably tell my students lots of things that they could tell me ... if I ever gave them the chance.'

Aim

To draw language, information and ideas from the students, rather than telling them everything.

Introduction

When there is some factual information that students need to know, simply telling them those facts may be the fastest and most efficient way of working. However, if this technique is used at length, repeatedly or exclusively, the amount of information may quickly become overwhelming for students. More worryingly, although the students have been present in a room where someone is telling them things, there is no guarantee that these things will have been heard, understood or learnt. As a learning strategy, just listening to someone else talking at you is not particularly involving or motivating.

Eliciting is the technique of drawing things from students, mainly by asking questions, rather than using teacher explanation. It leads to greater involvement, encourages thinking and nudges the learners towards making discoveries for themselves.

Technique: Learners tell you about a picture

One of the simplest, but most important ways of eliciting is when you invite students to look at a picture (perhaps in the coursebook, on the interactive whiteboard or on a flashcard – as part of a lead-in to studying a text or topic).

It would obviously be possible to say:

> Look at this picture. You can see a café in a busy city street. Three people are sitting at a table on the pavement having coffee, but inside, if you look carefully, you can see that something is happening. The manager is handing a lot of money over to the man with long hair. Maybe he is holding a gun. We can't see very clearly.

However, this approach is not very interesting or involving and crucially, it requires no thinking of any kind on the learners' part. They can just sit and nod.

To elicit instead of tell, we simply need to turn our statements into questions, leaving it up to the students to look, think, decide and say the answers. In this example, student responses are given in brackets:

Look at this picture. What can you see? (A café.) Where is it? (On a street.) Where's the street? (In a city.) Is it busy or empty? (Very busy.) What are these people doing? (Having coffee.) Are there any more people in the picture? (No.) Look carefully. Look inside. (Some people are inside the café.) What's happening inside? (Someone is giving money to someone.) A little money – change maybe? (No. A big pile of notes.) Why is he doing that? (Maybe the other man has a gun. Maybe he's a robber.)

By introducing the picture in this way, students are actively involved, looking carefully, noticing things, making hypotheses, drawing conclusions – and they will probably be much more interested in reading any follow-on text to find out if their interpretations and guesses were correct.

Techniques: Effective eliciting

1 Make sure the class can hear

When you elicit, it's important that everyone can hear answers given by other students. Make sure that students speak loud enough. Use techniques like Walking away (see Chapter 5 Unit 5). Summarise or echo if necessary.

2 Use a natural-sounding 'slightly puzzled' intonation

Questions sound more inviting if it sounds like you really don't know the answer (rather than sounding like a bored teacher checking answers to an exercise he or she already knows the answers to).

3 Elicit, then give feedback

If learners are speculating about a picture, it doesn't matter very much if there are a number of different ideas from different people, as none of them is 'correct'. However, if you elicit about something factual (for example, helping students to work out a grammar rule), then there is definitely a correct answer, and it is crucial that, at some point, you tie up the speculative discussion and give feedback. Often this will mean confirming what is correct. When not done, this can be a major cause of learner confusion and 'mislearning'. The following classroom excerpts show teachers confirming or giving feedback:

- 'So, three of you thought that the Past Tense is *drived*. Two students said *drove*. Well, the correct answer is *drove*.'
- 'The picture does look like a supermarket, doesn't it? In fact, it is a church!'
- 'Your answers are very close, but not quite correct. Think again about *why* he caught the bus.'

4 Wait a bit

After you ask a question, allow thinking time. Don't hurry them too much. Don't answer your own questions!

5 You can't elicit things they don't know and can't guess

Many things can be elicited, but not everything. I could elicit what students think I had for breakfast this morning (because there are some obvious likely answers they could try first, and because my students know me and might be able to make an informed guess), but it might be a waste of time to elicit my brother-in-law's name (as this would just involve a lot of random guesses) or a grammatical correction to a sentence when students have had no guidance or previous knowledge.

6 Be careful of asking too many hypothetical questions

'What happened?' is much easier to understand and to answer than 'What might have happened?'

7 Ask questions that move learners forward

If the learner already knows the answer to a question in full and learns or notices nothing new, the question simply leads to a display of knowledge, but not to further learning.

8 Remember that you have options in who you ask

Questions can be nominated (i.e. to a named individual) or open (i.e. to anyone). If nominated, the name can come before the question (e.g. 'Juan, What's the past of go?') or after it (e.g. 'What's the past of go? Juan?').

9 Avoid over-eliciting

Being asked questions all the time could become dull and counterproductive. Use eliciting as long as it is productive and enjoyable, but remain open to the possibility of varying your techniques as needed. Some things may be best told as information. You may also decide that students would benefit from other input methods, for example, to follow a lecture presentation and take notes.

Technique: Socratic questions

You can elicit in many ways (for example, by using pictures, gestures, gapped sentences on the board), but the most important way is with Socratic questions.

A Socratic question is one that has the intention of leading the learners to realise or discover something for themselves, possibly something that they already half know or are capable of working out for themselves, given appropriate help. The question may reveal a contradiction, inconsistency or false assumption in a student's understanding, which they can then be helped to clarify.

A common sequence of Socratic questions in language teaching might be:

Ask questions to find out what the learners already know about a subject –and to remind them about what they know.

Ask questions to help the learners focus on new things, leading the learner forward one step at a time, with each new question building on what the previous answer revealed.

The teacher will often need to introduce small pieces of new information into this sequence as it is revealed that the learner does not know something they need to know. For example:

Teacher:	So what do you think the past form is for the verb *blow*? (Writes *blow* on the board.)
Student 1:	Blowed.
Teacher:	Do we use -*ed* with all verbs?
Student 2:	No. Some are irregular verbs.
Teacher:	So ... is *blow* regular or irregular?
Student 1:	Blowed ... yes.
Teacher:	(Smiles and shakes head 'no'.) It's irregular. Can you guess what the irregular form is?
Student 2:	Blowed ... um ...
Teacher:	(Writes up *know* on the board.) What about this?
Student 3:	Knew.
Teacher:	(Nods and adds *knew* to board.)
Student 2:	Ah ... maybe ... blow ... blew?

It's not the formulation of the words that makes a question Socratic, but *why* it is asked. For example, the question, 'What endings can be added to this word?' could be used to elicit displays of knowledge or to assess or mark what the students know. However, if the teacher's intention is to encourage thinking, guide discovery, challenge assumptions or uncover new learning, then it is Socratic.

In asking a Socratic question, a teacher often needs to adopt the role of an enquiring person who does not know the answer. There is an element of fibbing in this: the teacher obviously *does* know the answers (in most cases).

Richard Paul suggested a taxonomy of Socratic questions. There are six types:

1 Questions to clarify underlying concepts.
2 Questions that probe assumptions.
3 Questions about reasons and evidence.
4 Questions about implications and consequences.
5 Questions about positions, viewpoints or perspectives.
6 Questions about the question.

Technique: Using Socratic questions to focus on grammar

The following are some sample questions that could all be used Socratically. They are classified according to Paul's taxonomy (see section above).

1 Clarifying underlying concepts
- What's the name of this piece of grammar?
- What words should be written here?
- What time are we talking about?
- Is this sentence correct?

2 Probing assumptions
- Are there any other words that you could use?
- Are any different endings possible?
- If I changed this word, would the sentence still be correct?
- Do you think this could be said in a different way?

3 Reasons and evidence
- Why does the word have this ending?
- Why do you think that?
- Why is the verb in this form?
- Have you ever heard anyone using this?

4 Implications and consequences
- How does this connect to what we learnt yesterday?
- Do you think you would use this language more in writing or in speaking?
- Why is this important?

5 Position, viewpoints and perspective
- What makes this difficult for you?
- Which part of this do you think you might make a mistake with?
- Will you use this grammar yourself?

6 The question
- Why do you think I asked you if it was in the past?

Techniques: Using sequences of questions – Guided discovery

The most effective questions will be ones that are just above and beyond the learners' current level of understanding, but for which they will already have the necessary understanding to be able to work out or make an informed guess about the answer.

Each question and answer can lead to a further question and answer, taking the exploration of a subject deeper and deeper. Sequences of questions like this are central to the teaching approach known as *guided discovery*.

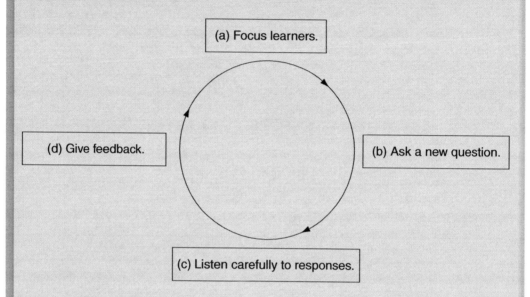

So, for example, if you are working on teaching a new grammar item, the cycle might look something like this:

1 **Focus learners** by writing up an example sentence or eliciting one from students. Ask learners to look at the sentence.
2 **Ask a question** that makes learners notice some aspect of the language or usage and forces them to think about it. Questions may also require them to remember other language they have previously studied and learnt.
3 **Listen carefully to responses**, remembering that you are not on a chase for correct answers, but are hoping to guide learners towards a better understanding.
4 **Give feedback on what they say**, for example, you could clarify, echo, write up, correct or summarise as necessary.

Finishing one circle leads you on to the next, so that the learner is taken forward, question by question, in a systematic and structured way towards new learning. To make the sequence useful, the teacher will need to have a clear sense of where the intended goal of the questioning is.

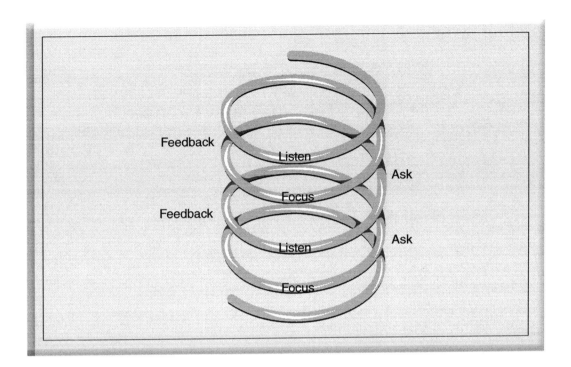

Technique: Hinting, nudging, suggesting

You don't always need to make your eliciting cues bold, direct and transparent. Sometimes a cryptic hint may give a gentle push that is more powerful than a piece of more direct guidance. Students don't always need to be led by the hand.

For example, try dropping in a single 'charged' key word or surprising idea – one that has the power to wake up a student's mind and make them think of lots of new possibilities, for example:

Student: I can't think of any interesting ideas to write in the essay about global warming. It's all, 'This is going to happen. That is going to happen'. Boring.
Teacher: Past Tense?
Student: What? Past Tense? How can I do that? It's in the future. Oh, do you mean that I imagine that I'm in the future and it all happened already? Hmm ... I can tell what the story was. Yes ... maybe that is interesting ...

Questions for reflection

- A colleague in the staffroom says, 'Eliciting takes too long. It's much faster just to tell students what they need to know, rather than wasting time guessing things they have no idea about.' Does she have a point? Would you argue back, and if so, how?
- Are there some things that you would typically never elicit (e.g. grammar rules)?

6 Questioning

> My questions are pretty dull actually. I find out if students know things – or don't – but not much more. But the questions never seem to get us very far.

Aim

To use a variety of question types effectively in class.

Introduction

→ *Socratic questions* are discussed in Chapter 4 Unit 5. *Catalytic questions* are in Chapter 4 Unit 8. This unit considers other kinds of classroom questions.

Questions are central to classroom life. Used well, they are one of the main engines of moving forward. Used poorly, they puzzle and demotivate.

By becoming more aware of the range of question types and the different ways that they can be exploited, we can select and use them more powerfully in the classroom.

Technique: Distinguishing degrees of openness in questions

Questions can be classified by how much scope they leave for the learner to answer in different ways. If there is only one possible answer, the question is significantly more closed than a question that allows an individual opinion to be expressed.

1 Polar closed questions

These are questions that are likely to lead to one of just two possible one-word answers, typically 'yes' or 'no'. For example, 'Did Juma buy the car?' 'Is my spelling of this word correct?' They don't have to be yes / no questions; they could offer choices between options (e.g. 'Is this correct or incorrect?' 'Is the sentence true or false?' 'Was the car new or second-hand?').

2 Closed questions

These are questions about fixed facts. They are often asked using a *Wh*-word (e.g. *who, whom, when, why, where, what, how, whose, which*). They are closed because there is typically one correct answer or a very limited number of possible answers, for example, 'When did Amina leave the office?' 'What is Sasha going to buy in Moscow?'

3 Open questions

These are questions that do not have a single fixed answer but leave scope for the person replying to answer in a number of different ways, e.g. 'Why do you think people visit the UAE?' 'How can we be healthier?'

Both kinds of closed questions demand very limited language output from the student. All the same, they can be very useful to help check whether learners have understood things. Open questions tend to encourage longer answers; closed questions, shorter answers.

Technique: Distinguishing different purposes in questions

We can also classify questions by looking from a different angle: by looking at what we want to achieve with them.

1 Real questions

In everyday life, when we ask a question (e.g. 'Has she bought it?' 'Did you tell him?' 'What happened?'), we are likely to be interested in the message contained in the answer. What is being said is usually new for us and adds to our understanding. We do not ask primarily to find out whether the person knows the answer or not.

2 Check questions

Teachers in classrooms tend to ask a lot of questions that they already know the answers to (e.g. 'Is this a noun or a verb?' 'Why did the ship sink?' 'What homework do you have to do?'). When listening to the response, the teacher is not mainly hoping to learn a new answer, but to find out if the speaker knows the answer the teacher already knows, in order perhaps to discover if something has been well understood or if it needs further teaching. Questions like these are known as 'check questions', or 'display questions' or 'test questions'.

Teachers tend to use more check questions than real questions in class. From the student perspective, there is sometimes confusion as to what type of question was intended. Many classroom communication breakdowns arise from learners answering what they think is a genuine question only to find out it was really a test question, for example:

Teacher: Where did you go on holiday?
Student: (Gives a long answer describing his holidays.)
Teacher: OK. Listen. I went to Spain. Repeat.
Student: Oh. OK. I went to Spain.

(The teacher wanted to practise past verbs; the student wanted to tell everyone about his holiday.)

If this happens too often, it can lead to students trying to predict what the teacher wants them to say rather than answering a question honestly.

3 Concept questions

These are a specific kind of check question used to find out if students understand the meaning and use of a piece of grammar or vocabulary. They break down the complex meaning of the language item into simpler component concepts that can be checked one by one, using closed questions in simple language. For example, if a teacher wants to check understanding of the grammatical structure *too ... to* in the sentence 'It's too wet to play football', she can distinguish the separate components: 'It's very wet. We can't play football … because it's very wet.' This leads to the concept questions (with answers in brackets): 'Is it wet?' ('Yes.') 'Is it very wet?' ('Yes.') 'Can we play football?' ('No.') 'Why not?' ('It's very wet.')

Techniques: Pitfalls in question making

Sometimes students look at you completely blankly when you ask a question, perhaps because your language is too complex, because they don't know the answer or because they have misread the intention behind your question, thinking that a check or concept question is a real one (e.g. Teacher: 'In the sentence, "Spain has won the World Cup", do we know when?' Student: 'Yes!' Teacher: 'Is it important information?' Student: 'Yes!')

Here are two common causes for misunderstood questions:

1 **Embedded questions**   (i.e. questions packed inside other questions) can be very hard for students to unpack, e.g. 'Have you got any idea what *horizon* means?' (= 'What does *horizon* mean?') 'Did you decide what the correct ending is?' (= 'What is the correct ending?').

2 **Rewording questions if not understood**   When a student looks puzzled after you have asked a question, it might seem helpful to reword that question to give them a new chance to understand it. In fact, rewording can often cause new problems, especially if the new sentence is as complex as the first version. It may offer an additional comprehension problem to the student, doubling the difficulty rather than reducing it, e.g. 'What solutions did you think about?' 'What sort of ideas have you come up with?' Remember that the student is already trying to understand the original question, so it may be most helpful to simply repeat that – maybe slower – in order to give them a new chance to unpack it. Alternatively, make sure that the rewording is at a significantly lower level of complexity than the original sentence, e.g. 'What are your ideas?'

Techniques: Who can I ask?

You can ask questions to:

1 **The class as a whole, expecting a choral answer,** i.e. lots of people speaking simultaneously.
2 **The class as a whole, expecting volunteers to offer answers,** e.g. by hands up.
3 **Specific nominated individuals,** e.g. indicated by name or by gesture.
4 **Location-restricted students,** perhaps those in a small section of the room that you indicate or call on, e.g. 'I'd like someone in this part of the room to answer'.
5 **Category-restricted students,** e.g. 'Boys only' or 'Only those who haven't answered a question so far' or 'Only students whose name begins with "s" can answer'.
6 **Random students,** e.g. you pick names one by one out of a bag for each question.
7 **Sequences of students,** e.g. each question is answered by the next person sitting round the room.

Technique: Nominate *after* the question, not before

If you say a name first and then a question (e.g. 'Marcel , What is the correct ending?'), all the other students can switch off because you have said someone else's name, and they know that they won't have to answer it.

If you say a question first, and then leave a longish thinking space, and then say a name, e.g. 'What is the correct ending?' ... (pause) ... 'Marcel?', you make the whole class think about the question in case you are going to ask them.

Techniques: Look for learning, not for correct answers

Read the short lesson sequence below. The teacher is checking understanding of a coursebook text that the class has just read. Decide if you think that the teacher felt happy at the end of it.

Teacher:	So, why did the sales team go to Delhi? Tom?
Student 1 (Tom):	They wanted to find new designs they could sell in England.
Teacher:	Very good. And what happened when they got there? Shari?
Student 2 (Shari):	Their hotel was booked up and they had nowhere to stay.
Teacher:	Excellent. So what did they do? Anyone? Yolanda?
Student 3 (Yolanda):	They slept in the street!
Teacher:	Brilliant. Well done, everyone.

The teacher asks questions. Students answer. The teacher might feel happy that she has found out that some students can give the correct answers. This helps her to feel that she is a good teacher and that her students are making progress.

And certainly, there is much that is recognisably good here, even in a short printed extract:

- The questions are clearly worded.
- Nominations are made rather than just 'first to call out' or 'hands up'.
- The nominations come after the questions, allowing all the class a little thinking time.
- A range of different students are asked.
- There's some evidence that at least some of the students have understood some of the text.

This sequence of exchanges is very typical of a lot of classroom work. But the fact that it is typical does not mean that it is as useful as it could be. There are some significant problems here, and they are ones that even very experienced teachers don't always notice.

The teacher is on a chase for right answers. He or she is collecting right answer after right answer. Teachers tend to ask more questions to those students who seem interested and active, and this makes those students seem more interested and active, which means that they get asked more questions. Teachers like to ask them because they get answers, and getting answers seems to move the lesson forward faster, and it feels like things are being achieved and their teaching has been successful.

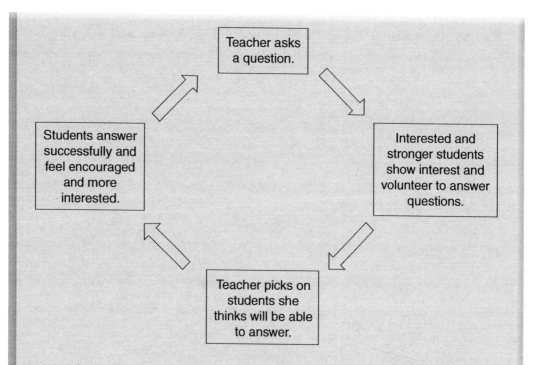

However, the fact that someone gives a right answer means that they have already found the right answer. That is where the learning has already happened, but not where the learning is still going on. The student who 'got it' is already OK, and the right answer is the surface evidence of that. But at this point of the lesson, the learning is now going on elsewhere. It is happening with the students who didn't get the answers. It's these ones that need our attention.

Collecting right answers is not enough. Our real job is to help those who don't have the right answer to feel their way towards it. In the case of the lesson sample above, this may mean that we need to send the students back into the text again, get them to reread, guide them to focus on specific words, to think out sections of meaning and so on.

Of course, it's much quicker to chase the right answers. Stopping to find out if others can answer, and working with them if they can't, will take longer, possibly much longer. In our new syllabus-obsessed schools with goals of so many units to cover in a month, teachers feel that they are often more comfortable with the illusion of learning (hearing some students giving correct answers in the room) than in the dirtier reality of finding out that quite a number of students haven't understood something.

Without discouraging the keen students, it's important to find ways of breaking out of this circle:

1 Nominate individual students to answer questions, making sure that you vary who you ask, and include all levels of students.
2 Find out if more than one student has an answer, e.g. ask students to compare answers in pairs before they say them to the whole class.

3 Use techniques that help you not to go at the pace of the fastest, strongest students, such as not hearing the stronger students (see Chapter 5 Unit 5).

4 Make sure that the stronger students remain engaged during slower moments when working with weaker students, for example, get them involved in giving help or explanations or preparing something for the next stage of the lesson. (See Chapter 3 Unit 3.)

Questions for reflection

- How can you improve your own use of questions in class? Is it more to do with the questions you ask, who you ask them to or how you deal with responses?

7 Checking learning and understanding

> *I keep asking 'Do you understand?' but I'm never sure if the answers they give me mean anything at all.*

Aim

To find out if learners have really understood and learnt something or not.

Introduction

An explanation or input of any kind that someone has not understood is patently useless. After any explanation, you need feedback of some kind to assure you that the message has been adequately conveyed and taken in. This feedback could be achieved in a number of ways, some more approximate, some more intuitive, some more precise.

Unfortunately, the classic teacher question, 'Do you understand?' is not hugely revealing, for the simple reason that students can say 'yes' when they don't understand, perhaps because of wanting to avoid looking stupid, because they *think* they understand, or for many other reasons.

We need more useful and more revealing ways of checking learning.

Techniques: Finding out if they 'got it'

1 **Notice reactions**   e.g. facial expressions that look positive or faces looking down at desks avoiding eye contact.
2 **Monitor close up**   If you ask students to take notes, wander round and have a look at what they write. If you ask students to do a task (e.g. 'Tick off each subject as I mention it'), look at what they are doing while the task is still going on (instead of waiting for the end).
3 **Ask check questions and concept questions**   See Chapter 4 Unit 6.
4 **Set listening tasks before each chunk of explanation**   It's very hard to judge understanding if students are 'just' listening. If you set a specific task, this not only helps to focus their listening, but also gives you a chance to see how well they are coping with understanding. For example, say, 'I'm going to tell you some different ideas for negotiating in business. Listen and note down three ideas that can help you to succeed in negotiation and one mistake you mustn't make.' At the end, you could let pairs compare their answers and then check in the whole class.
5 **Get students to summarise what has just been said**   e.g. 'So ... how is the causative formed?' or 'So what are the most important things you need to think about when writing a formal letter?'

---

6 **Get students to recode the information** Ask students to listen and draw a diagram (or fill in a table or complete a graph or sketch a picture) as they do (i.e. recoding the information from your explanation into a visual representation).

7 **Ask for a translation** Find out if students can put a piece of language into their own language.

8 **Test** Use a follow-on task to immediately find out if they have 'got it' or not. This could be a simple *True/False* or Multiple-choice exercise, a discussion task (that you can monitor to check what they are saying) or a more challenging activity that makes use of the explained content in some way.

9 **Encourage students to feel that getting things wrong is OK and normal** Ideally I want to create an atmosphere in class where students feel that it is absolutely fine to try out sentences and not worry too much about whether they are right or wrong. You achieve this mainly by showing that your own attitude towards attempts, errors and successes is balanced and that you respond with a light touch. Don't criticise mistakes; enjoy them. Similarly, don't overpraise successes. Encourage a general atmosphere of experimentation: trial and error is a perfectly normal way to move forward.

Questions for reflection

• Which method of checking seems to reveal the most useful insights to you as a teacher?

8 Being catalytic

> *I want to encourage learners to talk and explore their thoughts more, but I always seem to quickly steer the conversation back to myself and my own priorities.*

Aim

To encourage autonomous learning and self-exploration in your students: to help them to make their own decisions rather than telling them what to do.

Introduction

What is a teacher's job? Clearly, we have a responsibility to help our students learn certain quantities of language and become more capable in certain skills.

Beyond that, many (but not all) teachers would argue that the job is much more than that – that, as educators, we have wider responsibilities (whatever the nominal subject that we are teaching) for helping humans to learn how to learn better, to grow and develop, to become more rounded, more autonomous, more capable, more balanced, happier people.

But how to help best? In many teaching encounters, it is the teacher's agenda (or perhaps a school or government agenda) that leads the way and controls everything that happens. The teacher has planned the lesson and activities. The teacher structures and instructs throughout the lesson. It is the teacher's wish that guides and decides. What the students want will typically have no impact, or a very small one, on what happens in class.

As a result of regular agenda-deciding and agenda-imposing behaviour, teachers unintentionally find themselves continuing to operate in such ways even when it is inappropriate.

When a student comes to a teacher asking for help (e.g. 'Should I take the First Certificate exam or not?'), sometimes there's a fine line between offering informed, relevant, useful, actionable advice and making a too-quick decision about what's best for them, without taking the time to explore what it is they really want or need.

It may be inappropriate for the teacher's wishes and opinions to shape the conversation, or any advice that is offered. The priority here is to really hear the student's problem and to help them work through it. Many questions can be answered through a counselling-like process in which the individual is helped to explore and clarify their own thoughts.

Yet, it's all too easy to jump in with an instant answer. 'Should I enter for the First Certificate exam?' 'Yes of course. You're a good student.' A teacher giving such answers might assume that he or she already knows all the factors that have led the student to wonder about the question. But the teacher has not yet heard or explored the issues.

Giving generic solutions is a quick fix, maybe offering what we have said to other students in what we imagine to be similar situations. Yet every situation is unique. Even by asking a few more questions, we can dig a lot deeper and perhaps uncover something that could turn our snap response on its head:

Student: Should I enter for the First Certificate exam?
Teacher: What do you think?
Student: I'm not sure. There are some problems.
Teacher: Tell me what the problems are.
Student: Well, my mother will be in hospital next month, and I won't be able to work on my English so much.
Teacher: How will that affect your studies?

Notice that the teacher does not impose any of his or her own agenda here. The teacher is simply trying to help the student to explain and explore whatever it is that the student wants. The teacher in this conversation is being catalytic. It is a very powerful way to help.

Techniques: Catalytic helping

The five core strategies of being catalytic are:

1 **Pay attention** See Chapter 4 Unit 1.
2 **Ask supportive questions** Ask questions that encourage them to explore. Avoid questions to satisfy your own curiosity or to promote your solutions. (See Chapter 4 Unit 6.)
3 **Listen supportively** See Chapter 4 Unit 1.
4 **Stay with the speaker's agenda** Help them tell their story. Don't hijack it to your own.
5 **Beware of the urge to solve** It's so tempting to jump in with your own wonderful answers and ideas or to nudge the speaker towards these. Hold back. Work on letting the speaker find their own way.

By using these, we can work with a student and help them to explore their own story, help them to reach their own conclusions. This leads them to feel more capable, more motivated, more engaged.

Techniques: The catalytic toolkit

John Heron proposes a toolkit for being catalytic. Some of the tools are:

1 Summarising

At the end of a section of the student's talk, we can give it back to them in a summary. Not with added teacher opinion. Not with added advice. Just what they said, in a condensed form. This can help the speaker to review what they have covered so far and see if they want to add anything. A typical response to a summary will be 'Yes ... and ... ', as the speaker continues their talk into the next phase:

Teacher: So, you've told me that you find some of the students in the class very unkind to you. You want to stop this behaviour, but you don't know what to do.
Student: Yes. That's right. When I …

2 Organising the speaker's thoughts

We can use a variation on summarising to help organise what the speaker is saying, especially when they have presented their information as a spontaneous, rather disordered outpouring. We give back the content of their talk to them, but in a more organised way, perhaps by separating out issues, numbering points, etc.:

Teacher: So you felt that I marked three of your assignments wrongly. The first one was …

3 Checking for understanding

If you are not sure what the speaker meant by something they said, you can give it back to them as a question, without judgement or interpretation or opinion. These are not curiosity questions, but questions that seek to clarify:

Teacher: Can I just check? Did you say that Mr McGovern swore at you?

4 Echoing last words

When the speaker seems to have come to a halt, say their own last word, or last few words, back to them, perhaps with a slight questioning intonation:

Student: And so, I didn't know what to do …
Teacher: Didn't know what to do … ?

This echoing may provide just enough of a nudge to inspire the speaker to pick up their story again and continue it.

5 Selective echoing

You can also echo certain powerful words from the middle of a long turn. Perhaps you feel that there was something important that the speaker said, but hadn't realised was important and passed by. You are inviting them to go back and say more about it:

Student: And I got really angry about what she said, but, afterwards, I came home and had a cup of coffee, and then I watched TV a bit and did my homework.
Teacher: Really angry?

Questions for reflection

- When you next do a tutorial with a student, experiment with one or two catalytic helping techniques. Do you find that they allow you to hear more of what the speaker has to say?
- How difficult do you find it to be catalytic? Does the urge to 'hijack' a conversation take over?

▊9 Structuring and signposting

> *I thought I was very clear, but sometimes they just seem so confused – as if they have no idea where we are in the lesson or what we are doing.*

Aim

To help give shape and purpose to the learning experience and to raise learners' awareness about this: to bring learners into the *secret* of the lesson more by showing them clearly where we are, what we are doing and where we are going.

Introduction

Students often have particular difficulties with seeing how and why one thing connects to another. What the teacher views as a principled flow, leading to a useful aim, may come across as a series of apparently random activities – or a connected sequence, but with a totally different logic to what the teacher intended. Sometimes the teacher is working at such a pace (in order to cover the material or for fear of boring students) that the problem is exacerbated, with everything merging and smudging together into one amorphous unity.

Teachers can help students better understand what is going on by signposting more clearly. At its simplest, this just means being a little clearer in pointing out to students how separate pieces of the lesson start, stop and connect together – and to what purposes.

Technique: Mark stage ends and show how they link forward to the next stage(s)

When a stage comes to an end, pause. Take a count of five. Breathe. Don't feel impelled to immediately rush on. State slowly and clearly what has finished and how it links to the next part of the lesson.

What you say may seem so blindingly obvious to you that you might doubt whether it is worth saying. My own experience of observing many teachers' lessons suggests that (outside your own head), it really isn't so clear or obvious, and there is a great value in explicitly stating what is happening. For example:

> So … you have all finished the vocabulary task. Good. You collected a lot of words connected with cooking. (Pause.) In the next part of the lesson, you will use those words to make a story. OK …

Technique: Signpost the close of a lesson focus

When the whole focus of a lesson changes, it is important to explicitly state what is happening. Unless you say so, students will assume that the lesson is still flowing on from the previous activity, and they may be searching for links or a rationale (even if they are not aware that they are). Here is an example of signposting such a transition:

> We've been working all morning on the refugee article. You've done three different tasks, and I hope you have learnt some useful new expressions. OK, so is there anything anyone wants to say about the article before we finish this part of the lesson and start something else? ... OK ... So please put that article away now. (Pause.) We are going to work on something different now ... something new. The next part of the lesson is about helping you to speak more fluently.

Notice the five-part structure of this signposting:

1 Stating what has been done.
2 Checking if anyone wants to ask questions or say anything before moving on.
3 Orally and physically concluding the stage (e.g. closing books, changing seats, putting away texts).
4 Pause.
5 Announcing the next stage (maybe using a change of voice tone – perhaps brighter, more assertive, a hint of enthusiasm).

A sequence like this gives students time to take on board the change of focus.

It's surprising how rarely this is done in lessons, and the lack of it can lead to much learner confusion – the causes of which are often a total mystery to the teacher.

Notice in the examples above that the signposting comments are not instructions. The signposting comes in the spaces between things. The instructions will come as we move into the next activity: 'OK ... now get into pairs. Look at the words you listed and ...'

Technique: Involve and elicit for active signposting

Signposting doesn't have to be something solely for the teacher to do. In fact, it's much more useful if it involves students. This helps them to notice what they have done and achieved. For example, here is the signposting intervention (from above), reworked to involve students:

Teacher: So ... you've all finished the task. Good. What did you do in that task?
Student: We found words.
Teacher: Yes. What kind of words did you collect?
Student: Cooking words.
Teacher: Yes ... good. You collected a lot of words connected with cooking. In the next part of the lesson, what do you think you will do with those words?
Student: Exercise?
Teacher: Good guess. But this time ... no. In fact, you will use those words to make a story. OK ...

Technique: Signpost the methodology

A student can be autonomous, but still be wasting their time in out-of-class work if they follow procedures that are unproductive or unhelpful, for example, making long lists of every random word and translation they come across, or always listening to new recordings with the printed text open in front of them.

If we want to encourage our students to continue learning independently outside the classroom when there is no teacher, we need to make sure that they know something more about classroom procedures and their rationale. Think of it as teacher training for your students!

By doing this, you help them to gain important insights that inform their choices as to which techniques they will use when working on their own. Maybe a student who has noted the procedures, and understands the logic for task-based listening, is more likely to use a variation of that in their own independent study.

We help students to understand these things by *signposting* the *what* and *why* of our methodology.

1 Focus on the *what* of methodology and techniques by using questions that ask students to recall what happened, e.g. 'What was the first thing we did in the speaking activity?'
2 Focus on the *why* by asking reflective questions about the methodology and techniques, e.g. Why did I set a task before you started reading, instead of just asking you questions afterwards?

Here are two examples:

1 Teacher: We've been working on vocabulary for half an hour now. Do you remember the first thing we did?
  Student: We made a list of all words we knew about trains and stations.
  Teacher: Good. Why do you think I asked you to do that?

2 Teacher: In that listening activity, I told Mariel and Luisa to close their coursebooks. What was the purpose of that? Why didn't I let you read the text while you were listening?

Technique: Integrate personal review and reflection into signposting

A lot of classroom work proceeds, activity following activity, at a pace that allows little chance to pause and consider what has been learnt. Yet without a reflective gathering in of the harvest, many activities will be much less useful than they might have been.

When you signpost the end of a stage, it's a good opportunity to also encourage learners to look back and review what they have done, what they have achieved and what they still need to do. For example:

Well done! You worked hard there! So ... I wonder ... what do you think are the three most important things you have learnt from the work in this first 40 minutes? Look back over your notebooks and the coursebook. List three things that you definitely want to remember, and say why they are important for you. When you are ready, tell your partner, and find out what he or she has chosen.

Technique: Putting the day plan on the board

This is a basic structuring technique used by many teachers and actually required by many schools and colleges.

At the start of the day or individual lesson, the teacher writes up on the board a summary plan for the day. On a traditional blackboard or whiteboard, this is typically in one corner of the board.

> *Check homework*
>
> *Listening: People talking about whether they like sports*
>
> *Grammar focus: comparatives*
>
> *Exercises to practise the grammar*
>
> *Set new homework (project)*

On an interactive whiteboard, it could take up a whole page (which can be returned to and referred to at various points in the lesson) and, of course, could be prepared in advance, and hence be more detailed.

Why do it? The idea is that seeing such a plan will help the learners to understand the shape of the lesson and where it is going (which may not be as self-evident to the students as it seems to the teacher). Also, by being let into 'the secret of the lesson', the process of study is demystified slightly – and, in doing so, the same sort of procedural approach becomes more available to students to use for themselves when working on their own.

The plan you write up could be more or less detailed, as you prefer. Here are a few options:

1 **A statement about the topic of the lesson**   Today's lesson: Volcanoes and other natural disasters
2 **A statement about the focus of the work**   Today's lesson: The *Use of English* exam paper
3 **A statement about the aims of the work**   Today's lesson: By the end of this lesson, you will be better able to use some adjective-noun collocations to describe business successes and failures
4 **A numbered list of skills or systems work the students will do**
   • 1. Speaking: discussion about the sports day yesterday
   • 2. Listening: comparing abilities at sports
   • 3. Grammar: modal verbs to talk about ability
   • 4. Speaking: 'What can you do?' questionnaire
5 **A detailed outline of the lesson**   Listing topics, aims, skills and systems focuses and, perhaps, predicted timing or percentage of lesson

Refer to and annotate the lesson sequence though the lesson

Once you've written up a sequence, don't just ignore it through the lesson. Introduce it to the class at the start. Talk through it briefly. As stages finish or begin, come back to the plan, and tick or cross out the stage that has ended, and underline the upcoming stage.

Having written a lesson sequence up, you don't need to feel trapped by it. You can warn students at the start that you might digress from your plan, especially in response to finding out that students need something different from what you planned to do.

Technique: Signposting what has been achieved at high levels

There may be a particular need for signposting with high-level classes.

At low levels, students often assume that the teacher knows best and trust him or her to do things that might be of benefit to them (even though they often don't know why they are doing them). Progress is fast and tangible. It isn't always essential to understand why certain things happened in class because, in general, things seem to add up in the right direction.

But at higher levels, it can be much harder for a student to measure their progress, especially if they still equate usefulness of a lesson with how many 'new' things were learnt. At high levels, there is a whole pile of obscure vocabulary and itty-bitty fiddly grammar points. Sometimes at the end of a lesson, a student may say 'I haven't learnt anything useful', whereas the teacher may have seen the lesson completely differently as training and practice in specific skills and strategies – not a systems-focussed lesson at all. This is where clear signposting and drawing attention to the *what* and *why* can be very helpful.

1 Find points in the class (perhaps at the end of a lesson) to explicitly draw attention to what has been done, the aims and the achievements.

2 Get learners to keep a learning diary or learning blog in which they record what has been studied in each lesson, what they have achieved and what they still need to work on.

By understanding why they are doing what they do in class, students are more likely to stay motivated and feel their progress more clearly.

Technique: Planning as you teach

New teachers often feel bound into their pre-lesson plans and tend to follow them step by step, in the face of whatever actually happens in class. Once you are more experienced, it's important to find ways to work more with the live class, rather than just working through your route map. The job of teaching is not simply an application of a plan to a class. That plan was just your best guess as to what would happen in the lesson.

Once you start teaching the lesson, allow yourself to respond flexibly to whatever unfolds. You need to think and adjust and replan as you go, throughout the whole lesson. Listen to the students, check how easy or difficult they are finding the work, elicit feedback from them. Change what you do, and how you do it, in response. Stages can extend or shorten, as needed. Cut out stages, or change their focus. Don't always assume that emerging side roads are a waste of time; consider their potential usefulness, even if they don't match the original lesson aims. Speed up or slow down. Rejig activities for different group sizes or with different goals or working methods.

Questions for reflection

- Do you signpost in class? Would it help your students if you did it more?
- Imagine that you are working in a 'guided-discovery' manner with a pre-intermediate class when a student (using his L1) politely asks you why you keep asking them questions about grammar they don't yet know, when it would be much quicker, more efficient and less frustrating simply to tell them about it. How would you react and respond? How would you word your reply to the student?

10 Giving encouragement, feedback and praise

> *My trainer encouraged me to praise students all the time, and I still do. At first, I loved their excitement when I praised them, and I thought it really helped them to feel good, but recently I've started having a few doubts about whether it is really helping or not.*

Aim

To encourage students in appropriate ways and to avoid praising when it may be unhelpful.

Introduction

Language teachers often need to give feedback to students in class. Much of this is information about language and errors. (See Chapter 4 Unit 4.)

But teachers also need to give feedback on more personal things, such as achievement, behaviour, motivation, participation, attitude, engagement and so on. One key area is how we help our learners to feel encouraged and motivated, and at the heart of this issue is the surprisingly tricky question of praise.

In education, the term *praise* refers to the ways that a teacher approves, acclaims and extols a student for what they have done, typically for completing tasks successfully and to a high standard. It conveys to a student that you are pleased with them and their work.

But is praise a good thing or not? It is a much-argued topic in education, and there are strong arguments on both sides:

1 The argument for praise

For many teachers, it seems obvious and natural that praise must be beneficial. Praise is seen as encouraging and motivating. They believe that praised students will blossom and grow in the praise: When students feel noticed and encouraged, they try harder and earn more praise, so their achievement increases. Some children may have received very little praise or encouragement at home, so receiving it at school can have a substantial positive impact on them. In a classroom that is adopting a 100% positive approach to learners (see Chapter 6 Unit 1), there is a great deal of praise flying around, and this can have a very powerful role in creating the overall positive environment of a class.

2 The argument against praise

It could be argued that praising a student takes away their own ability to reflect on and evaluate their own achievements:

- It trains them to rely on other people's judgements and to devalue their own self-assessment.
- Students start to do things not because they see the purpose or are motivated to do them, but purely to receive the teacher's praise at the end. You risk creating a classroom of praise junkies who depend on the teacher to acknowledge and glorify what they do.
- Praising may be part of what prevents students becoming more autonomous. If at some point you start to praise less because you want to encourage them to become more independent, there is a definite risk that the learners will lose motivation completely and become disengaged – because all the earlier reasons for doing work have evaporated.
- Another problem may be that praise is often reserved for those who get correct answers or complete and achieve specific tasks, which means that some stronger students are likely to get a much higher dose of praise than others. Resentment might grow amongst others in class, and unhealthy rivalries grow. Competitive jockeying for the teacher's praise is possible, with stronger students trying to outdo each other in order to get the positive boost from the teacher.
- And if the teacher tries to balance praise to everyone, does that undermine the whole point of it? If students in the class hear the teacher saying, 'Well done! You wrote a fantastic paragraph' to everyone, do they believe her? Is the praise devalued? Is it possible that they will learn to distrust teacher assessments? Might excessive praise give the impression that you expect learning a language to be very difficult or impossible?

The decision on whether to praise or not must be up to you. It may be affected by a number of factors, such as the age of your students, their level, their current self-image and the experience they get in other classrooms. If you teach five-year olds, for example, the case for praise may be very different than that for a teacher working with young adults.

Technique: Giving supportive feedback

One alternative strategy to praising is to give supportive feedback on work. That may initially sound like the same thing, but we can draw a few distinctions.

Praise	Supportive feedback
Evaluates the person and the work.	Evaluates the work.
Tends to be generalised. Doesn't exemplify.	Tends to be specific. Uses concrete examples.
Comments are stated as if they are some objective, universal truth, e.g. 'That is really good.'	Comments are often owned by the comment maker using 'I', e.g. 'I really like the way you ended the story.'
Notices tasks completed well. Doesn't typically notice engagement and effort.	Notices work at all stages of a task. Acknowledges engagement and effort.
Compares a student's work with others in the class. Draws attention to achievement of the best class members.	Compares a student's work with their own previous work. Draws attention to achievement and progress for that individual student.
Doesn't give information about how to improve.	Gives useful information about how to improve.
Encourages trust in the teacher's assessment.	Encourages self-assessment.

Praise	Supportive feedback
Mostly reserved for the best, fastest, cleverest, etc.	Available for all students of all abilities.
Becomes a bit meaningless over time, as there is nowhere else to go after 'fantastic'.	Keeps its value over time as it addresses new issues.
Always good news.	Can be bad news given in a supportive way, as well as good news.
May come across as a habitual or token comment.	Sounds as if it springs from a genuine positive reaction.
May present a simplification or glossier version of the truth.	Tells the truth.

These are not cast-iron divisions. Any intervention may have a number of elements from both columns, but here are some examples that might help clarify the differences:

Praise:

- You're brilliant.
- You're great.
- You're so clever. The answers are fantastic.
- What a good girl!

Supportive feedback:

- I really enjoyed reading this story; the part about swimming made me laugh out loud.
- This exercise has 10 correct answers out of 10; how do you feel about that?
- You answered all the questions with well-written sentences. There were only three small grammar mistakes.
- I saw you working really hard to find the answers, but I'm afraid these four are wrong. What help can I give you to make the task clearer?

This is not to suggest that there is no place for 'good' or 'excellent' or 'amazing' or 'fantastic' in a teacher's feedback: simply that it's worth weighing up whether a diet that is mainly praise, rather than feedback, is as beneficial and useful in the long run as it might appear in the short term.

Techniques: Training students to notice what they have done well

An effective way to start weaning students off dependency on teacher praise is to help them become more able to look at, reflect on and assess their own work. This is a useful life skill, quite apart from any immediate benefits in your classroom.

You can introduce this gradually. Initially, start restraining your own praise a little. Before you give it, ask students questions that get them thinking about how they feel about their work: 'Are you pleased with that result?' 'Did you expect to get so many correct answers?' 'Is that an improvement over what you did last time?' 'How do you feel about your mark?'

Later, you can start using some more sophisticated ways to push them a little deeper into self-evaluation.

1 Reflective questionnaires

Devise a form that students can fill in after some lessons. It can direct students to thinking about what they have learnt and achieved. Word questions to help them notice the positive achievements and progress, as well as setting goals for future weeks. Sample questions: 'What are the most useful new things you have learnt this fortnight?' 'What have you got better at doing?' 'What was your greatest English achievement in the last two weeks?'

2 Learning diaries

Set aside a little time for students to write a learning diary or blog entry at the end of each day or week, summarising what they have achieved.

3 Can-do statements

It's a feature of many education systems (exam focussed, as they are) that they tend to draw attention to what students can't do rather than what they can do. As a result, it's not surprising that students tend to focus on what they got wrong or did poorly, rather than what they got right or did well. Try using can-do statements for students to self-assess against. These are simple descriptions of actions (real-world or language-study related) that require the use of English (e.g. 'I can give directions from the school to the station' 'I can name 10 different fruits' 'I can use the phone to invite a friend to my house' 'I can ask *Have you ever* … questions about people's experiences').

Questions for reflection

- How much do you use praise? Can you answer with certainty, or is it one of those automatic-pilot areas where you are unsure of exactly how much you do it?
- How could you research your use of praise and supportive feedback in class?
- How did you respond to praise when you were a school child? How much did you learn to evaluate yourself?

■11 Giving difficult messages

> *I had to tell one of my students that he needed a bath! I had no idea how to say this. I was unclear and never really got to the point.*

Aim

To convey 'bad news' or negative messages in a clear and supportive way.

Introduction

Teachers often need to pass on bad news to students: poor exam results, a change of class not possible, a special request denied and so on. Occasionally, a teacher has to tell students some very personal feedback that they really do not want to hear – about an aspect of their behaviour, attitude, dress, personal appearance, habits, cleanliness or hygiene. This can be the most difficult interaction of all.

There is a real skill in being able to convey true information (positive or negative) in a supportive manner. If you listen in while teachers give bad news, it is often much less clear and focussed than they might imagine. Sometimes the poor recipient ends up so confused that they can't even recognise that they have been given a negative message.

Because we are worried about the coming task of conveying negative information, our distress at what we are having to do can easily get in the way and interfere with the message we want to say. This may come over in these ways:

- The speaker avoids saying the key message and implies it, rather than stating it clearly and directly.
- The speaker wraps up the message within so many layers of words and side issues that it becomes very hard for the listener to unpack and recognise the essential information from amongst everything else.
- The speaker pussyfoots around the issue, minimising it and making it hardly seem worth bothering with.
- The speaker overcompensates for fear of the problems above and comes in much too harshly, hitting the poor listener with repeated restatements of the bad news and with minimal support.

Every teacher needs to find an effective way of conveying a negative message that retains a clear foundation of support: telling the truth with love.

Techniques: Telling the truth with love

Perhaps the best way to convey difficult messages is to be very upfront and clear, but never losing the undercurrent of support. A three-step approach can help to structure what you want to say:

Start:
Introduce the message clearly, e.g. 'There is something I need to tell you', or 'I want to tell you something. It may be important that you know this.'

State:
Give the difficult message clearly and concisely – avoiding any unnecessary wrapping – in one or two short sentences, if possible. Don't repeat it unnecessarily. Don't keep talking to no point.

When stating the core message itself, one approach is to first offer a factual description of behaviour, followed by your own personal impression and how you honestly feel about this, for example:
Behaviour: 'You were very rude to Margit in the group work. I heard you swear a number of times.'
Impression: 'This gives the impression that you dislike her and don't respect her.'
Feeling: 'And I felt upset when I saw this.'

Stop:
Allow silence and reaction time. Shut up and listen. Help the listener deal with what you have just said. Don't get into negotiation or argument. If the listener hasn't accepted the message, simply repeat it calmly.

Questions for reflection

- Do you find it difficult to convey bad news?
- Do you have any typical ways of doing this?

12 Permitting emotion

> *I saw a student today who looked really upset. I realised that I had no idea what to do or say. So I said nothing at all and ignored it.*

Aim

To create opportunities that allow the learners to express more openly how they feel about the course, lesson, activity, working modes and other aspects of their studies.

Introduction

We can think about what is experienced in the classroom under three headings:

- **The content** is the subject matter that is studied, taught or learnt. In our case, the main content is the English language and how to use it. In other school classes, it might be geography or physical education or whatever.
- **The methodology** is the way that the content is studied, taught or learnt: the activities, techniques and procedures used. In English language teaching, for example, teachers typically use pair work, information-gap activities, dictations, worksheets and so on.
- **The process** is the way that the course is experienced by the learner. This includes how they respond to the content and methodology, as well as to the whole experience of being in class and working with others. Emotions play a significant role here – how a student feels about the teacher, the other students, their work and place in class: positive, shy, bored, stupid, excited, disengaged, angry and so on.

When teachers elicit any kind of feedback from learners, it is most usually about the first of these, the content. This is the easiest to address and provides the least threatening kinds of answers, e.g. Teacher: 'Are these pieces of language useful for you?' Student: 'Yes. I can ask better questions when I meet a new colleague.'

Fewer teachers ask students for comments on methodology, but it can be very helpful to hear what students think about how teachers work, though this may feel 'riskier' as the comments students make may challenge the teacher's methodological decisions or beliefs, e.g. Teacher: 'What do you think about the way that we did that activity?' Student: 'It was too confusing with everyone speaking, and I couldn't understand which answers were correct or not.' If you can learn to listen to and reflect on such responses (without necessarily agreeing with them or implementing changes), you can improve your methodology very quickly.

It is very rare for teachers to ask for feedback on process, and, as a result, in many courses, this remains a crucial unaddressed area. Teachers are often wary or nervous to ask questions about how students feel, partly because they don't know how to and partly for fear that it may reveal some serious issues that they will not want to or be able to deal with. Yet, without attention to process, there is a real danger that anxieties, distress, resentments and other emotions may build up under the surface, only to explode as tears, complaints, walkouts or even violence at some later date.

Technique: Directing attention to process

Humans have emotions. We don't need to hide this in class. We can gently enquire when it seems helpful to do so, without being intrusive or inappropriately 'touchy feely'. But bear in mind that in English, the question, 'How do you feel?' does not typically elicit genuine responses about how people feel (though, 'What are you feeling now?' can be a powerful question). You need to make sure that your enquiry really gets home.

Address process by asking questions about how people feel, whether in the whole class, groups or privately, one to one. Ask directly whether they are enjoying the course, how they feel in the evening when they have lots of homework to do, what they find annoying in lessons, what bores them, how they feel about themselves as learners and so on.

Whatever is said, listen and restrain yourself from arguing back, justifying what you have done in class. The most powerful thing you can do is listen. Take notes if you wish. Help them to explore deeper if you feel able to (see Chapter 4 Unit 8 *catalytic interventions*). Thank them for their honesty at the end.

Technique: Process reviews

A timetabled process review is a simple, but powerful way to allow talking space – space for people to say whatever they want to. Build in five timetabled minutes or more each week. Introduce this as an unled, unstructured space where students can say anything they want to about their reactions to, or feelings about, the experience of the course (but NB not about the content). Introduce it clearly and then hand over. If there is silence, fine. Don't feel that you have to push people to speak. Stay relaxed and quiet, and try it again next week. Only intervene to point out that comments about content (e.g. 'Could someone explain about relative clauses?') are not appropriate for this part of the lesson. Once students start to realise what they can use the space for, it becomes an important and valued forum.

Your role is mainly to listen carefully and take notes. Don't view your main role as managing the discussion or responding to what is said. At the end, you could list or summarise what has been said and perhaps say 'thank you' and briefly say what you will do as a result (which may simply be, 'I'm going to take this list home and think about all that you've said').

If some students initially use the process review mainly as a space to express dissatisfaction or grouse, allow them to do so, without feeling that you have to jump in and defend yourself or the course. It's usually much better to get negative feelings out in the open rather than allowing them to fester unnoticed and unspoken. Simply having the chance to say negative things aloud can sometimes diminish the problem talked about without further action.

If a student repeatedly dominates or misuses the time, you may want to discreetly point this out to them and ask them to allow others a chance. You could also establish some ground rules appropriate to the group you are working with (e.g. 'Only make comments about what the teacher does' or 'No negative comments about other students').

Technique: Permitting emotional reactions

As an alternative to ignoring or passing over emotions in class, there may be points where it feels appropriate to open it up.

When you feel that you recognise a cue sign (e.g. body tensing, eyes narrowing or tears welling up in eyes) that reflects an important, but unstated feeling, allow yourself to intuit what emotion you think is being felt and to hand that to them in a question, said without a hint of criticism or self-defence:

• Do you feel sad?
• I noticed that you seemed upset just now. Am I right?
• You seem to be very angry with me.

By asking about an emotion, you give explicit permission to talk about it if the learner wishes to, though you should not pressure them into this if they choose not to. Whatever the answer, you will be a little closer to addressing the actual emotion that the student is feeling.

In response, they can, and will frequently, deny your intuition. If you feel confident, you could try handing it back again:

Teacher: You seem to be very angry with me.
Student: No, I'm not.
Teacher: Maybe you feel that what I said was unfair, and now you are angry.
Student: Well, yes. I think that you were unkind and that ...

In deciding whether to mention an emotion in open class, you need to be very sensitive to the impact your intervention might have. You don't want to embarrass the student or open him or her up to ridicule. Comments such as, 'You look like you are about to cry. Do you want to?' are likely to be more suitable for private interventions, e.g. in a one-to-one tutorial discussion or very quietly to an individual in class. One option would be to invite a student to step outside the room for a few minutes where you can ask your question.

Technique: Allowing humour

Teachers sometimes behave as if humour is slightly dangerous in class, especially if initiated by students. Perhaps it is seen as a threat to the hierarchy of teacher-student power, or there is a fear that it will undermine or damage something.

However, a classroom that is laughing and happy is a great place to be. And that doesn't come about just through polite student responses to a teacher's tired jokes. Humour can lightly pervade everything that happens, creating an environment in which people smile a lot, laugh a lot and enjoy being together a lot. The possible 'waste of time' can be more than balanced by the motivation created by the good atmosphere.

Try allowing humorous events to 'open up' as they emerge, rather than feeling a need to close them and swiftly move on. If, for example, two students start using silly voices to do a task, don't immediately jump in to order them to do it 'properly'. Instead, smile and enjoy what is happening, along with the rest of the class. Do keep an eye open to check if the joke is going on too long or is unkind in some way, but where viable, let it run its natural course. At the end, you can do whatever feedback you would normally do, but adding in a comment or question about the humorous element if you wish.

Technique: Dealing with anxiety, distress and other emotions

There are many stronger emotions that may surface in class time, and dealing with such issues should be outside the scope of a book like this. However, the reality is that many teachers are faced with situations where they need to support anxious, distressed or traumatised students without any immediate support, or where the student states that they will only talk to you. A teacher who is not trained in counselling may find that they feel quickly out of their depth, lacking the tools to really help – and there is a real danger that inexperienced counselling may offer inappropriate help or too quickly bring out issues that are too difficult or too deep.

Where you can and wherever it is appropriate, seek any professional help that is available, and strongly encourage the student to take up other support. If there is none, or you are in a situation where you feel that you are the only person who might be able to help, remember that perhaps the most powerful way any person can support another is simply by being a very good listener. Use Catalytic listening techniques (see Chapter 4 Unit 8) to help the speaker say what he or she wants to say and to explore the story for him- or herself. Resist the urge to jump in with advice and solutions. Offer these only once you are sure that you have heard all that the speaker has to say, and after they have really talked though their own possible answers.

Questions for reflection

- When a student comes to you saying that they are very upset about something, how do you respond?
- Do you think that it is valid to ask questions about students' feelings or emotions in class, or is this something best left untouched?

⓭ Being unhelpful

> '*I am always very literal, factual and exact with my class. I do sometimes wonder if I could be a little more playful in how I work with them – to provoke them a little and make them think.*'

Aim

To make deliberately non-truthful interventions in order to encourage different kinds of thinking and interactions.

Introduction

Despite the advice you'll find in the rest of this book to be authentic and honest with students, there are still occasions when it is good to do the opposite. Whether such working methods are appropriate for you and your own teaching style is something that you will need to decide for yourself.

Technique: Playing devil's advocate

When you play devil's advocate, you state things that do not necessarily represent your own opinion or beliefs, but you say them with a straight face, as if you do actually think or believe them. In other words, you are doing a sort of role play: making an argument from another person's perspective, as if you were that person.

This can be a powerful classroom technique, for example, to provoke a good discussion or to make students really think about a grammar point:

1 Example: Provoking a discussion

Teacher: I think that it's OK to steal things.
Students: (Quite shocked.) No! You don't think that!
Teacher: Yes! Some people don't have things and can't afford to buy them, so stealing is the best way to get them.
Students: But if everyone steals then … (And the discussion takes off.)

2 Example: Making students think about grammar

Teacher: So, what's the answer to Question 6?
Student A: Mohammed is taller than his brothers.
Teacher: Hmmm. I think it's … Mohammed is *more tall* than his brothers.
Student B: (Looks very puzzled.) Is that really the correct answer?
Teacher: Yes … More tall. Don't you agree?
Student C: (Uncertain.) I think that … with *tall* you have to make *taller* not *more tall*.

> Teacher: Oh ... (Pretends to look puzzled.) What do you think? (Looks at another student.) Is he right?
> Student D: Maybe. Yes ... I wrote *taller*.
> Student E: But, can we use *-er*? I'm not sure ... *more tall* ... it sounds wrong to me.
> Student F: I think that with short words you usually use *-er*, not *more*.
> Teacher: Ah, yes. Well done. Well ... I think you're right and I'm wrong. (Smiles.)
> Students: (Laugh.)
> Teacher: Let's just check that rule ...

The value of this is mainly in pushing students to think and react in more engaged and interested ways.

In the discussion example, imagine the resulting conversation if the teacher had started 'Do you think it's OK to steal?' There is a good chance that everyone would have agreed immediately ... end of conversation. By giving students something to bite on, something to react to, there is already the seed of a much more exciting debate. By taking on a new (possibly unpopular or unsavoury) role that maybe no one else would have taken, the teacher injects a new voice into the discussion and allows other arguments to surface. It's probably sensible not to try this until you are confident that you have a good rapport with the class.

In the grammar example, the teacher deliberately creates uncertainty amongst the class. This leads them to question and rethink their understanding, perhaps cementing the learning more deeply.

Of course, it's usually important that the teacher establishes clearly at the end that his or her role playing was role playing. Perhaps the ideal would be that students recognise what you are doing as role play from early on, but buy into the charade and play along with it. I sometimes aim to achieve this by responding to questions in this sort of way:

> Student: But, Jim, do you REALLY believe what you are saying?
> Me: (Serious face.) Yes. Definitely. (Followed by a smile, and perhaps a slow deliberate wink, before returning to the serious face.)

Any state of creative confusion and puzzlement that you create also needs to be clearly resolved. Puzzlement is useful for learning, but students shouldn't leave the room still puzzled.

Bear in mind that this technique may not be appropriate in cultures where it is considered very rude to contradict or argue with a teacher.

Technique: Being ignorant

A related 'unhelpful' technique is that of deliberately not answering when students have a question. Instead of role playing an opposite view, in this case, the role-playing teacher pretends to complete ignorance. For example:

> Student: So which is the correct answer? C or D?
> Teacher: I don't know. Is it possible that both are OK?
> Student: But ... in the exam, there is only one correct answer.

Teacher: Ah, so which is it?

Student: Well, I have C … but these students have D.

Teacher: So, we need to discuss this and find out which is correct.

In many classrooms, it would be normal for the teacher in Line 2 to simply state the correct answer. This would effectively end the discussion – and the learning. By refusing to immediately validate one answer, the teacher forces the students to think further and verbalise their reasoning. (This is related to 'not rubberstamping' in Chapter 5 Unit 6.)

This technique involves a degree of blatant lying (e.g. 'I don't know'). You'll have to decide whether or not you are comfortable with that and if it fits in with any of your own beliefs on authenticity and honesty. Personally, it seems acceptable to me, as I can identify this as a specific technique that is geared towards a specific purpose.

A variation on this is 'Playing dumb': You pretend not to understand students even when you do, in order to force them to try harder, e.g. correct their grammar or fine tune their pronunciation so that the message is more intelligible.

Questions for reflection

- Do you recognise techniques such as these? Are they already part of your repertoire?
- How uncomfortable would you feel 'lying' to your students? Would it be a difficult role to pull off successfully?

14 Vanishing

> *Do I need to be so visible and available all the time?*

Aim

To recognise times in class when the teacher's absence may be more valuable than his or her presence.

Introduction

In Philip Pullman's *His Dark Materials* trilogy, the witches have perfected the art of vanishing. It isn't a trick involving chemicals or special clothes. Rather, it is:

> *A kind of fiercely held modesty that could make the spell worker not invisible but simply unnoticed. Holding it with the right degree of intensity, she could pass through a crowded room, or walk beside a solitary traveller, without being seen.*

There is a place in the classroom for occasional invisibility. A spell worker (sorry ... *teacher*) is usefully present when he or she needs to speak, organise, correct and do any other things that will help the students to learn. Conversely, there are times when his or her presence might actually hinder learning. There are times when a teacher is most useful by not being there – or, at least, not being visibly, noticeably, there. These might include:

- When students need to work on their own.
- When students need concentrated thinking time without interruptions.
- When you don't want students to worry about what you think.
- When you don't want students to keep looking to you for help, ideas or language.
- When you don't want students to work in the hope of getting praise from you.
- When you don't want students to fear that correction is coming any moment.
- When you wish to discourage yourself from unhelpful or unnecessary interventions – countering that 'urge to teach'.

By vanishing, you give a clear message to students that you are not available, unless really needed, and are not going to interfere with what they are doing. It signals that this time is time for them to get on with their work.

Technique: How to vanish

A typical vanishing point would be after you have given an instruction for a task and then monitored and assured yourself that students are clear about what to do and able to do it.

You then discreetly withdraw yourself from the proceedings, finding a location and a way of being that, like the witches, does not draw attention to oneself: vanishing in plain sight.

One way to do this is to move to the back of the room or a corner, standing or sitting quietly out of the sight lines of the majority of the class.

Another way is to find a place to crouch or sit at the front, but below the sight lines of the room.

You can also vanish in full view, maybe sitting at your desk, by adopting a manner that shows your detachment from what is happening in the room: perhaps head down reading calmly to yourself (as opposed to looking anxiously and urgently around the room all the time).

You could even leave the room. This is particularly useful in cases where students don't seem to accept your wish for them to work without help. By leaving the room, you send the message that they are (briefly) on their own.

Some teachers I know leave the room, but then wait around on the other side of the door: out of sight, but able to monitor noise and behaviour – and to do that seemingly magical trick of reappearing just before there is a real problem!

However you choose to vanish, it's worth giving yourself a specific thing to do (reading, marking, etc.) so that you don't expend energy on constantly looking back at the students.

Vanishing is partly role play. You are pretending to be uninterested and detached more than you are genuinely uninterested and detached. You are doing this for a specific reason: to help the students work better and learn more. You are doing it because you understand that sometimes help is unhelpful, and learners need time to do things for themselves. So you advertise that you are not 'being a teacher' for a while. But part of you will continue to monitor the room in case there is a real problem that needs to call your attention back. Of course, if you do your vanishing skilfully and at the right moment, many students will not even notice that you have done it. Ask them after the lesson about how they felt when you left the room, and they might look at you in surprise and puzzlement, not having noticed that you ever left.

If you are working in a school culture where classes have a strong expectation of an 'up-front', controlling teacher, you may need to brief the students that you might do this at some points – and explain your reasons.

Technique: Silence

A variation on vanishing is making more use of your own silence. In whole class work, see what happens if you try to reduce the quantity and length of your interventions, saying less, but making what you say count more. Don't turn this into a strict vow of silence that can quickly become ridiculous. Just experiment with a more witch-like, more 'modest', less 'teacher-like' use of your own voice.

Questions for reflection

- Do you ever vanish?
- What do you think would happen if you left the room for five minutes? If your answer is a 'worst-case' scenario, what would the best-case scenario be?

5 | Facilitating interaction

Whole-class work

1 Encouraging students to speak

> *My students hate speaking. They say almost nothing in class, especially in whole-class work. So I end up speaking a lot. It doesn't feel right.*

Aim
To get students talking to each other as much as possible.

Introduction
Speaking is daunting for many students who find it hard to get the courage to open their mouths, especially in front of the whole class. They may be frightened of making mistakes, of saying things their peers will deem foolish, of not having anything to say.

Whereas you might (just) be able to get away with a physics lesson in which mainly (or only) the teacher spoke, it wouldn't be much of a language lesson if the only person to get practice using English was the teacher. Encouraging students to speak is an important part of classroom work, and it's important to find ways to encourage all students to take part.

Techniques: Creating the conditions for speaking

1 Build an atmosphere where people want to say things
For whole-class discussions, keep the mood relaxed, engaged and lively. Being asked to say something should feel like a great chance for students to give their ideas, rather than having a huge spotlight turned on them.

2 Create reasons to speak
Frame your topics as questions, puzzles or problems, rather than as plain statements.

3 Use picture cues
Show pictures to help inspire reactions and ideas.

4 Allow use of web tools
Let students use Google, Wikipedia, etc. to research a little before a discussion starts. This could be in class, or for homework the night before.

5 Work on vocabulary

Students typically feel more confident if they are not struggling to find the right words. Brainstorming useful vocabulary beforehand can make a difference – or just allowing some time for students to look up useful words for themselves.

6 Manage turn-taking

While it is sometimes fine to let whoever wants to speak to have their go, this can often lead to domination by a few louder, more capable students. You may, therefore, need to take an active role in deciding who should speak and making sure that a range of students have a chance (see Chapter 5 Unit 4.)

7 Scaffold where helpful

Support speakers by using conversational techniques that help them build what they want to say: asking questions, showing interest, echoing key words, suggesting words they can't find, discreetly suggesting corrections without focussing on them. Be careful to avoid hijacking the conversation or echoing so much that it means that no one else needs to listen to the speaker.

8 Don't jump on errors

If your main aim is to get students speaking, then don't keep taking detours to focus on errors. If you often pick up on mistakes and work on them, students will become more nervous to speak and might hide rather than volunteer to say things.

9 Allow thinking time

Don't expect immediate responses. The faster students can do this, but not everyone. Build in space after a question before you nominate someone to answer, or before you accept a volunteer to say something.

10 Let students make a few notes

With 'bigger questions' that require creative or well-thought-out responses, you may want to allow a short time for students to make some notes about what they think and how they could say it. Alternatively, allow a short time for students to tell each other what they think in pairs, before feeding back to you.

11 Listen to what students say

People speak most when they feel really listened to. Model good listening yourself.

12 Train students to listen to each other

(See Chapter 5 Unit 5.)

13 Talk less yourself!

Sounds simple, but this can be very hard for many teachers (see Chapter 5 Unit 3).

14 Avoid 'losing-face' moments

A major reason why students don't speak is that they are afraid of losing face, of seeming foolish, or uninformed, or incompetent, or uncool in front of their peers. You can't entirely change the culture you are in (see below), but you can do some things to avoid such issues. Whether a student's answer is right or wrong, you can still positively acknowledge the act of giving it, e.g. by thanking them for it. Make sure that any feedback you give deals with the message, not the person. In other words, the answer may be wrong (and it's fine to say that), but you need to show support and encouragement to the person who said it. Crucially, never be seen to dismiss a student's response as silly or stupid. Don't mock or give sarcastic reactions to what a student says. The impact of what you say may be entirely hidden in class, but can still have a long-term discouraging effect.

Techniques: Building confidence in individual students

Once you have started to get to know your class, you will soon notice which students tend not to speak. It's worth taking some time to support them and boost their confidence.

1 Nominate widely in class

Make sure you name quieter students as well as louder ones when you ask for people to speak. Whatever he or she says, acknowledge positively, and be encouraging.

2 Use 'choral-answer' questions

As well as asking individuals to answer, have some questions where you ask everyone to speak at once. You won't hear individual responses in the general mumble, but you'll get a general impression and, more importantly, lots of students get a chance to participate.

3 Ask open questions to stronger students and closed questions to weaker ones

Open questions are ones which require longer, fuller answers, such as summaries, opinions or interpretations. They are suitable for those who will be able to cope with the demands of forming longer, thought-through answers. While you are building confidence in weaker, less forthcoming students, ask them a lot of closed questions, i.e. ones that may only need short one- or two-word answers to convey fixed, concrete information. The most common closed-question answers are 'yes' and 'no'. Make up for the shortness of the answers by coming back to the same students often with new questions. Build their confidence by getting them to speak lots of times in class. (See more on questions in Chapter 4 Unit 6.)

4 Allow private turns

Students may not want to speak up in front of the whole class, but can still have a chance to word what they have to say. Sometimes when you ask a question, say that you don't want students to speak the answer to the class, but just to mumble or whisper it to themselves. This can help build confidence and courage for students to later speak in front of others.

5 Tutorials

Set your class some work that allows you to invite individual students to come and see you for short tutorial discussions. When you meet with quieter students, use the time to talk mainly about how they feel when speaking, why they avoid it, what would encourage them to speak more and so on. Avoid telling off.

6 Chat after class

If time (or quantity of students) doesn't allow you to arrange tutorials, find time after class for informal chats with the quiet students.

Technique: Consider and openly discuss cultural factors

There may be reasons why learners from some cultures do not interact in the way you expect or hope. They may have long-held assumptions or expectations about how it is right to behave with a teacher, or in front of other students. These ideas may be set in concrete after many years within a specific educational system. For example, Amy B. M. Tsui quotes the following research about how tacitly accepted, but unwritten behavioural rules governed Chinese students in Hong Kong, encouraging modesty in front of peers and avoidance of teacher criticism:

- *You should not demonstrate verbal success in English in front of your peers.*
- *You should hesitate and show difficulty in arriving at an answer.*
- *You should not answer the teacher voluntarily or enthusiastically in English.*
- *You should not speak fluent English.*

Obviously, you cannot change cultural factors overnight (or possibly at all), but it is still worth making them an open matter for discussion and reflection. You, as the teacher, can say quite clearly what you would like students to do and how you would hope for them to behave. You can encourage them to reflect on what their expectations are and if they clash or not with yours. By discussing such things, you do not solve the problems, but in bringing them out into the open, they immediately become less of a hidden volcano under the classroom floor. You all know where you stand and you have asserted your right to go on nudging, cajoling them, encouraging them to work a little more in the way that you think would be beneficial for them. You can encourage them to take part in little 'experiments', such as explicitly not following an unwritten guideline for twenty minutes (e.g., 'You should not answer the teacher voluntarily'), and then reflect on whether it was good or not.

Questions for reflection

- Which is the bigger problem in your classes: getting students to speak more in general or getting the quieter ones to contribute more?
- Which cultural factors have you noticed affecting speaking contributions in your classroom? Are any of them suitable for discussion with students?

2 Researching interaction

> *Lessons are sometimes so busy that, at the end, I have no real idea how much an individual spoke or even if someone managed to avoid speaking at all.*

Aim

To research interaction in your own class and to plan for improved interaction in future lessons.

Introduction

An important way of improving the interaction in your lessons is to first realise what kind of interaction you already have, but this is surprisingly hard to know. So much goes on in a lesson that, by the end of class, it can all blur in the teacher's mind, making it hard to be sure how many people talked, or how much. The teacher may have a general impression that 'students didn't talk very much' or that 'some students dominated'. However, the exact details and statistics of what really went on in the classroom might be very surprising if actually researched and revealed. Once the data starts to reveal what really happened, it becomes more possible to plan for things to go differently.

Technique: Mapping interaction

Prepare a simple sketch plan of your class, clearly showing seating and student names. Mark a T (for teacher), where you are most likely to stand, and a large W (for 'whole class'), somewhere amongst the students. Make a number of copies. Invite a colleague (or one of your students) to observe part or all of a lesson. Explain that this would not be a general all-purpose observation, but you just want them to notice one aspect of what happens: the interaction, especially in whole-class phases of work. Your colleague should choose two or three different parts of the lesson. During each of these, she should watch carefully for about three to five minutes and note interaction in one of these ways:

1 Quantitative

Each time someone speaks (student or teacher), mark a tally mark next to their seat on your seating plan, e.g.:

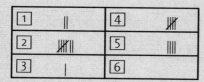

This will reveal who has spoken most and least over particular sections of the lesson.

2 Directional

Each time someone speaks (student or teacher), draw an arrow from them to the person they are talking to. If they speak to the same person again later, add tally marks to the arrow. If the teacher or student speaks to the whole class, draw the arrow to the W.

3 Qualitative

Each time someone speaks, write a number next to them, and on a separate page, make a note of the number, together with a short comment on what they said (e.g. 'Just said a mumbled "yes"' or 'Gave a long, useful answer to the question' or 'Spoke very slowly and wasn't easy to understand').

Technique: In-class research

If it isn't possible to get a tame colleague to undertake the data-collecting observation suggested in the technique above, one possible alternative is to collect your own data, keeping a tally of who speaks in whole-class question and answer sessions. Make a sheet with each student's name on it down the left side. Every time a student gives a substantial answer (i.e. something more than a basic 'yes' or 'no'), make a tally mark next to their name. After a few lessons, you should have a revealing picture of who does the talking – and who doesn't. Is there a dramatic imbalance? Do some students never or hardly ever say anything? Did you find that the act of doing the research already started to make you think and, for example, change how much you asked some students to speak? (The act of observing often subtly changes the thing being observed, even while that observation is still happening!)

Once you have collected some data about the interaction patterns in your class, you need to ask yourself some questions about them, such as:

- Who talked most: teacher or students?
- Did some students take a significantly greater role than others?
- How many students managed to hide, saying little or nothing?
- How well did you manage the interaction? Did you use effective techniques to get some to speak or to say less?
- Did you get in the way of student interaction at any point, e.g. talking too much, talking over students, interrupting, etc.?

Having thought about these, the next question is simply, 'How can I improve on that?'

Questions for reflection

- How do you imagine a map of interactions would look for a typical lesson of yours? Would it reveal that lots of different people spoke, and that the teacher did not dominate speaking time? Or would it be mostly you?

▣ Reducing unnecessary teacher talk

> *When I started teaching I equated teaching with talking. But now I suspect that the quantity of my talk is stopping students saying things themselves.*

Aim

To reduce unnecessary teacher talk.

Introduction

Most ELT teachers are familiar with the term TTT – referring to 'Teacher talking time'. On initial training courses, it is often drummed into new teachers that TTT is a 'bad thing': the more a teacher talks, the less space there is for students to talk. Of course, like all rough and ready guidelines, this contains both truths and simplifications.

In fact, there are many kinds of teacher talk that are extremely useful, such as good explanations, a teacher anecdote, a dictation or a piece of text read aloud in an exciting way. The problem is really with UTT: unaware teacher talk – the kind of talk teachers engage in when they open their mouths and fill the air with words for no very good purpose, seemingly oblivious to the fact that they are getting all the rich language practice rather than their students.

It's not only new teachers who do this. Many supposedly experienced teachers also talk a lot. And many teachers who don't think they do this, do it. This means that the first step may be simply to investigate whether this is true of you or not.

Technique: Researching how much I talk

Set up a microphone and audio recording on a mobile phone, computer or cassette recorder – or better still, set up video recording with a webcam. Record a short section of your lesson; ten minutes is ample. Then listen to or watch it.

You don't need any special tasks or forms to fill in. Simply check yourself out. For many teachers, a typical reaction is shock: 'Do I really talk that much?''Do I never shut up?''How on earth do the students ever get a word in?' If you feel at all uncomfortable with the quantity of your talk, look for techniques in this book to increase the space for students to interact, and reduce your own unnecessary talk.

Technique: Planning interaction

When you plan lessons, don't just plan what you will say and what tasks the learners will do, but also consider what kind of interaction there will be in each stage. If you make a written plan, leave a column for *interaction*.

You can use abbreviations such as:
- W: T > Sts (Whole class: Teacher to students.)
- W: Sts > T (Whole class: Students to teacher.)
- W: M (Whole class mingle.)
- Ps (Pairs.)
- 4's (Groups of four.)
- St > T (One student to teacher.)
- Sts > Sts (Students to students.)

When you have made the plan, check how much of the lesson involves students speaking compared with the percentage of the class when you are speaking. Over time, work towards moving the balance away from you talking and more towards them.

Technique: Finger lock

It can be hard to stop yourself speaking, even if you really want to. If this is a problem that you have, you may find that it helps to physically prevent yourself from speaking!

After you ask a question, try raising a hand to your mouth to cover it with a finger or two (as if you are about to say, 'Shhhh'). To the students, it should look as if you are musing thoughtfully about a student's response, whereas in reality, you are using your fingers to keep your mouth closed, symbolically sealing your lips. Some teachers find that doing this reminds them to stay quiet and discourages them from unnecessary talk.

Technique: Don't always top and tail

Acknowledge student contributions, but don't feel the need to say something after each one.

If you observe teachers at work in class, you will see a lot of them 'top and tail' everything any student says, i.e. before a student says anything, they will lead into it, introduce it, ask a question and so on. After a student has spoken, they will echo it, summarise it, respond to it, correct it or in some other way 'close' it or 'pass it on' to another student. How rare it is to hear a student reply to something that another student has said! How rare not to hear the teacher's voice every second turn!

If every time a student speaks, you say something in response, you are taking away opportunities for other students to react and respond themselves. When students speak, they need to know that they have been heard and that you are interested in what they said. But it's not necessary to comment on everything. You can still show some reaction, acknowledging their contribution; for example, you can say, 'Thank you', 'hmm', nod, smile or raise an eyebrow. You can invite others to continue the conversation on with a gesture (e.g. a 'passing on' hand), or just by looking in an interested way at other students and waiting. Often, the space and silence (i.e. the *absence* of the teacher saying something) is what students need to organise their own thoughts and find something to say (see Chapter 5 Unit 5).

Technique: Getting students to ask the questions

In most classes, it's the teacher who asks the vast majority of questions. Why not turn this around and get students to ask questions? It can make for a surprisingly exciting activity and builds a positive sense of students being in (at least partial) control of things.

One simple idea is to hold a question and answer session on something that you have just been studying (e.g. a reading text or a language point) or a general interest topic (e.g. the latest talent show series on TV):

> Ask the students to prepare (as pairs or in groups) a list of questions they would like to ask you. They can be any kind: factual questions, curiosity questions and so on. Monitor and help students word the questions well. When they are ready, sit at the front and let them ask you. Keep your answers brief and interesting. Remember that the focus is on their questions more than your answers. After each response from you, invite follow-on questions to explore the subject a little more.

Questions for reflection

• How much is your own internal image of a teacher that of someone who speaks a lot and 'tops and tails' everything a student says? Might it be necessary to think about and change the image you carry in order to successfully reduce your unnecessary talk?

■4 Should students put up their hands?

> *When we are working as a whole class, it always seems to be two or three people who put up their hands to answer. How could I get more students involved?*

Aim

To explore alternative ways for students to indicate that they have something to say.

Introduction

In many primary and secondary classrooms, students indicate that they want to speak by putting up their hands. Generations of teachers have found this a simple, but effective strategy. It allows students to indicate that they are keen to answer or contribute, while avoiding the potential chaos of everyone calling out simultaneously.

However, there is a danger with hand-raising that the teacher is consistently drawn to ask those who do raise their hands and because these are likely to be the strongest or fastest students, it becomes all too easy to go at their speed and not notice that some students never volunteer and rarely speak.

Is it possible that hand-raising encourages a few show-offs in class to dominate while the other students can hide and do little? Is it possible that the real, hidden working speed of the class as a whole is actually much slower than you have been led to believe?

In 2007, the UK Department of Education advised teachers to choose who to answer questions rather than asking for hands-up. Hands-up was deemed to allow 'invisible children' to remain 'quiet and undemanding'. These pupils were often 'anxious about taking risks and seeming to be wrong'.

Hands-up remains a controversial area, but in many schools is still absolutely standard practice – and teachers who don't go along with the status quo can get into trouble with colleagues. Putting up hands (or not) is one of the issues that turns up fairly frequently in popular newspapers and radio talk shows as a supposed barometer for how lax or over-liberal education has become. For tabloid writers, putting up hands is typically equated with good schools, discipline, and quality teaching and learning. But in language teaching, you need to check out carefully whether it may be more of a hindrance than a help.

Techniques: Using hands-up more effectively

1 Pick carefully

If you decide to keep using hand-raising in your class, it's important to check that you are not asking the same few students again and again. Deliberately choose different learners each time. Risk upsetting the two or three strong students who always want to speak. Sometimes pick on people who haven't put up their hand! (Don't be horrible to them! Help them to feel their way towards a good answer!)

2 Involve weaker students in strong students' answers

Sometimes pick a student who has put up their hand, but instead of asking them for an answer, ask them to ask the same question to a student of your choice (e.g. one you gesture towards). Now, of course, the reason the other student has not volunteered is most likely because they don't know the answer. But they can take their ideas and words by borrowing from the stronger student. For example:

Teacher:	Luis, don't tell me your answer. Ask the same question to Marisa.
Luis:	OK. Um … Marisa, why is the answer to Question 7 false?
Marisa:	(Shakes head.)
Teacher:	Tell Marisa what you think.
Luis:	I think he went to Rotterdam, not Brussels.
Teacher:	Marisa. Do you agree?
Marisa:	Um … Yes.
Teacher:	So tell me why it's false.
Marisa:	He went to Rotterdam.
Teacher:	Good.

There is, of course, a large element of prompting and leading here. It's entirely possible that Marisa didn't actually have *False – Rotterdam* as her answer (or have any answer), but she has managed to speak in the class and has had the boost of giving a correct answer. Maybe that makes it OK. It doesn't prove understanding, but it does bring her fully into the class interaction.

Techniques: Banning hand-raising

Many teachers have made the decision to ban hand-raising, either completely, or for certain lessons, activities or stages.

If students are in the habit of putting up their hands, and especially if other teachers in the same school use this technique, it will take some time for learners to get into the new habit of not putting up hands. There may also be some resentment, especially from the fast, strong students who have been used to getting attention and showing off what they know. You will need to stick to your guns and gently but firmly insist that this is the new way of doing things. But don't underestimate the difficulties of the transition.

Techniques: Alternatives to hands-up

If you decide to ban or restrict raising hands in class, what alternatives could you try?

1 Nominations

Ask students to answer questions by name. This could be a purely random choice, though over time you will want to ensure that a wide range of students get to answer. Nominating may have a powerful effect on students' attention and engagement. Instead of being able to drift off or hide in class, each student now needs to think of what they might say if they are asked.

- **Wait a little before nominating** Thinking time is crucial, so don't nominate immediately after asking the question. If you ask a question and then straight away ask a specific student to answer, you put them under pressure. Remember that the student needs to do a number of difficult things: understand and interpret your question, think about the question, come up with an answer or response, find the words and grammar to formulate that response, say the response. Asking them to do all these things immediately is very challenging. The strong students might well be able to do this, but if you want to start teaching the whole class, rather than the best few, build in thinking and preparation time. Try following these steps:
  1. Ask a question.
  2. Count slowly in your head while looking around the room.
  3. Name a student to answer.
  How long should that count in Step 2 be? In many cases, a count of ten would be effective. This may well feel like a long time to you, and may be much longer than you have typically expected for an answer in a hands-up classroom. But try it out. See if some students start to benefit from that extra time. See if more people are becoming more involved in your lessons. (And if that doesn't work for you, try counting to five!)

- **Nominations … then hand-raising** If you feel that you might alienate some keen students by never allowing them to volunteer an answer, you could try initially nominating people to answer and then, when one or two have spoken, asking anyone else who wants to contribute to raise their hands.

2 Hands/no-hands traffic light

On a large piece of card, design an indicator (such as a traffic light with a red hand on one side of the card and a green hand on the other) that you can hang on the wall or board and quickly turn over to indicate whether you want students to volunteer by raising hands or not.

3 Personal board – written answers

Invite *all* students to write their answers to a question, for example, by using individual student whiteboards, which they then hold up, or by contributing by WiFi or Internet to a collection of answers on the interactive whiteboard. Either of these techniques will allow you to see at a glance who has answered the question, who has the correct answer and who has problems.

4 Desk indicators

Give each student a desk indicator. Exactly what it looks like is up to you (or students could design it), but it needs to provide a simple feedback method that allows students to indicate whether they have understood or not, for example, a stand-up card that can be turned to show a smiley face or a puzzled face. Throughout an input section of the lesson, or when the teacher requests, students should turn their indicators to show if they understand and are happy or if they have problems. (This is, of course, just another variation on asking students, 'Do you understand?' and, as is discussed elsewhere in this book, students may say 'yes' for the wrong reasons.)

5 Pair or group buzz

Instead of asking for answers to be made to the whole class, ask your question, and then immediately tell students to turn to their partner (or speak with their group) and answer, agree answers or discuss the issue. This can be a very short buzz, maybe just 30 to 60 seconds. You can train students to make sure that they reach a compromise / agreed answer and are ready to report this back to the whole class afterwards.

Questions for reflection

• Putting up hands: necessary and useful for maintaining good manners and good order in class? Yes or no?

5 Training students to listen to each other

> *Students don't listen to each other. They talk over each other. When we have discussions, they wait for me to repeat things and then just respond to me, not to the student who said it.*

Aim

To encourage students to listen more to each other.

Introduction

In many classrooms, the only person anyone listens to or interacts with is the teacher. Many students may speak, but the others can't hear or don't listen.

However, to get a real buzz of communication in the room, we need to make sure that students not only speak, but also listen to and respond directly to each other, not always via the teacher.

Technique: Walking away

When a student is speaking so quietly that you (and other students) struggle to hear them, a teacher's natural reaction might be to walk closer to them. This would allow you to hear the speaker better, but does nothing to help the rest of the class. So, paradoxically, if a student is speaking too quietly, it is often more productive to move further away from the speaker (perhaps backing away while maintaining eye contact). You could then ask them to 'Say it again'. The distance will often encourage them to speak louder – and if you can hear them from across the room, other students will also be able to. In this way, what might have become a private exchange, excluding everyone else, is now part of the normal interaction of the whole class.

Technique: Avoiding echo

In many classrooms (when in whole-class mode), all interaction tends to always go via the teacher:

Student 1: I think that the answer is ... um ... he didn't get the job.
  Teacher: He didn't get the job. So ... you think he didn't get it. Do you agree, Idris?
Student 2: (Mumbles so that only nearby teacher can hear.)
  Teacher: Good ... so you agree, Idris.

(a) A student says something. (b) The teacher repeats it, then ... (c) The teacher asks another student what he or she thought of it. (d) That student says something in reply, which ... (e) The teacher then repeats ... and so on.

As a result, students never have to listen to what anyone else says; they can mentally switch off for a few seconds while any student speaks because they know that what the student says will be repeated pretty soon by the teacher. This kind of teacher repetition of things originally said by a student is known as *echo*.

But is it useful? In my class, I want students to learn to communicate with as many other people as possible, to listen to and speak with each other. I want discussions, exchanges of ideas, arguments – all interaction to be made directly, person to person, rather than always using me as an intermediary. In this way, the class stands a good chance of involving more people more actively, becoming livelier, more interesting and having a better pace.

One key to getting this to happen is simply to stop any unnecessary teacher repetition.

Teachers, when questioned about echo, often say that they have very good reasons for doing it, often because they feel that students wouldn't hear each other in class without the teacher repeating at a greater volume, or because they want the chance to correct any incorrect language before other students hear what was said.

Certainly, there may well be good reasons for echoing with a purpose. However, a lot of teacher echo is just automatic and unaware. The teacher does it without thinking, maybe because he or she has always done it. As with many classroom management areas, a key step towards making a difference is simply becoming more aware of what one does. Once one is clearer about that, change often follows by itself without much further conscious effort.

Steps to cut your echo:

1 When you are having a whole-class discussion and you ask a student to say something, listen with interest, but make a point of not echoing anything they say or responding with anything more than interested nods and noises. Once they have finished speaking, you can say, 'Thank you' or some other acknowledgement that avoids echoing or responding.
2 Look at another student and ask if they agree or disagree. They are very likely to say, 'But I didn't hear him', because they are not in the habit of listening to each other. In this situation, do not repeat what the first student said; this would just be a delayed echo. Instead, go back to the first student, and ask them to repeat what they said. If they say it too quietly, ask them to say it again louder. Avoid all temptation to say it yourself. Use the technique Walking away (see above) if necessary. Wait until the second student hears and responds.
3 Once again, deliberately avoid echoing. Ask a third student for their response. Continue in the same way.
4 Keep following Steps 1 to 3 lesson after lesson to slowly train your class in listening to each other.

When you work like this, you are facilitating a differently shaped interaction web, looking more like this:

 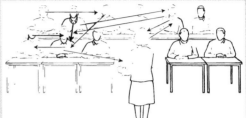

Interaction via teacher   Interaction web

Student 1:   I think that the answer is … um … he didn't get the job.
   Teacher: Thank you, Masha. Do you agree, Idris?
Student 2:   (Mumbles, 'I didn't hear.')
   Teacher: If you couldn't hear Masha, ask her to repeat it.
Student 2:   Masha, what was your answer?
 Student 1:   I said that … he didn't get the job.
Student 2:   (Mumbles so that only nearby teacher can hear.)
   Teacher: (Walks further away.) Sorry, I couldn't hear that.
Student 2:   Yes, I think Masha's answer is correct.
   Teacher: Do you agree with their answer, Danar?

This technique has huge potential for turning your lessons around. At the start, it can be a bit slow and painful, but after the class realises what you are doing, it quickly starts to work. Do this well and your class can go from a passive, quiet one where students hardly look at each other or communicate to one where there is a palpable buzz and excitement. One simple technique, consistently applied, can transform everything. Please try it!

Techniques: Drawing students' attention to their behaviour

Another strategy for discouraging students from talking over others is simply to point out to them what they are doing. They may not have noticed or seen the significance of their behaviour. Here are a few ways of doing this:

1   When a student talks over another, turn briefly to the interrupter, say calmly, 'You are talking over Ayda. I would like to hear her' and then turn back, avoiding any further discussion or disagreement about your statement. Give your full attention to the speaker.
2   After a conversation where such interruptions have happened, it may be useful to open this behaviour up for class discussion, particularly with younger students who may be less aware of appropriate ways of behaviour. You could say something like, 'In that conversation, a number of people talked over others. For example, when I asked Maja, she started to speak, but Tamas interrupted. What do you think? Is it OK to do this?' Let the discussion flow, and, at the end, see if you can get students to agree how they will behave in future.

Technique: Get students to speak to the whole class

When a student speaks, perhaps quietly and directed at you, try gesturing in a way that indicates, 'Don't just tell me (the teacher) but tell the whole class'. This could be one arm held out in a sweeping movement, palm flat, to indicate the other students in the room.

Technique: Intentionally 'not hearing' a loud student

When you ask a question in class, one or more faster, louder or strong students may shout out an answer, even if you have specifically named another student to respond (perhaps one who needs a longer thinking time). Because the stronger ones always call out the answers, the quiet ones never seem to get a chance.

In such a situation, it is very easy to find oneself drawn to look at the loud student who is calling out the answer, almost as if magnetically pulled in that direction, and then accepting their answer and moving forward with the lesson (while forgetting or ignoring the weaker, slower student who is still trying to formulate their own answer). This is one of the ways that lessons tend to start moving at the speed of the fastest few students, rather than at a speed more appropriate for everyone. This key technique addresses this problem.

When you ask a question to a nominated individual, consciously decide not to be pulled away from giving this person your full attention. Work on keeping your gaze relaxed, but steadily in the direction of the person you want to give an answer. If someone else shouts out, simply behave as if you don't hear them. Don't turn and look at them, even to say 'shhh' or something similar. Just let the other responses wash over you and have no effect. If the person you want to speak takes a while to form their response, don't look stressed or over-anxious about this delay.

Why might this work? When someone speaks to us, the natural response is to turn and look at them. This happens all the time in everyday conversation. We interpret being looked at as a show of interest, which also seems to give permission to continue speaking. Conversely, it is remarkably hard to continue speaking when the intended listener is not looking at us. We can use this reaction to our benefit in class. By simply not turning to make eye contact with a speaker, we quietly discourage them from speaking.

The first time you try this in class, it may feel rude. It isn't. It's simply an effective classroom management technique and a good example of one way in which classroom teacher responses need to be different from our normal out-of-classroom behaviour.

Questions for reflection

• Is it hard to stop yourself echoing? Do you feel an urge to speak even when you have decided not to? What do you think causes this? How could you reduce this urge?

6 Withholding validation of student answers

> *When a student gives a correct answer, my first reaction is usually relief. Phew! Someone actually understood my teaching! But after I've said, 'Well done', I'm left wondering whether that student was the only one who got it?*

Aim
To involve more students in answering questions, not only the fastest ones.

Introduction
When you get the chance to observe other teachers teaching, it's often noticeable how some race along at the speed of their best students, oblivious to the fact that the weaker learners are getting more and more left behind, more and more lost. The techniques in this unit can change that.

Technique: Not rubberstamping

I am sometimes asked what I think is the single most useful and important practical technique for a teacher to use. My reply is, 'not rubberstamping'. A surprisingly small number of teachers seem to use it, but when you do see it being used, the impact is astonishing. It is the one technique that makes all the difference between a class taught for the benefit of a few and one which involves and engages everyone.

So, of all the ideas in this book, I urge you to try this one. If it doesn't work for you first time, don't give up on it. Try it again. It can transform your classroom management, your teaching and your students.

When you ask a question and a student replies, it's tempting to respond immediately to what they say, perhaps validating their answer with a 'yes' or 'correct' or by indicating that they haven't yet got the right answer.

In doing this, you let the student know where they stand, but you also close down many possible ways that the discussion could expand to involve more of the class. The interaction is between two people, you and that first student, while the rest of the class may ignore you or drift off (especially if the interaction is quiet and hard to hear).

Look at this exchange in which the teacher is asking about a recording the class has just listened to.

Teacher:	So who do you think stole the purse?
Student A:	I think it was Petra.
Teacher:	Yes. Good. That's the right answer.

In answering like this, the teacher has confirmed that 'Petra' is the correct answer, and, in doing so, has completely closed the conversation. There is no point in now turning to another student and saying:

Teacher: Do you agree, Kamal?

It would be a bold or foolish student who chose to disagree or offer an alternative answer once the teacher has already put her 'rubberstamp' of approval on an answer. It's like putting a great big inky red 'CORRECT' stamp on a certificate. It leaves nowhere else to go.

Rubberstamping kills interaction. It ensures that you work at the speed of the first and fastest students to call out.

Train yourself to withhold the rubberstamp. When you ask a question, try these three steps:

1 Acknowledge, but don't validate

When a student answers, thank them or nod to acknowledge their answer or say something non-committal such as 'interesting', but don't give any response as to whether it is good or correct.

2 Get other students to comment

Look around the room, and ask another student, 'Do you agree?' or a similar question. Listen carefully, acknowledge, but, again, don't respond.

When the second student has finished (whether they agreed or not, whether they are right or not), move on to a third student and ask them, 'What about you? Do you agree with him or her, or neither?'

If you think it helps, you could objectively summarise answers given so far (e.g., 'So Nanami thinks that Petra stole the purse. Zainab also thinks it's Petra. Kamal thinks that it was the stranger'), but, again, make sure you give no indication as to which is correct.

You could obviously go on in this way, collecting different student answers and opinions, as long as you wish, but even if you stop after just two or three students have spoken, you will already have a much better idea of what the class as a whole thinks than by just asking the first student. In addition, you have encouraged them all to listen to each other and process what they are saying (rather than only listening to you).

3 Confirm and validate

At the appropriate point, after a number of answers, you need to confirm which are correct. Give credit to those who said the right answers, but avoid pointing out or picking on those who didn't.

If there have been a lot of incorrect answers (for example, in the listening example, if most people got it wrong), this is an indication that the students need more chances to get the right answer. In this case, avoid confirming which answer is correct; simply telling them (e.g. 'The right answer is Petra') wouldn't really help. They need to find it out for themselves (i.e. by listening again).

By using these three steps, you start to get answers and interaction *bouncing* around the class rather than getting caught in a permanent teacher–student loop.

Bear in mind that if your students are familiar with the 'first person wins' approach, they may be puzzled by your change of mode. You could explain what you are doing, or perhaps ask them what they think might be the value of this way of working.

Technique: Blank face

When using the technique above, watch out for indications you may unintentionally give as to whether an answer is correct or not – nodding your head, for example. Sometimes teachers are so relieved to hear a right answer that they cannot help *leaking* the fact that it is right as soon as it is given.

Try to practise keeping a *blank face* that does not give away the fact that an answer is correct.

Questions for reflection

- Think back over your own teaching. Do you think that you have a tendency to rubberstamp or not? If you believe that you don't, how can you be sure that what you think you don't do is what you actually don't do? (With this technique, there is often a significant gulf between what teachers imagine of themselves and what the reality is. It's worth checking out what the reality is for you. This would be a useful observation focus for a colleague to come in and comment on.)

Pairs and groups

◼️ 7 Making pairs and groups

> *The same students always seem to sit and work together. I want to form groups in more interesting or more useful ways.*

Aim

To divide students up into pairs or groups to work on a task.

Introduction

Learners often need to work together in pairs or small groups of between three and six people. The default option is that students get together with people who are already sitting near them. This has the advantage of speed and doesn't require much thinking or movement, but does mean that learners may always work with the same people.

The ideas below suggest some ways of forming pairs and groups in more interesting ways. Many of these will involve some language use (such as asking each other questions) in addition to whatever the intended language work of the main group task will be (e.g. asking each other what TV shows they like).

Techniques: Basic options

1 Say the instruction, 'Get into pairs' or 'Make groups of three/four/five'. You could let students choose who to work with, or indicate with gestures or further instructions who could be in which groups and where the groups should form.
2 Alternatively, go round the class, allocating a letter to each student (e.g. the first student gets 'A', the second 'B' and so on, etc.). When all students have a letter, give an instruction such as, 'Make a pair with an A and B' or 'All A's work together. All B's work together' Or 'A's come over here. B's make a group by the window', etc. You can allocate letters in order round the class, or you could pre-plan groupings by deciding beforehand who will get which letter.

Technique: Playing around with some basic variables

Here are a few things to think about when making groups:

1 Do groups all need to be the same size, or might it be interesting to have different-sized groups?
2 Would it be better to create groups around *similarities* (e.g. interests, language level, creativity, ages, gender, etc.) or around *differences*?
3 Do you want to engineer certain people to work together (or *not* work together)?

Techniques: Making random groups

1 'Make a group with people who have the same colour bag as you / were born in the same month as you / like the same TV show as you / enjoy the same style of hot drink as you.' (Instructions like this may require students to talk briefly with others before they can start on the main task.)
2 Get all students to write their names on a slip of paper and put them in a bag. Pull out names to form groups.
3 Tell each student to write down their favourite animal (or dessert/shop/song, etc.) from a short list you show them (e.g. ice cream, chocolate, cake, fruit). When students reveal their words, form groups of people with the same items.
4 Instead of using group letters, choose a set of words the class has recently studied (e.g. types of fruit). Allocate a different word to each student. When everyone has a fruit, you can ask all the oranges to make a group, all the apples and so on.
   - 'Tiger, cow, dragon, etc.: Wild animals meet up by the window. Imaginary animals meet up at this table.'
   - 'Renault, McLaren, Ferrrari, etc.: OK, all Ferraris drive over here and meet up; all Renaults race over there.'
   - 'Eiffel Tower, Big Ben, Uluru, Tower Bridge, The Louvre, etc.: Find partners from the same country.'
5 Make sets of cards. Each card should have one item from a lexical set (e.g. books: dictionary, encyclopaedia, coursebook, novel, atlas). Shuffle the cards and distribute one to each learner. Students should mingle, compare words and make a group that has one complete set of words.
   - 'Orange, purple, crimson, turquoise, etc.: Make a group with five different colours in it.'
   - 'Eggs, coffee, bacon, etc.: Get together and make a complete breakfast.'
   - Make sets of cards, but mix up lots of different sets of words (e.g. computer words, seaside words, food items, etc.) so that students must find others who have words that seem to be from the same set as their own word (e.g. 'mouse', 'monitor' and 'keyboard' will get together, but not in the same group as 'beach', 'waves' and 'pebble'). The group forming will take longer!
6 Prepare a meet-and-match task (e.g. different pictures, each cut up jigsaw-style into five pieces). Students mingle and try to find the other students who also have pieces from their picture.

Techniques: Making non-random groups

1 Ask learners to choose who they would like to work with.
2 Make groups based on results of a preceding activity, exercise or test (e.g. 'All students who got seven or more answers correct, work in a group over here').
3 Use a matching task, but don't distribute pieces randomly. Give out sets to people that you want to work together.

Techniques: Pairs

1 Tell students, 'Work with someone who … is not sitting in a seat near you / you think will have a totally different view to your own / you have never worked with before / lives far away from you / is waving to you across the room now.'
2 Ask learners to write an anagram of their first names on a slip of paper. Collect the slips and redistribute randomly. Students have to try to unravel the anagram to find their new partner's name.

Techniques: Making pairs with no big moves

If you decide not to ask students to move at all, you still have a number of ways of making varied pairs:

1 Sideways: work with a student on your left for one task, and then the next task with the student on the *other* side.
2 Front/back: work with a student in the seat in front of you for one task, and then behind you for the next one.
3 Diagonally: well … you get the idea!

Technique: Pairs or threesomes?

Consider the regular use of threesomes rather than pairs. Ken Wilson argues forcefully for this in his blog:

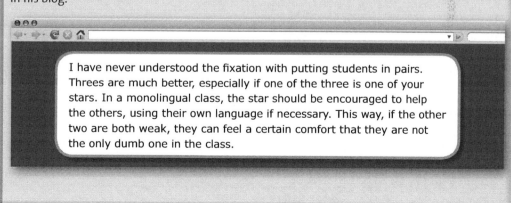

I have never understood the fixation with putting students in pairs. Threes are much better, especially if one of the three is one of your stars. In a monolingual class, the star should be encouraged to help the others, using their own language if necessary. This way, if the other two are both weak, they can feel a certain comfort that they are not the only dumb one in the class.

Questions for reflection

- Does the teacher have the *right* to decide who should or shouldn't work together? If one learner prefers to work with particular other people (and not with others), should we respect that?
- Do teachers have any responsibility to force learners into different working relationships?
- If you want to have same-sized groups and your group-making method produces uneven sizes, how could you quickly balance things out?

■8 Keeping pair work and group work interesting

> *I find that I keep saying, 'Get into groups', and they all huddle together and talk for 10 minutes or so – and it's sort of OK, but never very exciting.*

Aim

To add some variety and spark back into pair and group work that has become routine and predictable.

Introduction

Whether group work is a discussion, a problem-solving task, a shared exercise or whatever, teachers sometimes find that they need to add an extra element to help encourage students to participate fully and actively. One common way is to add a competitive element to work, calling the groups 'teams' and declaring the first to finish (or the team with the best answer or the most right answers) as the 'winner'. In the ideas below, I'll suggest some other ways that learners may find interesting.

Technique: Use different arrangements for pair work

For short discussion topics or *mingle* tasks:

1 Lines

Ask students to stand in two facing lines: Line A and Line B. Facing pairs from A and B talk about the subject. When you ring a bell or tap the table, everyone in Line A moves one place to their right, meeting a new person. (The person on the end of the line moves round to the other end.)

2 Wheels

The same idea works with two circles, an inner wheel and an outer one – the students in the inner wheel facing those in the outer.

Technique: Altering one variable

Sometimes altering just one variable (such as task timing or work position) can make a group-work activity different, for example:

1 Do an activity with a very tight, almost impossible, time limit. Ask students to do the task at speed, guessing answers or choosing the first answers they think of, not going back to check. Stick to the time limit (otherwise students won't take it seriously in future if you set a time limit for a task like this).
2 Do the activity standing up rather than seated. Or do it walking: keep moving around the room as you talk.
3 Do the activity, but only one person in the group can look at / read the task or text. This person has to read aloud or report to the others.
4 Do the activity, but only one person can write answers, make notes, etc.

Technique: Adding or changing ground rules

Adding or changing the ground rules for interaction, or adding restrictions, can be useful:

1 Set a new rule, e.g. after someone has spoken, the person on their right round the circle must speak next.
2 Give each group two balls made of material or some soft substance. Only students holding a ball may speak. They can throw it to another person at any time, but only after making at least some contribution to the activity.
3 Do the activity without speaking. Communicate with each other entirely using writing (e.g. using a shared large sheet of paper, notes on small slips of paper, via the whiteboard, or using technology such as emails, phone text messages, twitter, etc.).

Technique: Spies

This technique is particularly good for idea generation and creative problem-solving tasks.

After students have been working long enough in their groups to have come up with some ideas or solutions, go round the groups and theatrically whisper to one student of your choice in each group that their job is to be a spy – to go and sit with the adjacent group (pointed out by you) and find out what they have said, thought, achieved (but without joining in themselves). After a few minutes, the spies should report back to their original group with as much as they have learnt from their observations of the other group.

Technique: Pirates

This is similar to Spies (above), but the student from each group can browse around the other groups at will and steal anything he/she feels is useful or interesting.

Technique: Art gallery

This idea is good for activities that end with a creative, tangible product such as a poster, a piece of imaginative writing or a picture.

At the end of a group activity, invite each group to pin or stick their work on the wall or a noticeboard (or put it on a table) in different locations all around the room.

When the displays are ready, invite students to browse around the different exhibitions. You can also browse and chat with the visitors. At the end, you could lead a discussion standing by one or more of the exhibits (e.g. agreeing with students which was the most imaginative or most unusual item).

Technique: Carousel

An alternative to the Art Gallery (above) is a carousel.

This is a complex procedure to describe, but it's a great one to use in class as it really stirs things up and changes the challenge level in interesting ways.

1   At the end of an activity, ask students to lay out their completed work on their table or the wall. Ask one or two members of the group to remain behind at their table. The others move on to visit another group. The *old* group members welcome the newcomers and show off their work, explaining it and the thinking behind it.

So, for example, two people in Group A remain behind while the three other Group A members move on to visit Group B, where they meet the two members of Group B who remained behind when their colleagues moved on to Group C!

2 After a suitable amount of time, organise another move (and this one will surprise them!). Ask the people who have recently joined a group to stay there, but the original group members now move on to rejoin their original group at their new table.

For example, the three members of Group A who visited Group B now stay at Group B's table. The original two remaining Group B members move on to rejoin the other Group B students at C's table.

Now that everyone has shifted round one table, the explaining task becomes more challenging as the people doing the talking are not those who designed the poster or made the answers, or whatever, but are those who have just heard about it from the previous group.

Technique: Don't give up on pair and group work!

Sometimes, when teachers first try pair or group work, they may monitor and find many students doing the task poorly or incorrectly or in their own language or not doing the task at all. Teachers may sometimes use this as an excuse to dismiss such work as useless and a waste of classroom time. But as Michael Lewis and Jimmie Hill point out, even if half the students are not working as directed, that still leaves many who are: 'As a result, instead of one or two students doing something useful while the others sit back, 10 or 20 students are working constructively. Teachers must not drop pair work just because it is not successful for all students all the time.'

So, don't give up on pair and group work. Seek ways to make it more interesting, engaging and accessible for more students. Monitor to help the confused make more sense of the tasks and to help bring the non-participators in.

Questions for reflection

- Divide the ideas up into (a) I've used this, (b) I'll use this or (c) I'd never use this.
- Check out what holds you back from using the ideas in Category (c). Just to push yourself out of your comfort zone, can you plan a way of using a Category (c) idea next week?

▌9▐ Encouraging quieter learners to speak in pairs or groups

> *When we do group work, I always notice a few students who seem to hide and manage to say nothing in their group. I try to encourage them, but what more could I do?*

Aim

To find interesting ways to get reluctant students to speak in their groups.

Introduction

It's absolutely normal that some students will be shyer, less confident, weaker at English or less willing to speak – for whatever reason. Encouraging them to speak is part of our job, and part of that is to do with making sure that we allow space for them to participate. Often quieter, slower students simply get squashed out by the stronger, louder, more impatient students. Some of the time-honoured techniques, such as using a conch (see below), work on both managing the louder students and encouraging the quieter ones to speak up.

Technique: Conch

A *conch* is a shell which is either passed around person to person at meetings or is always returned to the centre of the circle, where whoever wants to speak next can retrieve it. Whoever is holding the conch can speak; if you don't have it, you can't speak.

You don't have to have a shell, but having some symbolic items to pass around (jewels, a shield, a rain stick, a horn, a cup/grail, an unusual stone, that weird souvenir you picked up on holiday) or to throw from person to person (a ball, a soft toy) can help give structure to speaking activities, whether in whole class or groups. It is most effective in situations where some individuals constantly talk over others and some never get a fair hearing.

Set the ground rules clearly (e.g. how long one person can speak, how many times each person can speak, the minimum contribution that each student should make); check that everyone understands and buys into them. If anyone breaks the rule, 'shhh!' them, or exclude them from the activity if it seems to be a deliberate act.

Once you have used your conch once, you will find that it becomes very usable in future activities. Everyone will remember the rules and how to behave, so with minimum set-up you can start the discussion.

I find that I sometimes introduce the objects that we will use for passing with a convincing (but entirely made-up) story of their ancient origins and deep mystical importance: 'These strange stones were found buried in the centre of Glastonbury Abbey in the year 1885. Some people believe that King Arthur ...'

Alternatively, if you like the idea of rewards in class, you could use objects (e.g. small packets of sweets) that will themselves become the prizes to the speakers who made the best contributions.

Technique: Discouraging passengers

In group work, some people tend to talk a lot whilst others say little, either because they can't get a word in edgeways or because they are OK with being passengers in the group. Here are some strategies for encouraging such learners to take a more active role:

1 Appoint quieter people as the chair

Give them some specific, stated duties. Putting learners in a facilitating role forces them to take a more active part.

2 Participation tokens

Hand out some tokens before a task. These could be coloured counters, money from a board game, pebbles, beads, Lego® bricks or anything that is small enough and which you have a quantity of. Each student would normally receive the same quantity, e.g. six tokens. When doing the task, each time a person speaks (for more than a short one- or two-word offering), they take one of their tokens and place it in the middle of the table. Once they have used up all their tokens they cannot speak again until everyone has also used up all their tokens, after which anyone can speak freely.

3 Participation tables

At the start of a group task, show students a table that they will have to fill in at the end (stating names and percentage of total participation in the discussion). At the end, all participants have to agree fair answers for everyone. See also Participation review below.

4 Close-up encouragement

Monitor group work and when you spot silent members, rather than tell off or persuade, try joining in with the group and saying, after a while, 'What do you think Ali?'

5 Set task guidelines

Before students start work, specify a rule, e.g. 'Each person in the group must state their views for at least one minute before you begin a general discussion.'

Technique: Random selection of who will speak in groups

Rather than allow anyone to speak at any time in group tasks, you can restrict speaking to randomly chosen students:

1 Wheel of fortune

Make little spinners with the letters A, B, C, D, E, F on them (for groups of up to six people. Each student takes a letter (e.g. C). When a person has finished speaking, the wheel is spun and the person with the letter pointed to can speak. If no one has the letter, anyone can say something.

2 Dice

Throw dice to achieve the same thing. (Students take numbers one to six. When the dice is thrown, the person with that number can speak.)

3 Lucky dip

Distribute a number of small pieces of card or paper to each group. Ask each student to write their name on five of them. When all names are written, they are turned upside down and mixed. A student picks one card, and that person can speak, giving their opinion. The next card is picked; then that person replies and continues the discussion and so on. The cards can be replaced and remixed.

Technique: Participation review

Help to raise learners' own awareness of their participation. After a group task, when you have dealt with all the issues arising and any language points that need work, invite one person in each group to lead a review of their group discussion. Hand this person one set of questions to ask the students in their group. Their task is to lead a discussion based on reflection and avoiding blame, recrimination, sarcasm and so on.

Which questions you offer can vary, but could include some of the following:

- Who do you think said most in our discussion?
- Who said least?
- Which people made interesting points during the discussion?
- Who did most to organise the group discussion?
- Which comments were the most exciting to discuss or argue about?
- What can be done differently next time?

Technique: Pyramid discussion – helping confidence to grow

This is suitable for creative or opinion-based discussion topics (e.g. a task where students have to rank things in order of importance).

1 Start by giving individuals a good amount of thinking time to make notes on their own.
2 Then get them to meet up and compare ideas in pairs. Require that the pairs come to a compromise decision/opinion that they can both agree with.
3 Now, form the pairs into groups of four, and once again ask them to come to a compromise answer that they all buy into.
4 Bring the whole class back together, and discuss the issues together.

By the end of this process, even weaker students might feel a little more confident in speaking. They have had lots of rehearsal time, saying the ideas again and again in pairs and groups. Also, they are no longer tied into their own original ideas, but can argue for the group view, which may be much easier to speak for and which they may have heard others saying. Necessary vocabulary, phrases and sentences will have been heard and perhaps learnt. Others from the same group might come in and support them in what they say, so they won't be entirely on their own.

Technique: Start in whole class; then hand over to groups

Try beginning a discussion in the whole class. Brainstorm possible ideas, headings, themes and arguments. Start discussing general issues. As it starts to get interesting or exciting, hand over to pairs and groups – who might (you hope) be fired up and ready to pick up from where you left off.

Technique: Use information gaps

An information gap is a much-used way of getting students to talk. Typically used in pairs: Student A knows different things from Student B (perhaps because they have read two different, but complementary short texts). This immediately creates a reason to communicate: They have something to say to each other. The discussion can involve comparing what they have learnt from their separate documents – and then maybe solving some puzzle or reaching a consensus or conclusion.

Technique: Community Language Learning

Here is an interesting 'slow' way of building up a fluent conversation. In the language teaching approach Community Language Learning, it is possible to create a whole conversation one sentence at a time. The technique may be worth trying with a low-level class or one that is lacking in confidence. You will need a way of recording individual sentences, spoken by different students at their seats, e.g. a dictation machine or a computer with WiFi microphone.

1 Explain what you are going to do to students; i.e. they will have a conversation about any subject they wish to (or on a subject set by you), and you will build it up sentence by sentence.
2 A student who wants to say something indicates this, e.g. by putting up their hand. When you come over, they use their first language to say what they want to say to you – or if you don't speak their first language, they say the sentence as well as they can in English. You tell them a good English version of what they want to say and help them to practise saying it. When they are confident that they can do it, you switch on the recorder and they say their sentence into it.
3 The next person indicates that they want to reply to the first student … so you go over … and so on.
4 Slowly, over time, you build up a whole conversation which has been recorded.

Questions for reflection

- Do you generally allow quiet students to remain quiet in your classes? If not, how do you encourage them to speak?
- Do you really know why they are quiet? Is there a tangible, known reason?

10 Monitoring pair and group work

> *When I did my initial training, I was encouraged to monitor students while they worked. But I'm never quite sure what to do. I either end up staring at them uselessly or interfering: overhelping and doing the task for them.*

Aim

To use a range of monitoring techniques, in order to make pair and group work as effective and useful as possible.

Introduction

Teachers have very different attitudes to monitoring. Some set up a task and then immediately sit back reading or marking. Others remain very visible in the room throughout the task, helping, encouraging, praising, correcting, criticising, interfering or even doing parts of the task themselves. Some newly qualified teachers tend to 'over monitor', perhaps because that was a practical suggestion overemphasised in their initial training.

The suggestions in this unit suggest a possible approach that varies monitoring, depending on what is happening in different phases of student work.

Technique: Varying monitoring through different stages of an activity

As tasks start

Do students know what they have to do? Immediately after you have given an instruction, as students begin work on their task, there is a vital need to check if they have really understood what to do and will be able to do it successfully. At this stage you need to:

1 Look

Move your gaze carefully around the room, checking if each pair or group appears to look confident, is leaning into the task, starting to talk, picking up pens or whatever they need to do.

2 Wander

Start walking slowly and unobtrusively around the room, overhearing various groups as they begin the work and watching what they are doing. Try to be a relatively invisible presence, rather than someone who is coming in ready to organise and demand things.

3 Support quietly

If you find that just one or two pairs/groups have misunderstood or have a problem, offer help on the spot: perhaps explaining again, showing them what to do, answering questions.

4 Stop and reboot

If you notice that there are a large number of misunderstandings or significant problems, it may be worth calling out for all groups to stop, getting them to listen to you giving the instructions again – perhaps with a worked demonstration of some sort, clarifications or questions from students – and then allowing them to restart the activity.

During tasks

Once you are sure that learners are working well on task, this gives you the chance to look more closely at what different pairs/groups are doing. This could be discreet or participatory:

5 Discreet monitoring

You can stay for a while near a pair/group, listening and watching to get a good idea of what they are doing. Don't hide, but stay a little out of their line of sight, for example, by crouching down beside a table or standing beside (rather than in front of) a student. Don't ask questions or intervene. You could make discreet notes if you wish to, for example, of student language that you could later give feedback on or turn into a future exercise. After a while, you can move on to another pair/group.

Some teachers find that they are able to do discreet monitoring by actually sitting down at the table where the group is working. This is a real skill; it might be difficult to remain uninvolved.

While doing discreet monitoring, you may find that learners have questions for you – maybe about the task or about language they need. You may also feel the need to give learners a *nudge* or two, to push them a little bit onto the right track.

You will need to find the right amount of support to give. While nuggets of helpful information can be very useful, if you start to give too much help, it can tip the balance of an activity. If you find the whole pair/group turning to you and becoming dependent on your answers, maybe you have made a takeover rather than supporting.

You can also use your monitoring to inform you as to whether it may be useful to drip-feed task adjustments into certain groups, perhaps adding an extra task for a stronger group, or simplifying the demands in some way for slower groups. (See Chapter 3 Unit 3.)

6 Participatory monitoring

Choose a pair/group, sit down with them and take an active role in the task, as if you were a student (rather than a teacher). This can be very useful, as the learners get a living example of how to do the work, and they may well raise their own game to match what you do. Of course, there is always the danger of your dominating or taking over completely, so watch out for this. After a while, move on and join in, in a similar way, with another pair/group.

7 Not monitoring

Once students are fully engaged on a task and a focussed sense of flow takes over, the teacher's presence may be a hindrance. Students don't want to constantly feel the pressure of the teacher watching and listening. In such circumstances, it is often appropriate for the teacher to *vanish* for some time. You could go to your desk or a seat in the corner of the room and quietly read a book (while bearing in mind that you do still need to keep alert to problems or needs as they arise). You show your detachment by not being a presence. If you have chosen the right time to do this, you will find that students are unlikely to even notice that you have done it. (There is a longer discussion of vanishing in Chapter 4 Unit 14.)

Questions for reflection

- What kind of monitoring do you enjoy most?
- What kind of monitoring feels most useful for your students?
- Are there any kinds of monitoring you avoid or never do?

11 Encouraging students to use English

> *Everyone keeps saying that students should be doing pair and group tasks. That's all very well, but what's the point if they just talk in their first language all the time while they are doing them?*

Aim

To encourage learners to speak in English when doing pair and group tasks.

Introduction

Teachers who work with monolingual classes, especially with school-age students, may complain that the value of speaking tasks is typically reduced because learners tend to do much of the communication in their first language (L1) rather than in English. This can sometimes be an issue in whole-class work, but is a particular problem when students do pair or group tasks.

One common situation is that the students use their own language (perhaps whispering or talking quietly) while the teacher isn't watching closely, but as soon as she wanders closer to monitor them, they switch (temporarily) into English (and then back again after she has left!).

Even when students are genuinely keen to speak English, they may find that the more interesting a task is, the more they find themselves reverting back to the other language. A slow dull task can be done in English, but an exciting race or competition takes over, and the desire to win or finish first or get the best answer supersedes all other aims.

Technique: Discuss the learners' use of English

When the issue of using L1 has caused a problem, raise it as a discussion point with the class (in L1 if necessary). Without blaming anyone, point out that you heard a lot of L1 being used. Ask them what they think: whether it is OK or not. Listen without pressurising them into an opinion. You may find students saying why it is natural for them to use L1, how it is hard for them to use English or maybe explaining that they don't see the point of speaking it.

After hearing them, you can also give your perspective, perhaps that it is your job to help them learn the language, that you believe that it will be very useful to them in the future, will help them get better jobs and so on. Ask for their advice: 'If I wanted you to use as much English as possible in future tasks, what would you advise me to do?' Note all their ideas. Ask clarification questions if you need to, but avoid arguing the points or dismissing them. At the end, thank them very much for their ideas, and say that you will try some the next few times you do tasks in class.

Technique: Dealing with the 'silliness' of talking in English

Some learners may feel foolish or self-conscious talking English to their peers, when they know perfectly well that they can understand their native tongue, and English just sounds so … frankly … silly! One way to deal with this may be by openly acknowledging how they feel and laughing together at the silliness of it all. For example, if you are a non-native speaker of English, you could say, 'Doesn't it sound strange for us all to speak this foreign language! Ridiculous! Right …. Let's see who can sound most like an English person [or an American, an Australian, etc.]!'.

This, and the preceding idea, pick up on a basic principle, mentioned elsewhere in this book: that when you meet a problem, it's typically better to face up to it directly, rather than to ignore it and act as if it doesn't exist – or respond to it as a 'naughty' discipline issue.

Techniques: Participation grades

Bear in mind that you can assess speaking and participation as part of the learner's overall mark for a lesson, a week, a month or the whole term. The higher a percentage that this mark contributes to the overall grade, the more likely your students are to take participation in English seriously.

Keep firmly in mind that this is a mark for participation rather than for quality of language or for correctness. Award grades for joining in, doing tasks in the spirit they are set, using English, neither dominating nor hiding. You may only need three grades each time: 2 = full, active, engaged participation; 1 = acceptable level of participation; 0 = limited, insufficient or no participation.

You do need to make sure that you grade fairly and accurately. Giving an overall impression mark after eight weeks' work is hardly likely to convince students of its fairness. However, if every time students do a pair/group task, they see you walking around, really listening and noticing what they are doing, and if you then make the cumulative marks transparent and public, this might well make a difference. How well people participate is naturally going to be a subjective judgement. Most students may well get a top grade, and this will motivate, but make sure that you do award lower grades for those who don't join in. Giving every single student in class the same high grade will not inspire.

Techniques: Rewards and prizes

Some teachers like to award rewards or prizes for areas of classroom difficulties such as this, e.g. everyone who speaks a lot of English gets a sweet at the end. Personally, I've never felt too comfortable with this, as it seems to be getting motivation to grow for the wrong reasons – but, all the same, you may well decide that it is worth trying with your class. For reward schemes, you might wish to try some of the ideas in Chapter 6 Unit 1 on rewards to do with behavioural issues.

Technique: Allow L1

One possible strategy is simply to allow L1 usage without prohibition or fuss, but just to gently cajole and encourage students to keep trying more use of English. In many ways, this more natural and more human response is the simplest and perhaps the most understanding of students' needs.

Technique: Time zones

Speaking English is very demanding and exhausting for many students. One way to encourage it to happen more is paradoxically to permit it not to be used.

Some teachers announce specific periods of the lesson that are 'only English', while taking a more relaxed attitude to use of L1 at other points. So, for example, you might have 10 minutes near the start of the lesson when only English is allowed. This might be followed by a long stretch where L1 was allowed, for example, while students were working on exercises. Perhaps near the end of the lesson, you might have another 10-minute 'only-English' section.

Of course, students will need to clearly understand when these time zones begin and end, which is where the next idea comes in.

Technique: Indicators

Indicate whether students are allowed to speak their first language, or only English, by using a clear indicator hung on the wall or board. This could be a large card with one side saying, 'Only English' while the other says, 'Italian allowed' (or whatever the language is). Traffic lights are another possibility: red and green.

Technique: Start tasks in L1 – finish them in English

Students often find the beginning of tasks and activities the hardest bit: 'What do we have to do?' 'How can we do it?' 'What are we supposed to write?'

In such cases, you can start a task off by permitting students to speak in their own language and only add in the need to use English later on – say after the first five minutes. For example, 'Get into groups, and start talking about the task. You can use Chinese, but when you hear this bell (teacher rings bell as an example), then you must stop talking in Chinese and start using English.'

Technique: Appoint monitors in groups

When you start group work, add an extra person to each pair or group, whose job is specifically to monitor language use.

1 Monitor as reminder
Whenever someone uses L1, the monitor can (gently) remind them not to.

2 Monitor as feedback giver
The monitor role/job could be expanded to a wider monitoring/facilitation remit. At the end of a task, monitors could report back on how the task went. There is some risk of this being seen as telling tales, and fear of blame or being put in the spotlight. To avoid this, monitors should be instructed to report on the general use of English in the group without naming any names.

3 Monitor as vocabulary recorder
An alternative use of the monitor is to keep a record of language that would be useful to learn. While students are doing the activity, if they don't know a word in English, they simply say the word in their first language. The monitor keeps a note of all first language use. When the activity has ended, everyone can look at the monitor's list and consult a dictionary to 'fill in the gaps' with all the English words they didn't know. Students can then redo the same activity, using the new vocabulary (and perhaps changing roles).

Technique: Do it twice

Try doing some activities twice (e.g. discussion and agreement tasks), the first time in the students' L1, the second time in English. This means that a lot of the difficult thinking and problem-solving can be solved the first time round, allowing them to spend more energy the second time on finding the best way to say things in English. The second time the activity is done, introduce some small variations to the task (e.g. with different materials or a very similar, but slightly varied, problem). This ensures that the students still have a reason to communicate with each other. So, for example, Task 1 (in their first language): Decide which historical character from a list would be good to invite to give a talk to the class. Task 2 (in English): The same task, but with a different list of people.

Technique: Speaking contracts

Ask learners to negotiate and agree a short contract about how they will use English in class. You could use a template, such as the one below, or devise your own format. The best format will be one actually planned and written by the students themselves.

Sample speaking contract:

We, Ms Ramirez's class C2B, agree that in English lessons ...

1 When we are working as a whole class, we will use English to ask or answer questions whenever the sign on the wall says 'English'.

2 When we are working in pairs or groups, we will use only English if our teacher says, 'Do this task in English'.

3 If a student speaks five or more words in Spanish at a time when English should be used, he/she will lose one point for their team.

Questions for reflection

- Do your students use their own language when doing tasks?
- Do you permit that, put up with it, discourage it or forbid it?
- Do you prefer the suggestion for a negotiated solution to the problems? Or is it better to choose a solution yourself and impose it?

🔢 Allocating group-participant roles

> *In most tasks, the same students always seem to lead while others are always silent. Even those who do speak tend to repeat the same sort of arguments and points of view. It would be good to force them out of all their comfort zones a little.*

Aim

To offer learners different ways of being within a group, extending and enriching the way they approach group tasks.

Introduction

Group work can easily become dull and repetitive if students always work with the same partners in the same sorts of ways. Some will naturally be more dominant, some quieter, some more engaged, some less interested. Some learners will behave like organisers, some like followers. This can make discussion-based tasks rather samey; everyone knows how everyone is likely to participate. Once a learner has found their place, it can be hard to break free of that.

One simple solution is to constantly mix up the students, reallocating membership of groups for each new activity, though this can lead to more seat-changing kerfuffle than you might wish and may frustrate students who prefer to work with friends. If you are happy with groups retaining the same members, there are other ways to inject some variety into how they work, by playing around with what roles people adopt.

You may be surprised at how much role allocation can transform classes and individuals. When given responsibility, many people take it up with enthusiasm. Instead of yet another, 'Oh we have to chat about global warming', learners may suddenly find new motivation and interest in their work.

Techniques: Choosing and supporting group leaders

Groups often acquire leaders, whether appointed by you or by group members: someone who simply emerges during the work process, someone who regularly adopts a leadership role or perhaps a person whose role outside class (e.g. the participants' real-life manager in company) propels them into position as a leader in class.

Having a leader may help in areas such as structuring and planning what to do, role defining and role allocation, interaction managing, consensus building, decision making, summarising and so on. The leadership role may be taken by different people over time, varying as tasks change or different requirements become apparent.

The following list suggests some key responsibilities and qualities of a leader. You might want to brainstorm a list like this with your students.

- Working democratically, consultatively and supportively, making sure that everyone participates and gets listened to.
- Keeping a clear, unambiguous task focus and a sense of progress towards a common aim.
- Organising, structuring and restructuring, as the task proceeds: forming subgroups, dividing up tasks, setting sub-aims, setting time limits, agreeing roles, etc.
- Maintaining a happy, engaged, positive working atmosphere.
- Pushing and nudging: encouraging people to think more laterally, feel more engaged, move forward and achieve even more than they believed they were capable of.
- Dealing with dissent, obstacles and failures in open, creative and supportive ways.

As the teacher, you need to encourage the things listed above to happen. Over time, you also need to ensure that it is not always the same people who become group leaders every time:

1 Appoint different people. Choose cleverly to match leaders to tasks.
2 Use random selection methods (e.g. picking slips of paper from a bag – whoever gets 'L' is leader).
3 Rotate leaderships. If someone has been a leader, they can't do it again until everyone has also done it. Keep track on a chart or list.
4 Invite students within groups to select their leader, but emphasising that the person they choose should not have recently been a group leader.

Help less experienced or weaker group leaders by sitting for a short time with them in their groups and *not* taking over, dominating or undermining them, but quietly showing support for what they are doing and helping to create a relaxed positive environment by doing things like smiling and nodding. You may sometimes want to intervene to support and echo what the group leader says even if you disagree or feel it unhelpful! Allow the group and the leader to go wrong, in their own way, if necessary. If a correction or redirection becomes really necessary, do so in as positive and unobtrusive way as you can.

Technique: Character role-cards

Allocate role cards to each person in a group. Students do the group task as their character described. The cards could:

1 Give real-life characters that the students will know, e.g. the names of some celebrities, local people, school staff, etc.
2 Give generalised job roles, e.g. politician, TV chat show host, pop star.
3 Outline attitudes or behaviour, e.g. 'You have one very good idea which you want everyone to listen to', 'You disagree with everyone', 'Ask questions to try and find out exactly what people mean', etc.

These role cards work particularly well with opinion or ideas-based discussion tasks, larger groups (e.g. six or more) and at higher levels, especially from Intermediate upwards. At lower levels, use of one or two simple one-word roles (e.g. politician, teacher) can be effective.

Technique: Procedural roles

Give roles based around the management of the group, the unfolding of the interaction and the completion of the task. These could also be simple one-line role cards:

• 'Try to make sure that everyone speaks; take notes of good ideas.'

Alternatively, you could make use of the more complex descriptions outlined in the table below (or you and your students can also devise your own). Which roles you allocate and how you allocate them (e.g. by your order or by learner choice) is up to you.

Remember that adding certain roles to a group will usually mean that your groups will need to be larger than just those taking part in the discussion, as some roles have a recording function and will not actually participate in the task itself.

NB Some of the active, participation roles (e.g. Ideas generator, Encourager) can be allocated to a number of people within the same group. It's probably not a good idea to put more than two people with a 'no' answer in the second column into a group, unless it is a large group of 10 or more.

Role	Active participation in task?
Manager Has the responsibility to lead the group. This does not mean talking most, but probably talking least. The manager's aim is to make sure as many people contribute as possible, that people listen to each other, that comments made by one person are taken into account by the next speaker (rather than just ignored). The manager can contribute and give his/her opinion and ideas, but needs to make sure that he/she doesn't dominate.	Yes, but is mainly managing
Librarian The librarian is the resources person. He or she collects handouts, paper, pens and any other resources from the teacher, makes sure that people are filling worksheets out correctly, collects documents when appropriate, returns them to the teacher and so on.	Yes
Ideas generator This person comes up with as many good ideas as he or she can.	Yes
Encourager This person's role is to see the positive in what each contributor says, perhaps by paraphrasing it and adding on reasons why it is a good idea.	Yes
Devil's advocate This role involves finding reasons why people's ideas and suggestions are not good or will not work. He or she must not simply contradict or knock down what others say, but must aim to find good arguments for his or her position.	Yes
Questioner This person tries to find out concrete information. If someone else suggests an idea, the fact finder will ask clarification questions that help to reveal more information and details.	Yes
Decision builder This person does not push through his or her own decision, but will try and encourage everyone else to reach a compromise answer that all can happily agree on. This may involve some persuasion, negotiation and argument.	Yes

Role	Active participation in task?
Reporter The reporter's job is to listen carefully to what others are saying and take notes. Every two or three minutes, he or she will give a very brief oral summary of what people have said so far, especially of any strong ideas suggested or any conclusions reached. Once he or she has spoken, people can continue the discussion (maybe even disagreeing with the summary). At the end of a further few minutes, the reporter again makes his or her report and so on. At the end, he or she provides a short summary report on what happened through the whole task. The report could be given both (a) within the group or (b) to the whole class.	No
Language monitor This person keeps an eye on whether people are speaking English (and reminds them if they are not – usually gently!). He or she can also note down a few (a) good examples of language used and (b) language that seems to have errors in it. The language monitor (like the reporter) reports back to the group at the end of the task. Students could then discuss if the language items he or she picked on *really* are good or problematic.	No

Technique: Long-term roles

Some teachers like to allocate roles for a longer period of time – i.e. the same student does the same role for all activities within, say, a two-week period. This allows students to become familiar with one way of working and to get better at it. The familiarity may be comforting and motivating to some learners.

Questions for reflection

- Imagine that you are working as a student on a teacher-training course and have to take part in a discussion. How would you react to being told to take on a role? Would you want to have a say in which role you had? Which of the listed roles would you enjoy, and which, if any, would you hate?

🖪 Justifying pair and group work to students

Every time I say, 'Get into pairs', they all call out, 'Do we HAVE to?'

Aim
To demonstrate some benefits of pair and group work to students.

Introduction
Nowadays, most teachers can see a real value in offering pair and group work. But even when teachers are convinced of the reasons for pair and group work, students may not always see the point. In some cases, they may complain and ask for less of it and for more teacher-fronted work. There may be genuine concerns about working with another student who is much stronger or weaker, or someone they don't get on with. There may be unspoken reasons such as the fact that teacher-fronted work is much less demanding on students and allows them to hide or relax much more. But it may simply be that they have not thought through or understood the value of it. The techniques below look at ways of bringing students closer towards that understanding.

The simplest argument for pair and group work is that it allows more learner talk in a class than if all interaction has to be with the teacher. This, in turn, is likely to lead to significantly higher involvement and engagement. Learners in groups may feel more like individuals, rather than being lost in the large mass of the class. They have more chance to say what they think and may feel that their opinions are listened to and count more. They might feel more confident talking in front of just two or three people than in front of everyone. Groups also have the possibility of working at different paces or on different gradations of tasks, which may make work more accessible for students.

Amy B. M. Tsui also points out another important reason for offering pair and group work: it offers the chance to talk in a different kind of way. She suggests that it:

> *Encourages students to take risks in the sense that they will verbalize their ideas even when they are not fully developed and coherent, and they will use the target language even when they are not sure whether it is grammatically right or wrong.*

She quotes Barnes (1976) who calls this kind of talk:

> *'Exploratory talk' as opposed to 'final-draft' talk, in which whatever is expressed is a final product presented for evaluation. Barnes points out that while teacher-fronted classrooms typically generate 'final-draft talk', small group work typically generates 'exploratory talk'.*

Language learning is a process that involves lots of attempts and errors along the way, and so it is very important to give learners opportunities to try out the language, to feel it on their tongue, to experiment with putting words together, to make attempts that turn out to be unsuccessful or only partially successful and not to aim all the time, unrealistically, only for supposedly perfect exam-ready sentences.

Techniques: Raising awareness of the rationale for pair work and group work

The following worksheet is for use with students. You could use it in different ways, but this is one possibility:

1 Hand out copies of the worksheet to individuals. Ask them to take a few minutes to write their own answers without comparing with others.
2 Form pairs or groups, and ask learners to compare their responses and to come to an agreed group compromise answer for each question.
3 Compare the different groups' answers in the whole class. Discuss with students, and give your own opinion.

Worksheet 1: Reasons for pair and group work

Choose the answer you agree with. Delete the other answer. Example: yes / ~~no~~

1 When we do speaking activities, the most important thing is to *communicate a lot / make as few mistakes as possible.*
2 I think we get better at English by *trying to speak even though we make mistakes / making sure our sentences are perfect before we say them.*
3 We get better ideas and say more interesting things *in pairs or groups / in front of the whole class.*
4 When we do pair or group work it's *good / bad* that the teacher can't hear everything we say.
5 When we do pair or group work it's *good / bad* that the teacher can't mark or check everything we say.
6 It is more stressful and difficult to speak *in a pair or group activity / in front of the whole class.*
7 We have more natural conversations when we speak *in a pair or group activity / in front of the whole class.*
8 It's *a good thing / a problem* that the teacher can't help us immediately whenever we can't find the right expression in pair or group discussions.
9 It's *a good thing / a problem* that we have to listen to lots of different people speaking in pair or group work.
10 Pair or group activities are *useful / a waste of time* because . . .

For Worksheet 2 below, work through the questions together in the whole class, filling in the numbers as you go. The end result should show a massive difference between the amount of speaking time in Calculation 1 and Calculation 2. For example:

1 Calculation 1: 50-minute lesson divided by 30 students = 1.6 minutes speaking per student in the whole lesson (i.e. very little).
2 Calculation 2: Out of a 50-minute lesson, 30 minutes is pair work; 30 divided by 2 = 15 minutes speaking per student in the whole lesson (i.e. more than 9 times more speaking).

Obviously these are very rough and inaccurate averages, but they should still make the point. At the end, discuss students' reactions and opinions.

Worksheet 2: Time calculations

Which of these two ways of working will help you learn most English?

a The teacher says a lot, and you say very little yourself.
b The teacher says a little, and you practise a lot, trying to use the language yourself.

Now do these two calculations:

Calculation 1 Speaking in the whole class

MINS

☐ = How many minutes there are in this lesson.

STS

☐ = How many students there are in this class.

SPK

Calculate: MINS divided by STS = ☐

SPK is how many minutes you could speak in a lesson if everyone speaks the same amount in the whole class.

Calculation 2 Speaking in pairs

MINS

☐ = How many minutes you do pair work in this lesson.

SPK

Calculate: MINS divided by 2 = ☐

SPK is how many minutes you could speak in a lesson if you do pair work.

Questions for reflection

• On in-service training seminars or courses, how do you and other teachers you know respond to working in pairs and groups yourselves? Is it something you enjoy and find useful, or something that you would prefer to avoid? Does what you like and find useful match what you offer your own students?

The world

14 Interaction beyond the classroom walls

> It's all very well having students chatting with each other in the classroom, but it's not 'real' and they know it. How much better if they could meet and talk with other people beyond the classroom walls!

Aim

To get students interacting with a range of English-speaking people.

Introduction

Classroom pair work and group work are useful, but they also have limitations. The students are only talking to each other. While this is good preparation for later real-life uses of English, your students probably also need at least some opportunities to interact with good language users from outside the classroom.

When teachers work in English-speaking countries with multilingual students away from their home countries, there is often a range of possibilities for taking them out to talk to English speakers in the surrounding environment. But it's much harder to engineer such speaking opportunities in a non-English-speaking environment. If you take your students out to the tourist information centre or the station, the people who work there can all speak your language, and few of them would want to have their time wasted by a group of students pretending that they can only speak English.

But, all the same, there are possibilities, and especially so with the growth and availability of the Internet. This unit collects some ideas for introducing spoken interaction with people beyond the classroom walls. Many of these ideas will primarily be useful with young learners in secondary or high schools.

Technique: Surveys in town

Unless you live and work in a very small hamlet, there are likely to be a number of users of English wandering around town, both native speakers and competent non-native speakers. In order to meet them and get your students talking with them, one basic approach would be to get the learners (in groups of three or four) to prepare a questionnaire with questions that they could ask people in town (e.g. opinions about the place itself, suggestions about improving facilities, etc.).

Arrange permission for students to wait in a suitable location where they might meet a number of visitors and tourists, as well as local English speakers, e.g. a museum foyer or the entrance of a local tourist site. Train the groups to ask visitors, 'Excuse me. Do you speak English?' as their first question and to continue only with those who respond positively to it. Students can then ask the questions from their questionnaire and collect the results. Encourage them to chat beyond and around the questions, as far as possible, rather than just reading from their form line by line.

Technique: Arrange English-language placements

This will take a lot of setting up (and probably some persuasion), but could be very fulfilling for competent, higher-level, older teenage students if it goes ahead. Write to local companies, radio or TV stations, tourist sites, magazines and newspapers, department stores and so on to find out if it's possible for students to take on an English-speaking placement on a number of occasions over a period of time. These might be jobs or roles that do not otherwise exist, but which would provide a helpful service if the students did them. The location would need to provide whatever basic training or induction is necessary.

Students could take on roles such as 'personal translator' (e.g. available to accompany shoppers round a department store or visitors to a company's offices), 'interviewer' (e.g. speaking to people for a local newspaper or TV show) or 'guide' (e.g. showing visitors round a museum or tourist site). The initial stage of negotiating with the organisations would primarily involve them discussing what placements might be genuinely useful and contribute to their work in a positive way.

Technique: Cooperate with other local schools

Try making contact with other schools in your area to arrange meet-ups where English will be the language used. These could be formal (e.g. take part in a series of organised games and activities, such as 'Board game afternoon' where people learn to play Scrabble and other games) or informal – just a chance to meet and talk, perhaps helped out and shaped a little by some guidelines or questionnaires to fill in.

If you have the chance to cooperate over a longer period of time, consider putting on a joint play or show – with some pieces performed by participants from both schools.

Technique: Plan an English-language day

Get all the classes you work with to plan and prepare an English-language day for the school. This could involve special events in break times, the lunch hour or after school. If possible, get other teachers and classes to get into the spirit and offer their own contributions.

Students could initiate, organise or run English-language word games, TV viewing of popular English-language programmes and films, a special 'English menu' in the canteen at lunch time, a karaoke competition, a 'treasure hunt' quiz that gets participants to look around the school for answers to a series of quiz questions, an English-language disco, an auction of donated English-language goodies and so on.

Technique: Enter (or initiate) English-language competitions

Many countries have some interschool English-language competitions. Amongst the most popular are formal debating competitions, poetry-reading competitions, quizzes and model United Nations. Entering these provides chances for those on teams to have an exciting experience, but, also, the whole class (and school) can enjoy following the team as they prepare and progress, and being hosts for an event can be a great English-language day for the whole school.

Technique: Arrange English trips

If you live in a larger town, there is a good chance that local sites (for example, a museum or gallery) will have guides that speak English. Book a guided tour of a location, but ask for an English-speaking guide. Explain the situation honestly in advance (i.e. that your students are not English speakers, but need the practice), and make sure that the site is happy with what you are planning. (It may even be beneficial for the site to have a chance to practise English guiding!) Prepare for the visit using any available English-language resources (e.g. an English webpage). Help students to prepare possible questions and comments that they might be able to use on the visit, as well as encouraging spontaneous interaction while on the visit itself.

Technique: Guest stars

Invite English-speaking guest visitors into the classroom. At its simplest, the guest could come into class, sit there and answer questions and chat with students. Such visits could be announced in advance and planned for (e.g. helping students to prepare questions to ask).

An alternative approach would be to have a 'surprise' guest and not give any introduction announcing who the person is or what they do, leaving the students to ask questions and interact to discover as much as they can in order to learn their story.

A willing guest might be able prepare a short speech or presentation, which will also lead to more questions and discussion. Some guests might be prepared to take responsibility for setting or leading a task with students.

If there are two or more guests, each guest can be assigned to a different group who interview them individually and then report back to the whole class. Alternatively, groups can be reconfigured so that each member reports on the person they interviewed and similarities/ differences are noted.

Technique: Web-based contact with distant schools

The Internet now allows us to communicate across the world cheaply and fairly easily, using video. Make contact with a likely school, perhaps one that your own school knows of or already has links with. Invite them to take part in regular timetabled communication (e.g. one lesson a month) with your students (though bear in mind that time-zone differences may make this tricky to set up).

Whole-class discussion or activities are possible, though technical problems (poor whole-room sound quality, limited ability to see all participants clearly, etc.) are likely to make these more problematic than one would wish.

More useful are small-group-to-small-group links, perhaps with groups or three students at one end talking to small groups at the other. To do this, you and your contact school at the other end will need a number of PCs equipped with webcams. You could design information-gap or discussion activities that will be done by the students working together.

Technique: Set up a real project/business

This is perhaps the most demanding strategy suggested here: for an adult class to engage with the outside world by initiating a real-life project (for example, an ecological campaign to tidy up an eyesore site in town) or a business (e.g. marketing something designed and produced by the class, such as an English 'what's on' magazine).

This is going to be time-consuming and demanding, but it is also task-based learning at its most powerful and exciting. Whatever you and the class choose to do, it will set the timetable and pace of much of your work for a long time to come, possibly for a whole month, term or year. The initial phases of work will be in class, creating the project or products and planning strategies. Beyond that, there will be the possibility of visits of all kinds outside, meeting people, talking to them, persuading them and so on. The risks are that the ideas never really take off and just fizzle, in which case you can always go back to more traditional study, or that some students get very involved while others take a back seat. But if it works, it will be one of the most memorable teaching experiences of your career.

Technique: Use virtual environments

As the Internet evolves, it will become increasingly possible to meet up and interact in virtual ways. At the time of writing, Second Life and similar programmes allow people to create an avatar (a cartoon-like character that represents you in the virtual world) and to use that to explore and 'live' within a virtual-world environment. Second Life looks game-like but is not a game, though it is immersive and believable in much the same way that a good game is. Schools and universities can set up their own bases within the world (a house, an island, a castle, a hotel, a cave, etc.) and create activities and tasks to encourage students to meet up and communicate with each other. Technology like this is still new, and there are glitches and dangers for the unwary teacher and student. However, it seems probable that this kind of interactivity will become increasingly usable and important as time goes by. I strongly suspect that the language student of the future will use something very much like this to get the bulk of their English-language practice.

Questions for reflection

- How much, if at all, do your students get practice outside the classroom?
- Which of the ideas in this unit would you never contemplate trying with your students? Why not? What might make you reassess them?

6 | Establishing and maintaining appropriate behaviour

This chapter mainly addresses problems faced by teachers who work with school children at secondary age. However, there are also many workable techniques and ideas that could be used for similar problems with young adults or with primary children.

1 Setting the stage for positive behaviour

> *I spend so much classroom time getting angry and telling students off. There must be a better way.*

Aim

To create the conditions in which good behaviour is likely to be encouraged.

Introduction

A common traditional approach to getting good behaviour in class was to instil fear in pupils, using threats of punishments that were tedious (write 100 'lines'), humiliating (stand in the corner) or possibly involving violence (corporal punishment). This resulted in a specific kind of motivation: motivation to avoid punishment, rather than motivation to learn for its own sake. The focus was on discouraging and stopping bad behaviour. Nowadays, most teachers would turn that approach on its head and mainly seek ways of encouraging and maintaining the desired good behaviour. Looking for the positive, rather than policing and punishing the negative, is also a more enjoyable approach for a teacher.

Children (and adults) do play around; it's absolutely normal and is part of a human's natural energy and creativity. While there is behaviour that is rude, unhelpful, unacceptable or dangerous, some of what teachers interpret as ill discipline may not even seem like that from the student's perspective, but as high spirits or a search for the humorous or the interesting. Sometimes, the fault may lie with the teacher more than with the student; bad behaviour can be a kind of feedback, the students defending themselves against boredom or perceived attack.

The most important single factor in encouraging better behaviour is in offering interesting and engaging lessons. Students who enjoy what they are doing are much less likely to be disruptive. Beyond that, the more buy-in you can get from students to whatever behaviour scheme you use, the better. Rather than applying a hierarchically imposed scheme on them, try to work one out with them – consulting and agreeing, making sure that the reasons for decisions are understood and agreed with.

Technique: Get students to devise the rules

Involve students in discussing and deciding how behaviour can be managed.

1 Choose or agree a method by which students can work out what the class rules should be. This could perhaps be done by starting with group brainstorms and discussions and then having a whole-class meeting to agree and finalise them.
2 Once the rules have been agreed, students also need to discuss and agree how they should be enforced.
3 Write up a final version as a contract and display it prominently on a poster or notice. You may want to ask students to formally show their acceptance of rules and sanctions by signing the document, or adding their thumbprint or a personal 'seal'.
4 Go back to the rules occasionally, maybe once a month, and get the class to review whether they are working and if they need to be added to or revised at all.

Even if you don't get students to design their own rules (as above), you probably still need to get them to fully understand and accept your rules. Propose the rules that you think are important, and explain the reasoning behind them. Ask if they agree that they are useful, and get them to say whether they will work to them. Make it clear whether there is any room for changing/rewording your rules, or if they have to accept your choices.

Technique: Build in chances to move, use up energy and let off steam

You can sidestep lots of discipline problems by addressing your students' natural need to let off energy, perhaps arising out of sitting still for a long stretch of time.

1 Add in occasional activities that afford chances to mingle, walk around a little, do some activities standing up, helping to move furniture or even just to change places. These have a real class-calming value, quite apart from any language learning aims they might involve.
2 Consider overtly physical activities, such as exercises, drama games, running dictations outdoors and so on.
3 Remember, if students haven't moved for ages, it's possible that giving them chances to move may lead initially to noise and a degree of chaos. Don't see this as a reason for not doing it; it's the opposite.

Techniques: Create routines

Some teachers would argue that establishing regular routines can help to give a sense of security and calmness to stages of each lesson; for example, always distributing exercise books in the same way at the start of each lesson, or always reorganising the room using the same procedures.

Work on getting students to understand the routines. Do this by simply repeating (again and again if necessary) what the routines are. Until the routine is totally established and habitual, work on the assumption that students not following it have not remembered it or are uncertain rather than deliberately misbehaving. Instead of telling off, simply restate as often as necessary what students have to do (e.g. 'You take your exercise book and pass the rest of the pile to the person behind you'), and if useful, restart the routine (e.g. 'OK, let's try that again and see if you can do it better').

Technique: Pace

Research seems to suggest that anti-social behaviour often correlates with activity transition points, lulls and pauses, for example, when the teacher is distracted, whether by technology, an individual student, the board or something else. One way of reducing disruption is to make sure that the lesson continues to engage students during transitions between stages, and maintains a strong flow of activity. (See Chapter 7 Unit 4.)

Technique: Work-focussed feedback

In this approach, the teacher only makes comments and gives feedback about work. He or she gives no reaction to, or comment on, any behaviour issues. There is a risk here that students get more and more badly behaved, but, paradoxically, it's not necessarily what happens. Some bad behaviour occurs precisely because it gets responded to. This approach works best with students who are attention seeking, as they slowly learn that the only way to get their teacher's attention is through their work.

Techniques: Find opportunities to notice positives

It's easy to get into the habit of noticing and attending to bad behaviour and not seeing or commenting on the multiple examples of good behaviour.

1 Train yourself to notice positive work and behaviour. Build the class up by giving lots of oral feedback on positive things. Keep the focus on specific achievements (in work or behaviour). Watch out that you don't slip into bland praise.
2 Keep a little pad of Post-it® notes or small slips of distinctive coloured paper. Write little notes and leave them in unexpected places: slipped into students' exercise books, on their desks, on their pencil cases. Pick on ordinary good behaviour that you noticed – the sort of things that typically go unremarked on, e.g. 'I noticed that you have kept your desk well organised the last two weeks! I was impressed!' 'You have participated very actively in all the group work today. Hope you enjoyed it!' 'Thanks so much for bringing in that photo I asked for. It was really useful in the lesson'.
3 Write messages home saying what students have done well (rather than only communicating with parents when there is a problem).

Technique: The 100% positive classroom

In Chapter 4 Unit 10, there is a discussion of arguments for and against praise: a much disagreed-about issue. Well, here is a praise-based technique that has many proponents. You'll have to decide for yourself if it's one that you could use.

The technique involves the teacher putting him- or herself in a mindset where he or she genuinely only sees the positive in what people do. Whatever happens in class, he or she comments only on the bright, good side. He or she seeks out positive achievements to comment on. Bad behaviour is ignored. With badly behaving students, the teacher looks for things that are positive and praises them.

In a classroom that is adopting a 100% positive approach to learners, there is a great deal of praise flying around, and this can have a very powerful role in creating the overall positive environment. Proponents would argue that, as a result, a lot of bad behaviour shrivels away and vanishes.

Technique: Track your own discipline interventions

If you can get an observer to come and sit in your class, even for 10 or 15 minutes, ask them to do a very simple task: every time you make a positive comment or encouraging intervention about a student, tick in column A, and every time you make a negative or telling-off intervention, tick column B, in each case with a quick note to remind you what was said or done. This data will give you a quick overview of what tone your classroom takes. NB Remind the observer that the term intervention includes actions, looks and noises, as well as spoken sentences.

Technique: Points and rewards

Many teachers use reward systems to encourage good behaviour. There are a number of variables that you can play with when devising a scheme to suit you and your students. Consider these questions:

- Should rewards be given immediately, or should points be given that can be saved up?
- Will points be recorded in writing? Where: in the teacher's book, on a wall poster or elsewhere? Will stickers, tokens or stamps be used?
- Are points/rewards given to individuals or teams?
- Do the points accumulate mainly to the glory of winning (e.g. 'champion team', perhaps with a certificate) or a tangible present of some kind (e.g. a box of chocolates)?
- Can your system successfully exclude cheating or falsely added points?
- Will rewards be given when points reach a certain total or at fixed points in time (e.g. at the end of each month)?
- Can everyone achieve points/rewards (not just the brightest students)?
- Is there a clear scheme for awarding points (but one that still allows some flexibility)?

Questions for reflection

• This unit mainly argues for a positive approach to discipline issues, but is this really viable in a large, misbehaving secondary-school class? What role (if any) is there for traditional tight teacher control and teacher-led punishment?

2 Dealing with small disruptions

> The most annoying things are not the big, obvious misdemeanours, but the constant flow of annoying little bits of naughtiness – like a continual soundtrack all through my lesson.

Aim

To find systematic ways to minimise any problems caused by minor cases of poor behaviour.

Introduction

Quite apart from serious bad behaviour (which we look at in the following unit), there are many small everyday disruptions and distractions that all teachers have to deal with: students arriving late, students shouting at others, students sending text messages under the table, name calling and so on.

This unit looks at some ways of dealing with these in a systematic manner.

Technique: Be consistent

Whatever you do in response to bad behaviour, try to do it consistently. It is confusing for students if something is dealt with in a certain way on one occasion, but then differently on a second occasion, for example, if a student punches another student in class and you give them a detention, but then, later in the lesson, a second student thumps another in a similar way, but you only tell them off.

Students need to be clear about where they stand. They need to see that you are being fair and applying rules and sanctions equally to all.

Technique: Don't threaten sanctions unless you mean it

The class need to see that you keep your word. Avoid empty warnings of dire consequences. If you threaten something that you would never actually implement, students will quickly see through it. Not following up has the counter-productive effect of training students to just ignore anything you say.

Similarly, if you promise something good to your class, make sure that you keep your word.

Technique: Minimal rules

Some teachers find it better to set one rule rather than lots. Can you state your classroom values clearly and simply in a sentence? This could be an idea such as, 'Everything is allowed in the classroom unless it hurts or disrespects another person or gets in the way of what they are doing'.

Technique: State and wait

This is a basic technique, but one that very often works to halt offending behaviour.

1 **State**   If a scene starts up (e.g. an argument), the first response is to clearly, concisely state an order to stop (or to do something else). Deliver it with a tone of un-angry total confidence that they will stop, speaking as loudly as necessary, but as quietly as possible. Do not start shouting, making threats or intervening. Be polite and avoid sarcasm.
2 **Wait**   Don't immediately start coming back with repetitions and louder orders. Look as if you expect them to do what you asked. Use eye contact (see *Wordless interventions* below) to firmly catch and hold the eyes of any participants who glance at you.
3 **Repeat**   Only if there is no response or calming down, repeat the original order in exactly the same words (perhaps prefaced by, 'I said …') as calmly and confidently as the first time. Wait again. …

The power of this technique is in the silence of your waiting and the confidence of your expectation that they will do what you ask.

Technique: Wordless interventions

Sometimes your message to a misbehaving child will be completely clear even without words. You could experiment with some of the following singly, or perhaps combine two or three together:

1 Raised eyebrows.
2 Head slightly tipped back.
3 Widened eyes.
4 A fixed stare at the person you wish to address.
5 A single clap of the hands.
6 A slow, small, discreet, slightly exaggerated 'no' shake of the head.
7 A cough, 'hmmm' or 'ahem' noise.
8 Using a noisemaker of some kind, e.g. a bell or a rainstick.
9 A raised finger, wagging 'no'.
10 An open mouth, as if you are about to say, 'Uh-huh'.
11 A hand raised in the direction of the offender, palm up, as if about to invite him or her into the room.

12 Tapping the table loudly and purposively (e.g. with a board pen), three times, slowly and with pauses between taps.

13 Placing your hand firmly and decisively on the desk/table of the person you are addressing.

And one to perhaps avoid: Repeatedly thumping your table with your clenched fist (which tends to look a bit cartoonish and exaggerated).

Technique: Get close

If you want to strengthen the power of other solutions, try moving very close to the person or people you are addressing. Right by their desk/table is a strong position for quiet orders.

Technique: Sit down with them

When one student or a number of students in one part of the room start getting disruptive, one great solution is to wordlessly, without any shouting or orders, simply wander over to their part of the room and sit down next to (or very nearby) the most troublesome person, continuing the lesson from there as if nothing unusual had happened. To do this, you could perch on the edge of their desk, sit on the desk behind, indicate to another unproblematic student that they can move to sit in a free seat, your desk or another empty location, thus freeing up a seat for you.

Technique: Distract rather than address

Another basic technique is to deliberately not address bad behaviour, but to create an immediate distraction that takes everyone's mind off it and makes the perpetrator forget what they were doing or why they were doing it. You might do this by starting a new task, showing a picture, saying something startling or unusual, starting to tell a joke, whispering something secret or interesting or behaving in some other unexpected manner.

Technique: Everyday nuisances

There are a number of regular daily problems that many teachers face: students repeatedly wanting to leave to go to the toilet (and staying there a long time), latecomers drifting into class and disrupting others, students packing up too early to leave, students reading and replying to text messages on their phones under the desk and so on.

Set clear rules and guidelines for these, and follow them consistently and fairly. You will need to adapt these suggestions to fit your school and situation, but here are some ideas to help you start:

1 Toilet visits

- If it's not a big problem for the whole class, don't make any rules.
- If one individual makes frequent visits, discuss privately with him or her. Don't assume deliberate bad behaviour; there may be other issues. Adjust your response accordingly.
- If many students regularly seem to be abusing things, set some guidelines, e.g. no visits in the first ten minutes or last ten minutes of class. You may also place a double-sided yes / no notice where all can see it, indicating whether toilet visits are permitted or not at different stages of a lesson (and turn it round as needed; e.g. do not allow toilet visits during key input or where it makes pair work unviable, but do allow it during larger group discussions or individual work).
- Discourage over-long visits by requiring students who miss classroom work to catch up during homework.

2 Late arrivals

- Distinguish between lateness that is genuinely unavoidable (e.g. the previous teacher let them out late) and dawdling or deliberate lateness.
- If you have a persistent problem with avoidable lateness, try initiating a system where you keep records of late arrivals (whether on the official class register or in your own record book/chart). Tell the class that you will mark them late if they are more than a certain time (e.g. three minutes) late to class. Ignore excuses. Be calm, consistent, tough and stick to your system.
- Require latecomers to sit in a special location, e.g. at the front of class. This could quickly teach students the advantages of coming on time.
- Rather than punishing lateness, make 'on timeness' part of any wider reward scheme of team points or individual tokens (see Chapter 6 Unit 1).

3 Packing up early

Some students insist on packing everything away six minutes before the bell, and this encourages others to also stop work early. Before long, you have a whole class who have given up four minutes before the lesson ends.

When you spot someone packing up early, make it a rule that you will hold them back to be the last to leave the room. Applied consistently, this will soon have an impact. You could ask them to unpack everything as well, and not restart before everyone else has gone.

4 Mobile phones

You may sometimes want to make use of phones in lessons (e.g. for speaking work or for looking up online dictionaries), but they can also be a significant distraction. Schools often have a general policy, but, if not, you may need to create your own rules. Consider:

- Ask all students to label their phones with their names. Make a drop box at the front of class for students to put phones in at the start of each lesson (and reclaim from at the end, perhaps with you checking them out). If security/theft are a real risk, ask students to put their phones in a locker, named box, shelf or folder.
- Appoint a phone monitor to collect phones at the start of each lesson and hand back at the end.
- Tell students that if they use their phone in class for anything unpermitted, there will be a sanction, e.g. they will be forbidden from taking part in the next game activity in class, or their team will lose points.

Technique: Set up a 'timeout' zone

Sometimes students need a chance to just get out of a situation, argument or problem, i.e. have a place to go that lets them cool down and get back their sanity. One solution is to create a part of the classroom set aside for this – maybe a chair at one side of the room. Agree a rule with the class, for example, that anyone is allowed to go there at any time once a lesson, for any reason, without needing to ask for permission, explain why they went or excuse themselves. Once there, they can stay for a set time (e.g. maximum three minutes) before going back to their place.

Technique: Quick crowd-control recoveries

Whatever you do, whichever systems and contracts you have in place, with some classes, there will inevitably be unavoidable temporary breakdowns in order. Here are some ideas for a quick recovery:

1 Stay calm. Speak loud and clear, but don't shout. Don't nag or beg. Do not lose your temper. Avoid physically intervening (unless it is absolutely essential).
2 Give clear directions. Say what you want them to do, not what they must stop doing. For example, 'Sit down', rather than 'Stop fighting'.
3 If there is no response, explain simply and clearly the consequences of not doing what you said, and the timescale, e.g. 'You have 20 seconds to do what I said. If you don't, I will …'. Sanctions warned about need to be applied absolutely as threatened, e.g. 'I will call your parents' or 'I will take you straight to the Deputy head's office'.

Technique: Don't be worried about apologising

If, when discussing a perceived discipline problem with a student, you realise that you have misinterpreted or overreacted in some way, apologise if it is appropriate, rather than covering up (e.g. by picking on another transgression and building that up). Students will usually appreciate the honesty of a teacher who has listened and can admit that they got something wrong. It will also make them less distrustful of future occasions when you really do have a case against them.

Questions for reflection

• What is your own most-used strategy for dealing with persistent minor disruptions? Does it work efficiently, or do you end up sounding like a broken record?

▪️3️⃣ Serious discipline issues

> *I'm a relatively new teacher. Most of the time, students are just naughty or get overexcited. However, occasionally a child does something appalling, and then I really feel out of my depth.*

Aim
To deal with serious behaviour problems in a firm, fair and clear way.

Introduction
When the British government proposed an initiative to encourage ex-soldiers to retrain as teachers, their idea was largely based on an earlier report which had argued that this would 'bring military-style discipline to tough inner-city schools ... (because) children from more deprived neighbourhoods often respond to raw physical power'.

I have worked with a number of ex-soldiers who subsequently became very good teachers, but it was not for these reasons. Is it right to respond to difficult children by treating them as if they were in an army, shouting at them, bullying them, using size and strength to exert power and dominate? If their behaviour problems have roots in violent or dysfunctional households, is bullying and aggression from the teacher going to solve the problems or exacerbate them? Might showing such strength only confirm and validate the badly behaving students' view of how life works? If a teacher can only win respect because he has fought and perhaps killed people, then there isn't much hope for education or our children's futures.

The skills that teachers need are very different. They have to be able to deal with bad discipline in ways that do not imply that strongest or loudest is best. They need to look beyond the immediate apparent issue (e.g. aggression or rudeness) to factors that may influence or cause it to happen (e.g. the students' insecurity or lack of self-awareness). Occasionally, a teacher may have to face a genuinely violent attack, but, more often, there is a need for care and understanding, as well as firmness, confidence, clarity and guidance about what to do.

However, while modern approaches to teaching tend to be more democratic and consultative than in the past, this does not mean that we cannot still exercise appropriate authority when needed. The teacher retains overall responsibility for the care and safety of everyone in the room. Sometimes the right thing to do is to give a clear, sharp order, perhaps to stop someone from doing something. This can be done without discussion or checking people's feelings. The trouble is that nowadays many teachers get limited practice in such interventions and sometimes feel under-skilled or uncertain as to whether they should do this, which leads to under-confident discipline and weak results. To be successful in such situations, the teacher needs to believe in his or her authority (i.e. feel confident that he or she has the right to intervene when needed) and remain calm and clear. Authority is best asserted in measured tones.

Technique: Categorising levels of behaviour

Be clear as to where you draw the lines about the parameters of acceptable behaviour, i.e. those things that you consider serious offences in school and entirely unacceptable – things you will always make a stand on, such as racism or bullying.

Some schools publish lists that clearly outline different kinds of behaviour in three or four categories, sorted from less to more serious. This would then cross-reference to an agreed scheme of sanctions. If your school doesn't already have one, you could discuss and agree a scheme like this with other teachers in your school, perhaps based on the example below. A system such as this would work most successfully as a school-wide approach that everyone consistently applied, though a simpler list could also work within a single class.

1   Poor behaviour
- Coming late to lessons.
- Using mobile phone, music player, etc. in class, unless permitted.
- Leaving rubbish or litter in class.
- Repeatedly using your first language when asked to use English.
- Continuing to be noisy or disruptive when asked not to.
- Deliberately behaving in a way intended to distract or annoy other students.

2   Unacceptable behaviour
- Missing lessons.
- Behaving rudely to the teacher.
- Cheating in tests.
- Being rough with others (e.g. shoving them or pushing).
- Arguing, swearing, shouting.
- Behaving rudely to other students.

3   Serious offences
- Serious or repeated cases of behaviour in the other two categories.
- Causing hurt to others (e.g. by hitting them, throwing things at them).
- Violence, bullying, harassment or threatening behaviour.
- Assault.
- Theft.
- Vandalising or writing graffiti.
- Missing school without permission.
- Illegal or banned activities (e.g. smoking, possessing drugs, weapons or alcohol).
- Making racist, sexist, homophobic or other discriminatory comments.

Technique: Break out of escalating cycles

It's all too easy to respond to an act of bad behaviour by shouting a command, getting a shout back or responding with a louder command – and, before long, finding yourself engaged in a full-scale battle in front of the whole class.

1 Avoid shouting other than in situations where there is an immediate need to give a warning (e.g. a physical danger such as something falling over about to hit someone). For everything else, it's usually better to be loud and project your voice as needed, rather than shout.
2 If you realise that you are getting into a quickly escalating showdown cycle, break out of it immediately. Don't get into responding to arguments. Switch to quiet or whisper volume. Or keep silent. Or do something that immediately changes the focus or distracts everyone.
3 Give the misbehaving students a chance to break out, too. In an escalating situation, all sides may wish that they could find a way out, but be so bound up in their emotions and reactions that it feels impossible to do so. Physical distance can be one way to achieve this (e.g. 'Anton, take a short while to calm down outside the room. We can talk in a few minutes').

Technique: Distinguishing between the presenting problem and the underlying problem

We may feel that we know our students quite well, but it is unlikely that we could fully know about most of them. We cannot know what depth of unhappiness, distrust, fear or tension they bring with them from home. They may be the main carer for an ill relative. There may be serious family problems. There might be financial problems that affect the quality of life. They may be witnesses to assault and abuse. They may themselves be on the receiving end of violence or mistreatment. Past events may have left them with a depth of trauma or emotional damage.

What we see in the classroom can be the tip of the iceberg. The child may behave poorly in class, but it is hard for the teacher to see behind this to what might be causing it. Doctors distinguish between the presenting problem, i.e. what the patient says is their problem when they come into their surgery, and the underlying problem, a much more serious problem that the patient cannot talk about and may not even recognise, but which is the real issue that needs to be addressed. For teachers, the problem is similar. When we see students misbehaving in class, or when we detect a problem with their general attitude or approach, we may often intuit that there is an underlying cause beyond whatever has been the immediate spark for some bad behaviour.

1 Deal with the immediate, visible, tangible bad behaviour

Don't make generalised statements about the person, their character, their 'always' doing things like this. If you need to punish, make sure that it is consistent with whatever you have said would happen, and with whatever another student doing this would get.

2 Follow up later

Once the immediate problem is dealt with and finished, arrange time to talk with the person. Make it clear that the meeting is not about punishment or discipline. In the meeting, use catalytic questioning and listening (see Chapter 4 Unit 8) to see if there is any way that you can help the student. Having a private word is an underused but very powerful tool, especially if the student clearly understands that you are not just extending the punishment, but are genuinely interested in them.

Technique: Seek support

You cannot do it all by yourself. Teachers bear a responsibility for creating the right working atmosphere in their room and for dealing with day-to-day discipline issues and a certain amount of basic crowd control. But there will always be some problems that are simply too difficult or time-consuming for a classroom teacher. In such cases, it is sensible to seek support. There is a fine balance here. You probably don't want to call for help on every issue that arises; yet you need to alert others and seek advice or intervention, as early as possible, in cases that need, or are likely to need, outside help.

1 Don't leave it too late

In most cases, the earlier you ask for support, the better. As soon as you realise that a problem is in some way beyond you, sound out who can help you. Problems that can sometimes be solved with a quick intervention early on can become huge and much more problematic as time goes on.

2 Think about how to word the problem and the specific questions you have

People are more able to help if they understand the problem well. The more accurate you can be in your description of the problem, the more they might be able to suggest strategies. The more precise your questions are, the more the answers are likely to fit your needs. Be specific about who the person you're having difficulties with is, what they did and when, and what you want to address.

For example, saying, 'Some of my students are so badly behaved! They're driving me mad! What can I do?' is so general as to be almost useless in soliciting anything more than the broadest kind of suggestions about dealing with bad behaviour. A more precise wording might be, 'In my lesson today, Robin and Abdul kept throwing things at each other and never seriously started work on their assignments. How can I stop them fighting and get them to work?'

3 Seek help from the staff room

The staff room is potentially a wonderful source of advice and suggestions. You don't need to make a big 'I'm having trouble' announcement. Try sitting down with a colleague or two over coffee or tea, people that you respect, and explain the difficulties you are having. If you feel confident, try asking a larger group and collecting a range of thoughts and comments.

Whatever they say or suggest, think it over carefully. Don't accept ideas without carefully checking them out for yourself: how much do they fit your personal style, your class, this particular problem? Don't worry about colleagues who join in and belittle your problem as something they solved long ago or which any capable teacher should be able to deal with. There are always teachers who like to take chances to advertise their own skills as being superior to others.

4 Seek help from your line managers or school support systems

This might mean your head of department, head teacher, subject leader, official mentor and so on. Part of their job description is almost certainly to support staff, so make good use of this! You could mention that you have a problem when passing them in the corridor, but it is often better to ask for a specific appointment to discuss the issue. This points out to the manager that it is something that you take seriously and that you wish them to devote some time to helping you. When you have your meeting, it's a good idea to bring along not just the problem, but also a list of possible ideas and solutions – both things you've tried and things you haven't. This gives a concrete starting point to start working from.

5 Seek help from parents

This is largely a pre-emptive solution. As part of getting your class started, can you involve parents in your approach to encouraging positive behaviour? Just as it's possible to have contracts with your class, you can also set them up with parents, bringing them into the process and encouraging them to share some of the responsibility for making the class successful. An example of some statements that might go on a parent-teacher contract:

- Every student in class will be given a contact book (or homework book). This can be used for two-way communication between class teacher and home. Both parents/guardians and teachers can make entries in this book.
- The parent or guardian agrees to read comments in the contact book at least once a week.
- If there is a behaviour problem at school, the teacher will note this in the contact book. The parent should make a written response in the book or contact the teachers directly, as appropriate.

Questions for reflection

- What was the worst piece of student behaviour you have ever had to deal with? How did you respond then, and did it work? Would you respond differently nowadays if it happened again?

7 | Lessons

■1 Starting lessons

> *When I arrive in class to start my lessons, it often takes a long time to get students to quieten down and pay attention.*

Aim

To make the starts of lessons more effective and engaging.

Introduction

The beginning of a lesson is crucial. You usually want to set a good atmosphere, re-establish contact with your students and then get onto the important work of the lesson as quickly, efficiently and enjoyably as possible. If something goes wrong at this stage, it can affect all the rest of the lesson.

Teachers use different terms to talk about these sorts of activities:

- **Lead-ins** are part of a single flow connected to your main lesson focus. So, for example, if your lesson has the aim that 'students will be better able to use Conditional Type Two', your lead-in would be something that directly 'leads into' and starts *that* part of the lesson.
- **Lesson starts or 'warmers'** are slightly different. They are typically stand-alone and outside the main flow of the lesson and usually have very different aims, i.e. often group-building rather than linguistic (though this is not to say that a cleverly planned lesson start couldn't segue neatly into the main flow!).
- **'Icebreakers'** are activities used right at the start of a course to help a new class of students get to know each other and feel more comfortable working together. They might include 'Getting to know you' activities and name games (often involving mingling), where students meet and talk to a large number of other students.

Technique: Gatekeeper

With teen classes and younger learners, position yourself just inside your classroom door as students come into class. Meet, greet, chat and welcome students warmly and individually as they arrive. Being there as they come in allows you to quietly assert that they are arriving at your shared classroom. You can take the opportunity to immediately direct which part of the room they should go to, where to sit, what task to start working on and so on. Students will get the message that the lesson starts as soon as they arrive.

Technique: Don't wait for the right time for the 'lesson to start'

Teachers sometimes sit uncomfortably for a minute or two at the lesson start time, looking around, waiting until most students have arrived in the room, perhaps asking questions like, 'Is everyone here?' or 'Is there anyone else?' before finally sighing and saying, 'Shall we start now?' This always feels uncomfortable to me, and I get the impression that I then have to do something big or impressive to actually 'start' the lesson. It works much better if you:

1 Think of the lesson beginning as soon as one student is in the room.
2 Start chatting with the early arrivers (and make late arrivers feel they have missed something).
3 Segue (i.e. move smoothly) from the chat into the lesson's first main task as seamlessly as you can (completely sidestepping the clunky 'lesson-start' moment). Some teachers do this by subtly manipulating the conversation so that they can drop in some of the grammar or vocabulary points that the lesson will focus on. They can then seamlessly stand up, write one or two sentences that have just been said on the board and proceed with the language focus work they wanted to do.

Technique: Greet individually

Try to say, 'Hello', 'Welcome back' or another greeting to as many individuals as you can, while they arrive. This is a far more powerful and personal welcome than saying 'hello' to the class as a whole (and hearing, 'Hello, Mr/Ms Kim' called out in chorus).

Technique: Don't hide in plain sight

It's good to be able to make eye contact with students as they arrive. If you are writing on the board with your back to them, or rummaging around in your desk, you miss that chance.

Technique: Start at the very beginning

Try setting immediate, simple tasks from the first moment that students arrive in your classroom. This could be achieved by directing them from the door as they arrive (see above), by writing task instructions on the board (and training students to always check this as they come in and settle down), by leaving a task sheet or exercise on each chair or desk or by establishing and following a regular routine, such as, 'When you come in, always start by comparing your homework answers with the person next to you'.

Technique: Board welcomes and running themes

Take a minute before students arrive to write a short welcome message on the board. This could be partly greeting, e.g. 'Welcome back', partly informational, e.g. date, weather, the day's lesson plan and/or partly starting to focus students for the lesson itself.

Some teachers choose a running theme to add to the board each day. Students look forward to checking this as they come into each lesson. Themes might be:

1 Quote of the day (use the Internet to find some interesting comments by famous people).
2 Proverb of the day.
3 Funny news headline of the day (you could hand out a related article for students to read in the lesson or later).
4 Joke of the day.
5 Anagram of the day (or other word puzzle).

You could add in a puzzle or language-learning aim to any of these ideas. Do these regularly, and students will start looking forward to the next day's puzzle. Discussing them and possible solutions can be a great lesson opening.

Here are some examples, for variations on a quote of the day. You could write it:

- In a mixed-up word order.
- In phonemes rather than ordinary letters.
- With a spelling mistake.
- With a missing word.
- With one word substituted with a word that is completely wrong in this context.

Techniques: Focussing starts

Some things seem to attract interest and focus attention especially well at the start of lessons. Here are a few ideas that you could use to lead in to the main activity of the lesson. Many of these will be easiest to do if you have an interactive whiteboard in your room.

1 Hidden → revealed

Introduce one or more hidden things that are speculated about and then slowly revealed. For example:

- The teacher has a large picture on the board, but it's covered up. She invites students to guess what it is and then slowly uncovers part of it … for more discussion … and so on.
- The teacher writes up some unusual key words on the board. She explains that they all come from one text. What do students think the text is about?
- The teacher projects a text on the board (e.g. a website), but covers up large parts of it. Students try to guess what it is about.

2 Broken → reconstructed

Show students something that has been broken up, and invite them to reassemble it. For example:

- A printed text that has been cut into pieces.
- A sentence on the board that has had its words mixed up.
- A picture that has been cut up like a jigsaw.

3 Mystery → solution

Creating little mysteries that students have to think about and solve can draw attention and focus minds. For example:

- The teacher shows an odd, blurred or unclear photograph and asks students to discuss and decide what it shows.
- The teacher gives a one-sentence statement about something strange that happened, perhaps in his or her own life (e.g., 'Last night I woke up screaming'). Students may only ask yes / no questions to try and work out what it is all about (e.g., 'My neighbour's cat climbed in my window and sat on my face while I was asleep').
- The teacher has a large bag and explains that a stranger – before running off – came up to him or her, pushed the bag into the teacher's hands and said it was vital to look after it. The teacher asks students who they think it belongs to, whether to keep it, etc. On their suggestion, the teacher decides to look into the bag. He or she then extracts an (unexpected) item from the bag and invites speculation about the owner, and the purpose of the item. The teacher then takes a second item … and so on.

Techniques: Quiet starts

ELT can sometimes seem to encourage buzzing, active, noisy starts to lessons: discussions, pair-work speaking activities, mingle tasks and so on. If this sounds like your typical lesson, you might want to experiment with the opposite, just to see how it feels. Instead of lots of activity and speaking, try a really quiet, atmospheric, even mysterious start. For example:

1 Storytelling

The students arrive, making their usual noise. The teacher is sitting in some central location, with a book in his or her hand. The teacher smiles a greeting at the students, but doesn't say anything. When everyone has arrived, the teacher starts reading, surprisingly quietly, but with feeling. Students 'shhhh' each other so that they can hear what the teacher is saying. Very quickly, the class settles down, and their attention is fixed on the teacher and what he or she is saying. The teacher is reading a rather exciting vampire novel, and the students find it interesting. The teacher continues to read without explanation or tasks or comprehension questions for ten or more minutes, then stops, smiles and puts away the book. Even now, there are no questions or tests from the teacher. Some students ask what happens next. The teacher asks if they would like to find out. If enough say 'yes', the teacher replies that he or she might read more … tomorrow … or another time.

2 Puzzle

Throw out a slightly odd fact, perhaps from an upcoming text (for example 'Charles Lindbergh only took four sandwiches with him'), and then keep silent. Students will initially be puzzled, but might soon come back with questions – and will start to learn about the story (Lindbergh was the first man to fly solo non-stop across the Atlantic!).

Techniques: Energising starts

Most ELT teachers quickly collect a number of favourite movement-based activities and games, especially for use with younger-learner classes. These can be handy at the start of a lesson (or at other points) to help wake sleepy students up and give them a chance to stretch their legs – and perhaps laugh a little. There may not be any specific language aim, but working together and speaking in English may help to get students re-engaged with using the language. Here are just a few examples:

1 Sequence memory

Ask the class to stand up. Explain that you will do a movement, and they should copy it (e.g. your first movement could be rubbing the top of your head). Ask a student to do the action, and add a new action (e.g. rubbing the top of his or her head and then waving to a friend), which everyone (including you) should copy. Indicate a new student who must repeat the previous two actions and add a new one. Continue in this way until it becomes impossible or too funny.

2 Mirroring

Pair students up, standing eye to eye, directly opposite each other. Explain that A is standing in front of a mirror, and B is the mirror. Every time that A moves, B should copy it exactly. Encourage students to start with very slow actions. Swap roles after a minute or two.

3 Acting out a story

Tell the class to stand up. Start telling a short story that has a number of distinct actions in it (e.g. taking a box off a shelf, catching a ball, waving to someone, etc.). As you mention each action, mime the action, which students should copy. After you have finished, go through the story again, but don't do the actions yourself. See if the students can.

4 Secret passing

Ask students to stand in a wide circle. Pass out some hand-sized objects (e.g. an orange, a glasses case, a toy car) to different students. Any student who has an object should discreetly pass it round the circle in either direction. Any student who doesn't have an object can pretend to be passing an object. After thirty or forty seconds, stop the passing and pretending. Invite a random student to take three guesses to try and find where the objects are. Then restart the passing, and play it again a few times.

Questions for reflection

- Which adjectives would best describe your lesson starts? Organised? Noisy? Chaotic? Focussed? Efficient? Engaging? Time wasting? Inspiring?

2 Using the board

> *When I look at my board at the end of a lesson, it always seems such a mess. I have no idea whether the students managed to copy anything useful down, or if they even knew what some of the things I had written were meant to be.*

Aim

To make board use clearer, more organised and more useful.

Introduction

The board (whether black, white or interactive) is, in many classrooms, the crucial central teaching tool, yet it's also one that gets little thought. The board has been so omnipresent through our childhoods and working lives that we almost forget that it may be possible to get better at using it. Even a few minutes of quiet practice in an empty room, with a little self-checking (from the back of the room) and reflection on how we might be able to improve what we do, can make a big difference. Some very small changes can make your use of the board much clearer and more effective.

Techniques: Using the board

1 Divide the board into sections

At the start of the lesson, draw dividing lines to create distinct sections on the board. How many will depend on how large your board is, but many teachers typically use four: a column down the left and right sides of the board, and a horizontal division of the middle section. You will now be able to keep different kinds of board work organised into these separate areas, for example, the right-hand column for new vocabulary; the left-hand column for administrative information, student names, homework, etc. The top and bottom middle sections can be a 'working zone' for the teacher – perhaps with illustrations or texts in the top half, and explanations and examples for students to copy in the lower part. However you use them, simply having your work clearly divided up will make it easier to access and easier to keep organised. It also means that you can erase one section while leaving another part still visible.

2 Plan your board use

Before your lesson, make a sketch plan of your board usage. Draw a rectangle, divide it up into sections and number them. Use the numbers to make a list of exactly what will go in each board section. Of course, if you have an interactive board, then you can prepare some of the actual pages of the board. Beware of making fully complete pages in advance, as this can take away some of the 'live' lesson and risks turning the lesson into a slide show.

3 Use handwriting and sentence case

Avoid writing everything in separated block capital letters. Evidence suggests that rather than making things easier to read, it is actually harder. Using cursive handwriting, with normal usage of big and small letters, helps train your students to read handwriting in the real world.

4 Check out the clarity of your writing

Writing with chalk or a board pen on a vertical board is very different from normal handwriting. The thickness of the pen/chalk can make some letters hard to read as the lines merge into each other. It is also surprisingly easy to find yourself writing at a slant, with all your sentences rising to the sky or sinking to the floor.

Check yourself out when there are no learners present. Go to the back of the room, and take a good critical look at what you have done. Do you need to write everything bigger? Do your A's and O's look distinctly different? Could things be straighter? Might the writing look clearer with more spaces between the lines? Is punctuation clearly visible, and unambiguous? Can you easily work out what layout was intended? If in any doubt, try it all again, but bigger. You will be able to write less, but the gain in clarity and usefulness may be significant.

5 Use graphic organisers to help structure text

Wherever you can, use graphic organisers such as tables, flow charts, bullet points, mind maps, diagrams and so on to help give a shape and a structure to text. It makes it easier to see, read and copy.

6 Use colour to a purpose

Some whiteboard pen colours, for example, green or red, can be tiring or difficult to read from the back of the room or in poor lighting conditions. If you write a whole text in these colours, it can add to the difficulty and extend the time needed for reading or copying. Try to write all key items in strong colours such as black or dark blue. Use other colours for specific purposes such as underlining, adding a phonemic transcription or highlighting some problem letters when spelling a word. Colours are also useful for helping to structure the board – drawing those initial section dividers, drawing boxes round important elements, shaping tables, drawing lines and arrows to connect things on different parts of the board and so on. Of course, colours are also great for illustrations.

7 Stand back to check

It's amazing how easy it is to write up nonsense. Writing close up, you don't get a clear view of the whole text. Students interrupt with questions and clarifications. Quite often, the result of this is that some of your writing has simple errors (spelling, missing words), or sometimes there is a glaring piece of incoherence, such as missing out an entire line you intended to write. Students may spot this and alert you to it, but, as often as not, they won't recognise that there is a problem and will happily copy down whatever you wrote (because 'teacher is always right').

When you have written something, make sure that you take some time to stand back and quietly read it through again to check. Try to see it with your eyes, rather than your memory. By this, I mean try to see what you have actually put up, rather than filling in from what you know and think should be there.

8 Review post-lesson

At the end of a lesson, get out your phone and take a snap of the whole board. Have a look at it later on and see how readable it is: does it still make sense to you?

9 Ask learners before erasing

Don't just rub out content as soon as you need space. Make sure that everyone who needs to has finished reading, copying or whatever. Ask and double check that it isn't only the fastest students that you hear.

10 Use the board creatively

Don't just write *everything* up. Don't just get students to copy. Don't only put up the 'boring' stuff. You can use Blu-Tack® to put up pictures, students' work, notices, flowers and other objects.

Technique: writing 'game-show' style

Most teachers need to write on the board at various points through a lesson. However, when this is done with the teacher's back to the class, possibly for a period of some minutes, it can have quite a distancing effect. Students cannot clearly see what the teacher is doing, and the teacher cannot keep in eye contact with the learners. Even if the teacher asks questions or tries to involve students, they often have to give their answers to a back, rather than to a face.

1 Stand facing the class to the left or right of the board, with your back to the board at an angle of about 45 degrees (as in this figure, seen from above).

2 Keeping your body at the same angle, you can now turn your head to the board and either reach out to write with the arm closest to the board or bend the furthest arm across your body to write on the board.
3 Vary your eye contact between the board, where you are writing, and students in the class. Turn your head a little to look at the board, and write a few words; then turn back, and shift your eye contact to talk with students; ask a question; then shift your attention back to the board and so on.

The position will probably feel quite odd and contorted the first few times you try it, and it will take some practice to feel comfortable and be able to write easily. Practice in an empty classroom before doing it in front of students. Before long, it should become quite normal and natural. The value of staying in active communication with your class outweighs the slight effort involved.

(This technique gets its name from the fact that the position is reminiscent of a TV game-show hostess facing the audience and smiling at them while pointing out winning numbers or letters on a game board behind her.)

Techniques: Using an interactive whiteboard

Having an interactive whiteboard (IWB) in your classroom allows you to use many interesting and useful features beyond basic writing and drawing. For example, you can hide and reveal screens or items on the screen, project images or documents you have prepared earlier, save pages (and return to them later on in the lesson or another lesson), access interactive materials (perhaps prepared specifically for your coursebook), add notes on top of texts and view internet pages, video clips and so on.

Here are a few basic ideas for using an IWB:

1 Use it as an ordinary board

Just because it's an IWB doesn't mean that you have to do fancy digital magic all the time. It's most important use is still as a board to write on. Certainly, use any special features when they are useful and appropriate, but don't feel impelled to do so.

2 Show pictures

One of the best uses for an IWB is also its simplest: showing images. ELT teachers often want to show their class a picture, for example, as an introduction to a reading text or as a context for a grammar presentation. The IWB can project a large clear image that has far more impact than a traditional small flashcard does. You also have the option of hiding parts of the picture, revealing it slowly, zooming in on a section or writing over the top (e.g. to label vocabulary items). It's also easy to track down the images you want, using an image search on the Internet.

3 Don't assume that the board will do all the teaching

It's not enough to prepare a great set of screens and then simply read them aloud, one after the other to the class. This can make for a terribly dull lesson. Find ways to exploit the technology to inspire. You need to interact with the students as much as ever.

4 Project texts

When students have done some reading work on printed text, it's very useful to be able to project a copy of the text onto the board. Use it to point out which section of the text you are looking at, and for close-up work on sentences and details. Use the IWB's facility to zoom, underline, annotate and so on to help the students make sense of complex parts of the text.

5 Use the Internet together

If your IWB has a web connection, you can integrate planned or spontaneous use of the Internet right into the heart of your lessons. Do a Google search on an interesting person who featured in a coursebook text. Find out if there is a video on a current topic of interest. Check the synonyms of a word on a web thesaurus. Practise listening to the live news.

6 Prepare screens that are only partially filled in

When you prepare your lesson, it's possible to create screens that you can show on the board in class. Resist the temptation to write down everything that students need to see in class. This can lead to 'dead' feeling lessons. Instead, it's often better to prepare partially complete boards (e.g. with the framework of a table, but not the contents). This leaves you the opportunity to work with the students and fill in the missing information as part of your 'live' teaching in class.

7 Revise using boards from earlier lessons

It's great being able to save boards and return to them later. Use this as a great revision tool. Remind students of the content from a lesson a month ago. Try hiding part of a screen and seeing if learners can recall what was on the missing half. Do problems or tasks again quickly. If your board is full of answers, get students to think of the questions.

Techniques: Students using the board

In primary schools with traditional chalkboards, being 'board monitor' was often a prized responsibility role for children – though it didn't often call for much more than cleaning the board at the start or end of the lesson. In most schools, the board has remained essentially the teacher's property. As part of democratising our classrooms, we can help learners to become far more active users of the board.

At the very least, inviting students to use the board gets one or two up from their seats for a few minutes. Beyond this, students may start to feel that the board is a shared resource and not just the teacher's property. They could get used to writing on it, doing exercises together, coming up in a group to prepare an idea together, lead presentations using it and so on. Students may quickly start to initiate work themselves using the board, perhaps writing up a problem sentence or helping to explain something for another student. Try some of these techniques:

Suitable for all kinds of boards

1 With younger learners, appoint students to set up the board at the start of each lesson, making divisions into sections, writing up the date, copying headings or information from your notes.
2 When you need an illustration, invite a volunteer to do it for you.
3 When you have some simple text to write up from a book or document, invite a student to do this.
4 When students do a group task on paper (e.g. design a poster about a topic), get one or two of the groups to come up and use one half of the board as their 'paper'.

5 When students do a task (individually or in groups), monitor and ask some or all of them to write their text on the board when they have finished.

6 Write exercises on the board, and get students to come up and add the answers.

7 Teach interactively, getting students to come up frequently to add information, complete timelines, point out things in pictures and so on.

8 When you play a game on the board, ask students to do any writing up or score keeping.

9 Make the vocabulary column a student responsibility to maintain. For example, when there seem to be some useful words (for example, in a text you are working on), ask students to select the most useful ones to write up in that column. The word column can grow though the lesson, even when the rest of the board is cleaned.

10 Leave a column on the side of the board for students to add their comments, questions and thoughts. Encourage them to add things at different stages of the lesson.

11 When students prepare a report or presentation, encourage them to plan board use into what they do.

12 Completely hand over part of your teaching to your class. For example, if you have to teach 16 words in a word set, ask different groups to each prepare to teach the meaning of two of the words or phrases. When ready, invite each group in turn to do their teaching up front, using the board as appropriate.

13 With smaller classes, establish an environment in which everyone feels able to use the board at any point in the lesson – for working on, for putting up thoughts and so on. Frequently gather students round the board and work on it together, passing the chalk/ pen from person to person as you solve problems.

14 Try an experiment in which you make the board a place that *only* learners use … (which means that you'll need to find an alternative!).

Suitable for the interactive whiteboard

1 Invite students to send texts to you (for example, by email or SMS mobile text message), as the lesson proceeds. Show some on screen, and let the students come up to talk the class through them. You may wish to check texts before displaying them to the whole class, in which case you will need to plan in some moments when you will get a chance to review them before putting them up on the display.

2 For certain parts of your lesson, use a window on your board to show Twitter, TodaysMeet or a similar messaging service, with a live stream of comments on screen. Your class, using netbooks or mobile phones, can react to the lesson as it unfolds, asking questions, adding comments, answering questions and so on. You can keep a check on understanding as you go.

Questions for reflection

- Is your board easily legible? And what about from the back of the room? What is the least clear, untidiest, least successful aspect of your board work? How can you immediately improve on that?
- How much do you feel 'ownership' of the board? How much do learners use the board in your lessons? A little? A lot? Never? Is getting students to write a few things on the board perhaps just a token nod towards democratisation – whereas you still keep all real control?
- Some teachers use writing on the board as a way to get a 'break', take a breath and briefly avoid the need to interact with students. When you maintain eye contact with students, do you find that you miss any of this 'time out'?

■3 The coursebook

> *Every day I go in and say, 'Open your book at page ...', and every time I know they are going to groan.*

Aim

To better exploit the class coursebook.

Introduction

Coursebooks can seem to encourage you to start on page 1 and progress steadily through exercise by exercise, page by page, unit by unit. Many school syllabuses require that teachers 'cover the book' in this sort of way. Teachers are asked to finish a specific number of units by a certain date and test students' learning at the end of this time. But coursebooks can be a flexible resource.

Technique: Get to know your coursebook

It's worth taking some time to familiarise yourself with the coursebook you'll be using, both by flicking through the pages to get general impressions and, also, by looking carefully at units in different parts of the book. Consider questions such as these:

1 Is the book's appearance appealing? Are there good illustrations, diagrams and tables? Does it make you feel keen to read the texts or yearning to close it as soon as possible?

2 What is the thinking behind the book? Does it have a particular angle (e.g. a strong lexical focus), and, if so, are you comfortable with that? Do the authors set out a convincing case for the book in their introduction?

3 Is the syllabus mixed and balanced? Is there enough vocabulary, grammar, pronunciation, listening, speaking, reading and writing? Is there a predominance of one system (e.g. grammar) or skill?

4 Do the units look suitable for your students? Do they match their needs? Do they match their expectations? Are the topics relevant and interesting? Is reference information (e.g. about grammar) clearly given? Are there summary sections?

5 Are there lots of opportunities for useful practice (e.g. communication activities)?

6 How is the book divided up? How long do you think a unit will take to do? Do you think you should do the whole book, or will you pick and choose units, sections and exercises? What sort of things will you need to supplement it?

7 Does the teacher's book seem helpful? Does it provide more than just a repetition of task instructions from the student's book? Are there supplementary ideas, activities and materials (perhaps at the back)? Does it have photocopiable worksheets? Tests? Online resources? Interactive whiteboard resources?

Techniques: Introducing your class to their coursebook

When first starting to work with a new coursebook, many teachers would jump straight in at the first page of the first unit, but it can be worth taking some time to introduce the book to the class, for example:

1 Ask students to look at the cover and quickly flick though the book, without reading anything. Let them discuss their impressions and expectations. Spend a little time looking at the back cover, helping them to understand any difficult bits. What do they think now? Do they think the book will be interesting or useful? Get students to spend a longer time browsing through the units. What topics jump out at them? Are there any interesting illustrations? Which bits are they looking forward to?

2 Design a treasure hunt activity, i.e. one that forces students to look through the book to seek out certain things. Students could work in teams to find the best set of answers. You could include tasks (whose answers would all be in the book) such as: 'Write three page numbers where you can find a picture of a fish or sea creature', 'How old is the waiter at the Los Alamos hotel?' 'How far away is the Andromeda galaxy?' 'Find the names of three instruments you can find in an orchestra', 'Does this book have work on the grammar area Passive Voice?'

3 Do two or three discussions, tasks or exercises drawn from very different locations in the book. This can help to demonstrate to students that learning a language isn't necessarily linear (i.e. they *can* succeed with material that comes from later in the book and don't have to study every page that precedes it). It also makes the point that you will not necessarily work through page by page in strict order.

Techniques: Ways to work with your coursebook

As alternatives to starting on page one and going through linearly, unit by unit, here are some ideas to try:

1 Take ownership

A good starting point for working with a coursebook is to take real ownership of it. Rather than a factual change, I'm thinking of a subjective shift in your relationship to the book: an assertion to yourself that you control the book and how it's used, rather than that the book is running your course and making all the key decisions. Take the view that the book is just a resource (and one of many) that can help to create a good course. It is available to use as and when you want to, but it does not need to dominate. The book is not the course. Believe this, and you are off to a sound start in the relationship!

2 Be selective

You don't have to do everything. Pick out sections that are interesting and useful.

3 Leave bits out

Omit things that don't seem useful. Just make sure that you are not only omitting the bits that you find hard to explain or teach. Make sure there's a balance; avoid missing out all the skills in favour of all the systems (grammar, vocabulary and pronunciation) work.

4 Divide and allocate

Not everyone needs to do the same things. You can ask some students to do one thing; others to do different bits. You could allocate on the basis of learning differences, such as level or work speed, or for other reasons, such as what they might find interesting.

5 Democratise

Ask learners for their opinion as to what they (as a class or as individuals) want to do, the order they want to do it in, how they want to do it (e.g. fast, slow, with the teacher, in pairs, individually, with answers to check as they go, without answers, etc.).

6 Reorder

You are not restricted to the order pre-defined in the book. Feel free to jump ahead or double back or pick out a useful feature from a much later unit.

7 Adapt

Use material from the book, but in a different way. For example, exploit a good picture for a discussion, use a text intended to teach grammar as a reading-skills resource, give different instructions for an exercise.

8 Exploit

Don't feel you have to rush through a whole page of activities in one lesson. Take just one activity and see what you can do with it, e.g. a grammar exercise which you get your students to complete, compare, cover up, try to reconstruct from memory, personalise, add to, search for expressions to put into a dialogue and so on.

If you choose to do some of the ideas above, students may well ask why you aren't 'following the book'. You will need to be prepared and able to explain your rationale (which might include the fact that the coursebook writer doesn't know this class and that he/she wrote the book to work in a range of very different situations, but that it is your job to make the best course for your students here and now – and that means adjusting and selecting as you go).

Technique: Don't panic about 'covering the book'

One constraint that may hold teachers back from using a coursebook creatively in class is the feeling that the school (or department or education ministry) requires them to 'cover the book' or 'complete the syllabus'. While such impositions are probably set from the best of intentions, they can feel most unhelpful and may display a misunderstanding of the nature of learning, assuming that a language-learning syllabus can be divided up and learnt piece by piece in the same sort of way that a geography or physics syllabus can. Teachers often feel that they are being asked to 'turn the pages' of their coursebook, often at a ridiculous speed, being satisfied with the illusion of learning simply in order to report, at the end of term, that they have 'done it', rather than focussing on the real learning needs of their class or working at the actual pace their students need. This encourages teachers and schools towards being satisfied with an illusion of learning.

If you work in a school where you are asked to 'cover the book', see if you can find the confidence or courage to politely:

- Argue the case (with whoever makes the decisions) that this is not really appropriate for language learning. It's not an item-by-item accumulation of knowledge.
- Explain that you wish to get away from 'lockstep' teaching (i.e. where all the class work at the same pace on the same thing).
- Point out that you are differentiating work for individuals in order to help each to achieve the most they can, and that this makes the whole concept of 'covering the book' redundant. If you are going to genuinely differentiate work for students, this will inevitably mean that not all students will do all the work and that you will observe and adjust work demands and pace as you go, taking your cue much more from the students than the pace that the coursebook sets.

And if your persuasion and informed arguments fall on deaf ears, I'd suggest that you could still try doing what you think is best anyway, though this is not necessarily an easy decision. The wrath of managers or parents asking, 'Why hasn't Hassan done all the book?' can be a tough one to argue. Even if you strongly believe that a token 'finishing' of the book is less useful than really becoming good at language, it's not easy to convince less-informed others. But students will not pass exams any better, simply because they have been sitting in a room where the class have looked quickly at every page. The best test results are more likely to come from students who have worked thoroughly on a smaller number of areas.

Questions for reflection

- Is your coursebook the heart of your course? How much of lesson time do you spend with it? Would there be any value in escaping a little more from it?

■4 Time and pace

> *My lessons often seem to plod along at the same speed, but I don't know if this is just my impression. What is the right pace for a lesson?*

Aim
To set and vary the pace as appropriate through the lesson.

Introduction
Whereas time is a factual element of the world that we can't change, pace is subjective. It is how we perceive time and what we do in time. There are many variations on the old report of the theatregoer watching a Wagner opera who found that, 'After two hours, I looked at my watch and saw that ten minutes had gone by'. For a student listening to a dull lecture about grammar, ten minutes can also feel like two hours.

It can be hard for a teacher to know if a lesson is too fast or too slow, or to engineer a change of pace if she feels that it's currently wrong. Yet it is clearly a crucial skill: 'The pace was too slow' is a very frequent student complaint.

Technique: Discovering what your pace is
Because you usually teach in similar ways that seem natural to you, it can be very hard for you to recognise or assess aspects of your teaching such as pace or atmosphere. This is a really useful thing to get an observer in to watch. Even seeing 10 or 15 minutes of your lesson should be enough for an observer to be able to answer some useful questions. Ask them to watch a part of your lesson where you are working with the class, rather than one where students are mainly working on their own in pairs or groups. Here are some suggestions for questions that you could ask a colleague to give you feedback on:

- Compared to your own teaching, do you feel that my lesson moves faster or slower or about the same pace as your own lesson?
- Can you name some bits of the lesson that seemed to be done faster than you would have done them yourself?
- Can you name some bits of the lesson that seemed to be done slower than you would have done them yourself?
- Choose one strong student and one weaker one. How do you think the pace of the lesson seemed to them?

As with all such developmental observations, there are no right answers. The hope is that when you meet up afterwards to talk about the lesson, you will be able to have a useful discussion about things noticed and both of your thoughts about those issues.

As an alternative to getting a colleague in to observe, you could ask for direct feedback from students. Useful questions might include:

- Did the work in this lesson seem too fast, too slow or about right to you?
- Name one part of the lesson that you would have liked to go faster.
- Name one part of the lesson that you would have liked to go slower.

Another option would be to monitor yourself in some way. For example, when planning the lesson, write down an estimated time for each stage or activity. In class, note the actual time taken for each stage/activity next to your predictions. This will provide some data for you to reflect on after the lesson. Consider whether the activities really needed the time you predicted or the time they took? Decide whether you would aim to go faster or slower next time.

Technique: Playing with time limits

It's often a good idea to state a time limit for a task. This gives students an idea as to how long they will have, and whether they have to work fast or can take more time to think about things.

But remember that the fact that you have given a time limit doesn't mean that you have to keep to it! In a few activities (e.g. tests or quizzes), fairness may require that you absolutely stick to what you said, but, in other cases, time is flexible. If students are struggling to complete the task, extend the time; if it's proving easy, reduce it. Neither of these negate the usefulness of stating the original time limit, as that gives students an idea of what to expect and how to plan their work. If they have been fully engaged, it's unlikely that any of your class will notice that you have played with time.

Whether you alter time limits or not, it's still useful to give indications and warnings as to how much time is left, for example, 'You have ten more minutes' or 'Just two minutes left'.

Technique: Playing with pace

Students can get locked into dull working modes, perhaps always attacking tasks too slowly and lazily, or too fast and carelessly. The more that either happens, the more it becomes the norm and starts to set the tone of everything that happens in class. The teacher can address this by deliberately engineering changes of pace through a lesson – gradually, or perhaps with a sudden, sharp variation. Try these ideas:

1 Set contrasting tasks. Follow a slow one with a much faster one. Follow a sitting-down, heads-down task with one that involves a lot of movement and interaction.
2 Change the amount of concrete outcomes required from a task. If students have to produce one agreed answer to a question, this allows for a slower, more thoughtful approach to finding it. Conversely, a large number of answers will require attention to be paid to many different things and may encourage faster, less thoughtful work.

Techniques: Using empathy to judge pace

Remember that pace is both a subjective and a relative concept.

1 Subjective pace

This is closely connected to how engaged you are with what you are doing, and how unpleasant what you are doing is for you. When we are interested, involved and enjoying ourselves, we hardly notice the passing of time. When we are bored, it seems to drag.

2 Relative pace

Different people have different perspectives. What may seem too slow to you may seem too fast to learners.

A common example is in listening lessons, for example, when a teacher plays a recorded conversation. The teacher hears and understands the whole recording in full the first time he or she plays it. By the time the teacher replays it a second time, it already starts to feel dull for him or her, and the teacher finds it hard to believe that it would be interesting or useful for it to be played a third time; to the teacher, that would seem to reduce the lesson's pace to a crawl. But for many of his or her students, the content of the recording may be a total fog for the first or second time of listening, and only as they start to work on it does it clear a little. For them, engagement may be increasing as they start to get an understanding of the contents and wish to learn more; repeated plays may cause them to get more involved.

Einstein summed it all up quite neatly: 'Put your hand on a hot stove for a minute, and it seems like an hour. Sit with a pretty girl for an hour, and it seems like a minute. *That's* relativity.'

- Use your empathic skills to try and feel the pace of an activity from the learner's perspective rather than your own. Imagine yourself as them, with their current skill levels and faced with the task they are supposed to be doing. How does it feel now?
- Seek feedback from learners as to how they feel about the pace, and adjust accordingly. Don't dismiss students' wishes to do something again as simply efforts at avoidance or time wasting.
- Remember that teachers may often have an instinct to go faster than the natural pace of their students' learning. Perceived pressure from the school, syllabus or 'get-through-the-book' requirements may push them to go faster than learners actually need. See how much you can match the real pace that learners are learning at, rather than forcing an externally imposed pace.

Techniques: Getting to the 'meat'

Training courses sometimes encourage teachers to include a 'lead-in' as part of their planning for systems lessons (e.g. on grammar). A lead-in is an introductory activity designed to help make students readier to engage with the work and draw connections to previous studied lessons. However, such introductory activities often prove interesting in their own right, more challenging than expected, take longer than predicted and may even take over a substantial part of the lesson. That's not necessarily a bad thing if the work is useful, interesting and relevant. But if you really want to work on something important later in the lesson, it can also be a problem. A common reason for failure in high-level practical teaching tests is that observers watch 'lead-ins' that take far too long and steal time that could have been used more productively to focus on the intended real aim of the lesson. A common complaint from examiners is that crucial practice or use of the language being taught never happened (or will supposedly happen in some future lesson) because the candidate spent a lot of time on a relatively useless lead-in.

Apart from the language-related uses, teachers may use lead-ins to fill time while late students arrive (though this might be counterproductive since if students know that there will always be a warmer, there is less pressure to arrive on time). A few teachers even use lead-ins as a deliberate avoidance tactic, to prevent themselves from having too much time to focus on aspects of language that they are not comfortable with.

1 If you are happy with a free-flowing, flexible, spontaneously evolving lesson, it may not matter how long your lead-in takes and where it leads. If you have a substantive, planned language point that you want students to focus on, then you may need to make the lead-in short and to the point. Get to the 'meat' of your lesson as soon as you can.
2 Question whether students really need to have their engagement turned on via a lead-in. If the language point is interesting and the main work tasks challenging in their own right, consider going straight to the meat of your lesson without any lead-ins.
3 Plan lessons backwards. Start by thinking of what you want students to be able to do at the end of the lesson. Plan the tasks that get them doing that. Work back to the task or input that has to precede that. In that way, you can find out if you have any time to do a lead-in and how long it could be.
4 Observe and time limit your lead-ins. Be prepared to stop them if they are taking too long.

Questions for reflection

• Are you fast or slow? Do you know?
• Which kinds of activities in your lessons tend to take much longer than you expected?
• Choose an engaging whole-class activity (e.g. a single coursebook discussion point). Estimate how long it would typically take you to cover it (e.g. two minutes). Consider: What might be any benefits and drawbacks if you allowed it to take five times that normal time? For example, would a wider range of different students get the chance to speak? Would you be able to listen more carefully to what they were saying? Would other students be able to respond and react more? Would the subject get boring if extended too much?

▊5 Handouts

I'm not very good with handouts. I've been reusing some of mine for years; they do look a bit scrappy and tired. And I always seem to make giving them out far more complicated than it needs to be!

Aim

To produce better, clearer, more usable handouts, and to use them more efficiently and effectively in class.

Introduction

Most teachers use handouts at some point. They often fall into one of three categories: work tasks to complete (e.g. supplementary exercises, homework); a record of language items or other content that came up in the lesson; and further reading on what has been studied in class, often as a resource for revision.

Techniques: Preparing better handouts

Poorly designed handouts can cause many classroom-management headaches. If the activities or tasks on them aren't clear, the teacher has to do a lot of extra instructing, guiding and monitoring. Here are some ideas for making more effective handouts. These are hints rather than rules; feel free to use them selectively!

1 Where possible, prepare handouts on a computer. This allows you to easily save and edit text for future reuses.

2 If you are going to handwrite handouts, consider pre-printing a number of computer-printed frames (e.g. plain rectangles or possibly decorative borders) as a starting point; it can really help to smarten up a handwritten page. Similarly, if you photocopy dull exercises (e.g. from a grammar book) onto a handout, consider placing them mid-page inside a printed frame. Last-minute handouts (i.e. you've suddenly realised that you need to write something and copy it just a few minutes before class is going to start) can be especially scrappy; having some ready-made frames works very well to quickly improve these.

3 If you regularly need the same header or footer on handwritten handouts, try printing that text onto a transparent sheet. Lay this over each handout before you photocopy it. You can reuse this again and again. You could also let students use the template to smarten up any of their own work that is going to be distributed.

4 Text sometimes looks better in two columns; you may want to try this. If you don't know how to do this on your word processor, ask for help. It's a simple trick to learn. Similarly, using tables really helps to organise text on the page; you can always make the lines marking the edges of the table invisible.

5 Don't fill handouts with text alone. Add lots of white space into the page: wide left and right margins as well as top and bottom. This space makes the whole page less intimidating and leaves room for comments, vocabulary notes, translations and so on.

6 Help the reader to navigate the handout by good use of headings and sub-headings. Don't go mad with lots of different fonts, but carefully use a limited range of sizes and bold style to help headings stand out.

7 If your handout has multiple pages, number them clearly and repeat headers/footers. This helps the handing-out process, as well as the filing and later reuse.

8 Use memorable graphics (e.g. diagrams, charts, cartoons, photos). Difficult information can often be better conveyed in diagrams than in dense text. Consider sometimes letting the graphics take up more space than the text.

9 Consider using coloured paper if your school has it. You could even colour-code themes, topics or handout types by colour. It doesn't cost a lot more than white paper, but can help students when sorting and filing.

10 Avoid that ninth-generation photocopy look: when a page has been photocopied and re-photocopied many times, it often gains dark stippling and phantom-edge marks from earlier copies that look fairly ugly. A quick way to smarten up the page is to cut out just the text of the page, avoiding all these marks, and paste it down onto a new blank sheet of paper before copying. Better yet, scan the text into a computer and start with a completely fresh new copy.

11 If your handout is a summary of some lesson content, think about how much detail you want to use to convey that information. Here are three options:
   • Type one: Just the key points summarised. Note form, possibly using bullet points. It aims to jog memory rather than provide comprehensive information.
   • Type two: Detailed notes. Text paragraphs sorted under headings. It aims to provide a fairly complete summary of the content the student needs.
   • Type three: Texts with tasks (e.g. gap-fills or diagrams to complete). It aims to give comprehensive information, but also makes the student work a little to recover and recall the content.

12 If your handout is purely a reading text, perhaps as a record of something studied in class, it's worth including a short introduction saying what the text is and why it's useful – as well perhaps as a question or two, or a thinking task. When the revising student comes back to the handout in a month or two's time, long after they have forgotten what the lesson was about, this will help them to find a way back into the text. Another option is making the text a gap-fill activity. Don't do it in class or set it for homework, but when students come back to the text months later, they will need to work a little to reconstruct the text, and this might just help them learn the contents better.

13 Instead of preparing a handout yourself, get students to design it after you have taught something. Select the best, copy or print them and distribute to the whole class.

14 Consider using electronic handouts, e.g. emailing texts to your students, rather than printing everything out. If your institution has a Learning Management System (e.g. Moodle®), handouts and lesson summaries can be made available there.

Techniques: Distributing handouts

With only a few students, it's easy enough to give handouts out yourself, but the larger your class, the more thought you need to put into working out efficient ways of doing this. Here are a few ideas to try:

1 Appoint handout helpers. Pass all the handouts to them, and let them do the distribution. ('Helpers' such as these are not just for primary school; it works just as well with a group of managers in their company classroom!)
2 In a classroom with rows of seats, give out a pile of handouts to students at the end of each column at the back of the room. They each take one and hand the rest of the pile forward.
3 In a class with groups around tables or seats in a semi-circle, give a third of the handouts to one student/table on the left of the room. Explain that they must take one and pass the pile on. Use your finger to clearly point out the direction in which they must pass. Go to the middle of the room and then the right, handing out the other thirds and pointing out which direction to pass. At the end, ask anyone who has still not got a handout to put up their hand.
4 Place handouts in a pile at the front of the class. Ask students to come up row by row (or however your class is arranged) to collect one.
5 Decide the best time to give your handouts. Would it be more useful at the start of the lesson or before they study the work so that they can refer to your notes while you are doing input? Or as they are needed during the session? Or all together at the end of the lesson?

Technique: Using sorting envelopes

Some activities require you to prepare a number of cut-up small materials. These slips of paper often need to be kept as separate groups of items (for example, when each group of five students needs five different role cards and a task instruction card).

Sometimes these can be very problematic, especially if there are a large number of slips of paper. Keeping the sets separate can be fiddly. Teachers may spend a long time cutting them up pre-lesson only to find that, by the time they get to class, they have somehow all become mixed up, rendering the task undoable without a massive resorting operation.

A related problem is that the slips are easily lost, hard to collect in and sort and are, therefore, not easily reusable for future lessons, requiring the teacher to remake all the materials each time they are required.

At the time of preparing the slips of paper, use paper clips to hold sets together, and then place each set into a separate envelope. Label the envelope clearly with the name of the activity and the precise contents (e.g. 'set of five role cards and one task card'). In class, hand a whole envelope to each group, and ask them to distribute the contents within their group.

At the end of the activity, ask each group to replace all the items in their envelope. Collect in the envelopes. These sorted sets will now be easily reusable in future classes.

If your school has a laminating machine, consider using this to make your materials smarter and more durable.

Technique: Comb cuts

If you don't have time to sort items into envelopes, one quick solution is to use a *comb cut*. This is a way of partially cutting up materials, but still keeping them together until the last possible moment (and thus reducing the potential for confusion).

You do a comb cut by cutting the slips almost all the way to the edge of the page they are on, but stopping just before they are separated, leaving a 1 to 2 cm edge. The resulting slips of paper will all still be attached to the page – looking something like a comb:

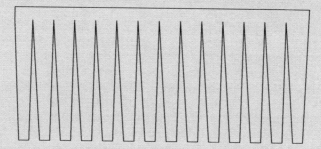

In class, tear the slips away from their page at the very last moment, as you hand them out. In this way, you are sure that the slips you distribute all came from the same set.

The diagram above shows a comb cut used by a teacher for an activity in which she needed two identical sets of fourteen cards. She had divided the class into two groups of fourteen students, and each student in a group needed to have a different slip. She prepared two comb-cut pages, each with fourteen slips on it.

Questions for reflection

- What is the most useful and least useful handout you have given in the past month or two? What made them good or weak?

■6 Low-tech resources

> *Nowadays, I spend a lot of classroom time using the interactive whiteboard. But I sometimes yearn for the old hands-on teaching stuff we used to do.*

Aim

To make good use of simple resources for lesson preparation and in class.

Introduction

Is there still a place in teaching for magazine pictures, scissors, correction fluid, flipcharts and all those traditional pen-and-paper resources that have suddenly started to look a bit old-fashioned? In the modern, digitally connected world, young people are constantly online and using screens, both in their studies and in social interaction. Won't they roll their eyes at being asked to look at a torn-out picture, make a hand-written poster or collect ideas on a flipchart?

I'd argue that such traditional resources still have an important place in language classrooms, and, interestingly, they are starting to feel increasingly engaging, perhaps because they are simple and different – a hands-on contrast to the staring at screens that makes up so much of our 21st century days. In being different from much of the separated, individual computer work students do, pen-and-paper resources often bring people together, working with tangible, shared materials, in a way that feels surprisingly alive and engaging.

Techniques: Posters

What do you need? A stock of very large paper (e.g. from a flipchart pad) and a good collection of coloured pens of varying thicknesses. Optional extras would be a stock of old colour magazines, glue and scissors so that students can cut out pictures and use them to brighten up their posters. Here are some ideas for posters:

1 Get students to work in pairs or groups to make posters on current topics or language points. Display round the room.
2 Posters are good for needs analysis, planning courses and tracking progress. Try starting the year with each pair making a poster of what they need and want from the course, together with plans as to how they will try to achieve that. Come back to the displayed posters later in the year to compare aims with actual progress.
3 Try using posters to encourage more personal reflections on life and learning. Set tasks to make posters on topics such as 'highlights of my life' or 'English and me'. Leave creative legroom by not being too explicit about exactly what students have to do or how they should do it.

4 Use A3 poster paper as a sharable 'whiteboard' that students can work at on their desk (for example, when they have a group task to discuss and come to some shared conclusions), and then display the results to the class afterwards.

5 Ask groups to prepare a poster. Then request that half the class stays by their posters while the other half circulates to look and ask questions (then the other way round).

Techniques: Flipcharts

Flipcharts (i.e. a very large pad of paper, usually on an easel) are a useful tool, especially when used by students working in groups, for example, when brainstorming ideas, planning projects, discussing ideas and so on. The old-technology feel of felt pen and large crinkly paper works well. Pens appeal because students have something tangible to hold, to work with and to pass or grab off each other. Another advantage of flipcharts is that you can track back over old pages and see what you wrote a few minutes, hours or days earlier.

1 Have one flipchart set up at the front or side of the classroom. Use this to note down key things studied in the lesson. Revisit this at the end of the lesson, or later in the course, to help review and revise.

2 If possible, have a flipchart for each group in class, set up in different parts of the room. When students do group discussion or planning work, the chart provides a focussing role, drawing people's eyes to notes being added and encouraging sharing of ideas.

3 Exploit the 'secret' potential of a flipchart. The chart can easily be turned away from the class so that one or two students can write on it without everyone seeing what they put. This could be the basis of guessing games of various kinds.

Techniques: Flashcards

A flashcard is a picture that a teacher can show their class. While many teachers nowadays use the high-tech version – a projected image on an interactive whiteboard, there is still an immediacy to the low-tech version – a simple 'hold-uppable' printed picture cut from a magazine, perhaps stuck onto a piece of card or laminated.

Flashcard images need to be quite large so that they can be seen and recognised from all over the classroom. Flashcards could also be made showing words, letters or phonemic symbols.

1 Use flashcards to introduce grammar presentations, teach vocabulary, provide a starting point for stories and so on.

2 Give a small number of flashcard pictures to students, and ask them to find a connection or make a story with them.

3 Build up a personal set of flashcards by collecting good pictures from magazines or the Internet. Laminate them so that they don't get dog-eared over the years. Keep in mind that pictures can date quickly, especially ones with fashionable clothes in them! You might want to have a 'cull' of outdated pictures occasionally.

When using flashcards, make sure everyone can see the key details. This may involve:

a   Holding them at chest height or higher.
b   Taking care not to cover up important parts with your fingers.
c   Making sure that students have long enough to really look at and interpret the picture (with a complex picture, this may take longer than you expect).
d   Angling the picture towards different parts of the room for a reasonable time in each direction.
e   Walking round the classroom to offer more students the chance of a close-up view.
f   Asking a question or making a crisp statement to draw students' attention to what they need to notice.
g   Not talking all the time. Allow some 'just-looking' time without constant background noise.

Techniques: A vocabulary box

Keep a small box and a set of blank cards. When interesting or tricky vocabulary items come up, the teacher or a student can write them on a new card: word on one side, notes on the other (meaning, pronunciation, difficulties, etc.). As the collection of cards grows, they can be used to revise and recycle the items.

1   When you need a three-minute filler at the end of a lesson, pick out a few cards and test the class using them.
2   Pick out a selection of cards when you need items for vocabulary games.
3   Encourage students to use slack minutes to pick out a few cards and review them.
4   Consider getting every student to make and use their own personal vocabulary box.

Techniques: Real stuff (realia)

The term realia refers to any real-world objects that you might bring into class to use in your lessons. They could be toys or models of things.

These could be used to:

1   Teach the names of objects as part of a vocabulary lesson (e.g. a range of vegetables).
2   Show things that will help understanding of a topic or text being studied (e.g. an opened electrical plug to show the wiring).
3   Provide vivid illustrations for an anecdote or story that you tell or read (e.g. a postcard from your friend).
4   Inspire students to create their own stories (e.g. some unusual souvenirs and puzzling objects).

Technique: Correction fluid

This white liquid used to be one of the most important items in a teacher's bag, crucial for making gap-fill exercises or removing items from photos for spot-the-difference activities. Although teachers are likely to find both tasks much easier on computer, there is still a value in getting students to make their own handmade exercises using it. For example:

Hand every pair the same text and some correction fluid. Ask them to read it, and choose words to gap out. You could set different word classes (e.g. verbs, nouns, pronouns, adjectives, prepositions) to different pairs. Collect them in; photocopy and distribute the exercises to new pairs to solve (without looking again at the original text!).

Technique: Keeping materials for reuse: cardboard and lamination

If you wish to reuse pictures, example texts, instruction sheets, reusable exercises (e.g. to stock a self-study area) and other materials, it's well worth laminating them. Lamination involves placing the page you want to keep into a transparent pocket which is then passed through a small machine (a 'laminator') which heat-seals the paper inside. Laminators can be bought cheaply these days and are quick and easy to use. An alternative would be to stick pictures or texts down onto a cardboard backing with glue, though this tends to be messier to make and often looks uglier.

Techniques: Audio (on CD, computer, podcast/music players or interactive whiteboard)

Even though much audio and video content is now played over sophisticated equipment (e.g. interactive whiteboards, digital music players), there is a place in many classrooms for the humble CD player, DVD player – or even the ancient cassette recorder. There are a few guidelines which help make these (or their more contemporary equivalents) work better:

1 Place the equipment well, and find the best volume. It needs to be loud enough to be clearly audible through the room, but not so loud that it is painful. Watch out for this: many teachers play recordings too loud. Rather than pushing people into listening more carefully, it tends to have the opposite effect, encouraging them to switch off and try to avoid the noise.
2 Learn how to efficiently rewind and replay short sections of the recording (e.g. a single sentence) so that students can re-hear and work on understanding parts of the longer text.
3 If you have the equipment, consider using separate devices with individual headphones so that listeners can work at their own speed.

Questions for reflection

• Have you left behind many of your old low-tech techniques and resources over the years as new technology arrived? Which would be most exciting to revive?

■7 Working with computers

> *I've found that it's quite hard to integrate computers well into English teaching. I'm never sure what the best arrangement for the room is – or how much control I should take over what the students do.*

Aim

To find efficient solutions for classroom use of computers.

Introduction

An important part of contemporary classroom management is to do with successful use of computers and high-tech digital equipment. Many language teachers want to use new technology, but they are often based in classrooms that are unequipped or only partially supplied with the devices they need. The alternative may require a time-wasting move to a different room or a complicated distribution of equipment (e.g. from a locked cupboard or portable trolley). It's important that when schools set up computer rooms, they don't only consider the technical needs of science and content-based subjects, but also think about how language teachers might use computers (e.g. the need to have space for using computers, but also to get away from them in different interaction, all within the same class!) Some of the ideas in this unit may be useful for discussing and planning computer use with the decision makers in your school.

Techniques: Room arrangements for fixed computers

How can fixed computers be best placed in the classroom? Here are a few basic choices:

1 Standard rows

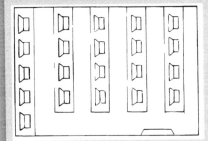

A space-efficient way is to use traditional rows without any fixed teaching area. This allows the teacher to constantly wander around, monitor and view work being done, as well as, by standing on the other side of the desk, make face-to-face conversation with many of the students.

2 Rows with teacher space

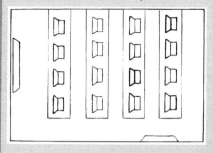

Many classrooms also have a space at the front for the teacher who has his or her own computer and a projection screen or interactive board so that any examples or work the teacher has on his or her screen can be seen by the whole class. The catch with this arrangement is that the teacher is looking at student faces, but cannot easily see if they are doing the set work, checking their email or watching YouTube® videos.

An interesting option here is to make the teacher space at the *back* of the room, thus allowing him or her to continually monitor what is on students' screens without needing to wander round all the time. When the teacher wishes to call the class's attention to his or her input or demonstration, he or she simply asks them to turn their chairs around *away* from their screens.

3 Around the edges

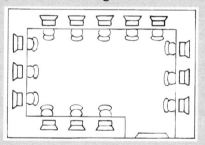

A common alternative arrangement is for computers to be placed around the walls of a classroom. This allows the teacher to easily browse and monitor all work being done, but it can make face-to-face teacher-student communication more difficult.

4 Separate computer/non-computer zones

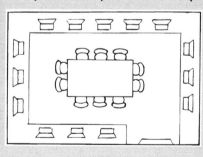

One problem with many computer rooms is that students tend to have their heads locked onto the screens through entire lessons, even in phases where the teacher wants to talk with them or do some upfront input. In language classes, we will typically not want to spend the entire lesson on the computer. Lessons will often benefit from having the opportunity to get away from PCs for a while, to enable other kinds of interaction and grouping for certain stages.

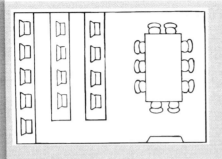

In a large-enough classroom, it's useful to have a distinct area (e.g. a table in the centre of the room or at one end of the room) for students to move to, away from their computer screens. This creates two separate areas (computer/no computer) and two different ways of working. In the centre-of-the-room variant, if you use wheeled or easy-to-move chairs, the class can keep their same chairs and assemble or disperse quickly when necessary.

5 Islands

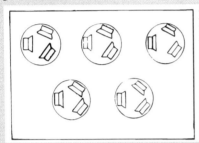

Grouping two, three, or four computers onto separate tables around the room can look attractive, though it does make continual monitoring difficult, as screens will be facing in many different directions. There is no single place in the room that the teacher can easily get a quick at-a-glance overview of what everyone is doing.

Techniques: How many students to a computer?

Some variations to consider:

1 One student per computer

Naturally, this allows the maximum time per person per computer. It is efficient for work that is individually driven, e.g. a personal essay or project. Focussed help to individuals can be given effectively, though it also becomes harder for the teacher to help so many people working separately. This work mode can lead to a sense of individuals working in isolation and is likely to reduce interaction in class and the sense of group identity. There is also the risk of students wasting time on the computer when they are not being closely watched.

2 Two students share a computer

For many tasks, this is the optimum arrangement. If two students work together on one screen, they will need to collaborate: sharing ideas, discussing what to do, correcting errors and so on. Ideally, both students would equally share all work, but it may happen that one student regularly becomes the typist while the other takes on more of the thinking and checking work. You need to watch out for pairings where one person dominates and does all the work while the other just sits back and watches. In terms of class time available per student, it is more efficient for the teacher to help two students at once than to help an individual working on their own.

3 Three students work on a computer

It's possible for three students to work at once on a PC, with one typing and the other two sitting either side, but often it feels uncomfortable, and at least one of the watchers tends to withdraw or get sidelined. One consideration to check before you make use of this arrangement is how wide the viewing angle of the monitor is. Some can easily be seen if you are seated far to the left or right of the screen, but some have very tight angles and are useless for shared viewing. Having three students working at one PC may be most suitable for short bursts of computer work, e.g. typing up results or reports following an earlier activity where the students have already been working together and now need to consolidate or write up their work.

4 Groups work with a computer

Once you get beyond three people on a PC, the natural way of working is for the majority of people to discuss and work *away* from the computer, while one appointed person acts as a sort of secretary, typing up what he or she is told to. The group can move over to the computer to look at the work when helpful, or text can be printed out as needed.

Techniques: Working with and away from the computers

Using computers in a lesson isn't an all-or-nothing decision. It is entirely possible and often desirable to use computers in a fluid and integrated way, moving into computer work when important and then out again as the lesson moves on. (A course that contains a mix of face-to-face and computer work is sometimes referred to as 'blended learning'.) Similarly, it is possible to work with changing and different-sized groupings, just as it is with any normal classwork.

1 Try using different work groupings within the same lesson (just as you would do in a normal English lesson), e.g. individual work, pairs, small groups, whole class.
2 Try using periods of time at and away from computers. You can manage these yourself by calling out instructions to finish stages or start new stages; or you can set a task and outline the working methods, and then allow students to manage their own movement through the stages, to and from the computers.

Here is an example lesson description:

Writing

1 Set a writing task for students. Make groups of five. Each group appoints one secretary. The others brainstorm ideas together on the writing topic while the secretary takes notes on the computer.
2 The ideas are either printed off and circulated to the class for discussion, or the notes are shared by displaying on the interactive board.
3 Pairs are formed who now discuss (away from the computers) how they will tackle the writing task.

4 After a while, the teacher invites them to move to a PC to write up an outline in their pair. When finished, the teacher reads and approves it, perhaps adding some advice.

5 The students then sit at their own individual computer to write up their individual response to the task, based on the outline.

6 When finished, the two members of each pair swap computers, read each other's texts and comment, while their partner sits with them.

This lesson moves as follows: (1) group with secretary, (2) whole-class discussion away from computer, (3) pairs away from computer, (4) pairs at the computer, (5) individual work, (6) pair work.

Techniques: Tablet computers

Many of the well-known problems associated with using full-size computers in class are resolved by using tablet PCs. Desktop computers take up a lot of space and often need fixed locations in the room. Students need to move to them (perhaps in a different room), away from their normal desks – with all the potential palaver that this leads to. In contrast, tablet computers are light and completely portable. They can be used on the student's own normal desk. Students can write and share messages or documents easily. If enabled by the teacher, it's also possible for students to send messages directly to the teacher, other students, or for messages to be shown on the interactive whiteboard. Students can research the Internet at their desks and take notes directly on the tablet while they work. Teachers can distribute tasks, worksheets, texts, documents and links directly to each individual student's device. Because of all these advantages, it is entirely conceivable that the future of coursebooks is on tablets and mobile devices.

The main problem for many schools with tablet PCs is likely to be their potential for being stolen. They are small, light and easily slipped into a bag. Keeping careful track of them will require some thought and might possibly involve physical security attachments, such as electronic tags, cable locks or fixed enclosures; however, with all these, there is a trade-off between security and the potential for flexible use. Simpler, cheaper measures would involve engraving tablets with school names and tally numbers or requiring that students bring their own tablet to school.

Techniques: Discouraging distractions and misuse while on computers

Whenever students (of any age) get the chance to work with connected computers, there is likely to be misuse. Instead of working on the task they are supposed to, some will surf the net for subjects they are interested in, some will spend their time in social chat with online friends, some will go shopping, some will download inappropriate or illegal material – and, quite often, one or two will actively seek to hack, modify or bypass programmes, settings or operating/security protocols you have in place.

The best protection against most of these is active monitoring: simply walking around and keeping an eye on what students are doing. If a pair always goes into a fluster of activity every time you get nearby, it might be worth checking what else is running, minimised on their screens.

1 Time wasting and distractions

Talk with students about the ground rules for using computers and agree a code of conduct with them. Be clear what you consider acceptable or unacceptable. It may be that you don't mind use of some non-work-related sites or programmes if students still manage to complete their work. In many ways, being scattered and unfocussed, hopping around here and there, may all be part of using computers successfully. We no longer read, write or think in quite the linear way that old school classrooms persuaded us to do.

If you definitely want to restrict student use, you could:

- Create individual accounts for each student. Set up usage trackers on each account.
- Remove any programmes that you don't need students to use, e.g. messenger programmes or games.
- Set up filters so that only certain websites can be visited, or, perhaps more usefully, blacklist sites that you really want students to stay away from, e.g. popular social or email sites.
- Block peer-to-peer file sharing.

2 Hacking and reprogramming

- Get your IT department to advise how best to protect your computers against deliberate attempts to harm them. If settings can be password protected, this is often a good first option. It also might be worth asking an IT specialist to prevent local installation of new programmes. Make sure the high-level administrator username and password are kept secret, and change them if there is any doubt as to their remaining secret.
- When you need to do any of your own work on computer in lesson time, do it randomly at different machines in class, rather than always using the one at the front. In this way, you get to notice firsthand if there are any alterations or reprogramming at work on individual machines.
- Keep records of who uses which machines in different lessons. This can be useful to help you track back and find offenders if a malicious use is discovered.

Questions for reflection

- Which are the biggest organisational headaches for you when you want to make use of new technology in classes? Are there any simple ways to alleviate or resolve these problems?

8 Post-task

> *After students have finished an activity we go through each question, one by one, and it always feels so predictable and boring.*

Aim

To use feedback stages after exercises and activities in a more productive way.

Introduction

When students have finished working on an exercise or a task, teachers often want to check answers or give feedback on the answers students have come up with. This lesson stage is often curiously underexploited. Many teachers use it purely for validating correct answers, for example:

Teacher:	Question 1?
Student 1:	Have eaten.
Teacher:	Good. Number 2?
Student 2:	Has gone.
Teacher:	Good. Number 3?
...and so on.	

All this is achieving is confirmation of the correct answers. At times this may be sufficient, but, in many cases, this has the potential to be one of the most important opportunities for classroom work. Chapter 5 Unit 6 looks at some techniques for involving more people in answering questions and especially avoiding immediate teacher rubberstamping of answers. In this unit, we look at ways of making use of varied styles of post-task feedback and reports.

Techniques: Checking answers after exercises

Your students have just finished doing a standard exercise (e.g. 12 multiple-choice vocabulary questions). Here are some ideas for various ways of checking (or not checking) the answers:

1 Traditional: whole class
Go through the answers, question by question, in the whole class, asking different students to call out the answer to each question, and then have the teacher confirm them.

2 Led by students
Ask one or more students to lead the checking and feedback.

3 Hold-ups

Ask each student to write their answer on a piece of paper or tablet computer and hold it up. You can get a quick sense of whether the majority of students are right or not and spot students who have problems.

4 Student response

When students call out answers, don't confirm or comment yourself. Tell students that the class as a whole has the responsibility of saying whether they agree or disagree, and if they think it's wrong, discuss and decide which answer is correct. Or choose an individual to confirm or challenge a student's answer.

5 Nominated nominations

Ask the individual student who is answering a question to nominate the next student who has to answer the following question.

6 Read out other people's answers

Just before you start checking, ask students to pass on their answers to someone else. Students then call out answers from the page they have been given, rather than from their own (NB If you think that bad handwriting or poor answers might make this embarrassing, best avoid this option).

7 Don't check everything

Although out of habit as much as anything, teachers typically check through every answer to every exercise, it may not always be necessary. Try: 'OK, let's check only the answers you are really not sure about. Which ones shall we look at?' or 'Choose the three questions … yes, just three … that you really want to check or discuss'.

8 Traditional read to check

Students look up answers in the back of their books or on a handout you give. They use the answer sheet to check their own or another student's answers.

9 Lay bets – then read to check

Rather than the checking becoming a rather dispiriting affair as students realise how much they have got wrong, this variation both adds a light touch and allows even weak students to feel good about their achievement. When students have finished an exercise, but before they check, ask them to make a bet as to how many they will get correct. For example, 'Piotr thinks he will get only four right out of 12 questions.' Everyone should write down their bet or tell the teacher who can note it on the board. Students then look up the answers and see how close they got to their prediction; the closest is the winner. And perhaps Piotr will feel quite pleased at getting seven right – three more than he expected (whereas in a normal post-exercise check, he would only have felt bad about getting five wrong).

10 Monitor, and then don't check in whole class

There are times when your monitoring will inform you that an exercise was no real problem and that students can do the task without errors. In such a case, further checking is just a waste of time. Move on!

Techniques: Getting students to present reports

When groups do discussion tasks (e.g. puzzle, problem, planning or other types), at the end, there can sometimes be a sense of 'What was the point of all that?' Students may feel that they have spent a long time working together, discussing and agreeing, but then the teacher just brings the task to a close and suddenly moves on to the next piece of work. One important way of giving added value to such work is to add on an extra post-task stage: a report-back or presentation from students. This gives them a chance to show others what they have done (and find out what the others have done). It is also a good chance to reuse language that has been in circulation during the task, but with the useful added pressure of having to upgrade it a little for a more public, less-informal audience.

1 Preparation for a report

In order to be able to prepare a good report after a task, it is important that students can recall what they discussed and agreed.

- At the beginning of a task, appoint (or ask students to appoint) a secretary in each group. The secretary's job is to make notes about what is discussed and concluded. At the end of the task, these notes can help the group review how they did the task and prepare a report.
- At the end of a group task, allocate some extra minutes for students to prepare an oral (or written) report back on the task process and outcomes to others. Make sure they have enough time to review how they did things, to think about what they have discussed and concluded and to make notes if they need to.
- Prepare a template to help students review their task and draw conclusions. The template could have questions (such as, 'Which point did most people in your group have strong feelings about?') or headings (such as, 'Our three most important suggestions').

2 Students report in groups

It is often useful for students to report group findings directly to other students. There are various ways of doing this:

- Go round the groups, allocating a different letter to each person in a group, i.e. within one group of five, the students would be given A, B, C, D and E. When all students in the room have a letter, say, 'All A's meet up over here … all B's make a new group over here … All C's …'.
- Ask two students from each group to stand up and move on (clockwise) to join the next group, while the remaining students stay seated. The students who moved report to their new group on outcomes from their old group and then hear the report from the students they have joined.

3 Students report to the whole class

You may decide that you want groups, taking it in turns, to give an oral report back to the whole class.

- Make sure that they've had a chance to prepare and that they have agreed which members of the group will speak.
- Alternatively, you could appoint the speakers yourself or require that every member of a group has to say something in their report.
- Listen positively. However many mistakes, make sure that your feedback includes positive encouragement and acknowledgement of their achievement in making the report.

Technique: Following on from role play or dialogues

A 'public performance' can seem the natural way of ending a sequence of activities involving role play or dialogue practice. Invite students to come up to the front to show what they have been working on. If students are embarrassed about performing before everyone, you could divide the class into two 'theatres' at different ends of the room, with each group performing to the other students in their half. The fact that students know that this will happen may help 'concentrate their minds' during the 'rehearsal' stages.

Questions for reflection

• Could you get more learning value out of what happens after a task has finished?

9 Closing lessons

> *My lessons always seem to end in a bit of a muddle and anti-climax. I usually get my timing wrong, so we finish up doing six or seven minutes of Hangman.*

Aim
To find satisfying and useful ways of closing lessons.

Introduction
Closing your lesson well may be as important as starting it well. You might want to avoid any sense that it is rushed, chaotic or confused – or that you have run out of things to do after an activity finishes earlier than you expected. Perhaps you'd like your students to leave feeling that they have had an interesting, enjoyable class, that they have achieved something useful and that they are looking forward to the next lesson.

When you watch experienced teachers, the way that their lessons conclude neatly and on time, with everything tied up, can seem almost magical. But a lot of this is simply to do with being able to predict how activities will go from much earlier on in the lesson, and adjusting as they work.

Another aspect is to do with use of specific closing activities, such as revision games or a review of the lesson.

→ For ways of dealing with students misbehaving at the end of lessons, e.g. packing up too soon, see Chapter 6 Unit 2.

Technique: Teacher summary
For many students, the lesson that you have just taught will be forgotten as soon as they are through the door. I don't just mean the taught content of the lesson, but even what it was that happened. You may be able to help later recall of lesson content by helping recall of the actual shape, structure and flow of the work. The memory of activities done might just help to revive and anchor memories of the language used.

At the end of class, take a minute or two to simply state what the lesson has been about and perhaps to answer any short questions that arise. The summary could be a teacher monologue, or it could involve some eliciting from students. The teacher could note key points on the board, as he or she says them, or refer to a projected list of items.

In this lesson excerpt, Izolda is summarising the lesson she has just taught:

So, I hope you enjoyed that activity. Let's finish by looking back at the whole lesson. First of all … do you remember what we did first of all? How did we start the lesson? (A student responds.) Yes, that's right. We looked at vocabulary about the environment. Can you remember some of the words? (Students call out.) Good. And after that, what did we do? (Students respond.) OK … We read a story about Paolo who lives in Brazil, and we answered questions about the story. What grammar did we study? (Students respond.) Yes, words like 'slowly'. What do we call them?

Techniques: Encouraging student reflection

A good way to close a lesson is by initiating learner reflection on what they have studied and what they have learnt or not learnt.

1 Board sentence

Write a sentence head on the board, e.g. 'The most difficult thing in today's lesson was …'. Invite students to write their own ending for the sentence in their notebooks. Hold out the board pen, and invite different students to come up and write their version for others to see and discuss. Alternatively, for a more anonymous response, hand out a large pile of paper scraps and ask students to write answers on the scraps (which you can then collect in and read a sample from, which might be helpful in informing your planning for the next lesson).

Here are a few more ideas for sentence-heads:
• The most interesting thing I learnt today was …
• I'm sure I'll forget …
• The bit of today's lesson that really bored me was …
• Next lesson, I hope we …
• I need to spend some time revising …

2 Quick individual reflection

Ask every student to look back over the coursebook pages, handouts, tasks and exercises used in the lesson and make a note of:
• The three most interesting or useful things that were studied.
• One important thing they have learnt and will try to remember from this lesson.
• A question that they want to ask about something in the lesson.

Encourage them to be specific rather than general, e.g. naming a specific set of words they learnt rather than saying 'new vocabulary'. When students have written their answers, pair them up to compare notes. If you have time, you could ask for some students to tell the whole class.

3 Pair or group buzz

Put students into pairs or small groups. Ask them to answer your questions as quickly as they can. Call out a series of questions, allowing about a minute for students to spontaneously say everything they can think of in response to each one, without reference to books, notes, etc. Questions could include things like:

- List all the new words that came up today.
- Name some surprising things in today's lesson.
- What did people laugh about in today's class?
- How did your personal energy levels rise and fall though the lesson?

4 Pair/group letter to absent students

Ask students to write a short summary of the lesson for any student who happens to be absent. This could be a letter or email, or any form you choose, perhaps even an immediate update on a class website or Facebook® page or a series of Tweets on Twitter.

5 Closing address

At the start of each lesson, appoint two or three people to take on the responsibility of making a summary speech at the end of the class. As the lesson unfolds, they make notes about what everyone is doing, interesting things that happen, etc. Before the end of the lesson (perhaps instead of a final task), allow the two or three students to meet up and decide what they are going to say. Invite them to the front and let them give their 'closing address' to the class. When you first do this, students will probably give a fairly factual summary of the lesson. As they become more familiar with the task over time, the style and content of reports will change, and you'll probably get more amusing and creative interpretations.

6 Reflection tennis

Pair students up, and seat each partner some distance from the other. In turn, each person has to recall something specific from the lesson (e.g. a word, a grammar point, a fact, part of the story, etc.). They call out their answer and, as with a tennis match, the imaginary 'ball' goes over to their partner, who must now name a new thing to 'hit the ball back'. The game goes on, back and forth, until they run out of ideas. One reason for sitting pairs slightly apart from each other is that this forces them to speak a little louder, which allows others to overhear their ideas, which, in turn, gets more ideas in circulation around the room. It also makes for a jolly, noisy and pleasantly chaotic end to the lesson. If you want a quieter version, simply seat the two students in each pair close together. You could focus the game more tightly by setting a specific question (drawn from the lesson content) at the start of each game, e.g. name words that you can find on a farm.

7 Reflection against a syllabus

At the beginning of a course, give students a copy of the syllabus they are following (e.g. a list of can-do criteria statements). This could be in a folder, diary or book, or perhaps digitally stored on a local computer or online. Ideally, each syllabus statement should have space to allow students to add comments, dates and other information and to grade their achievements (e.g. 0 = Not achieved yet; 1 = Partially achieved; 2 = Fully achieved). At the end of each lesson, ask students to compare what they have studied in the lesson against that syllabus, self-assessing as to what they can do well now (and what they still can't do). As time goes by, students will very clearly be able to see their progress and get a sense of what still needs to be studied.

8 Reflection feeding into action plans

Whatever form of reflection you facilitate, it's also useful to get each student to combine this with preparing an action plan, i.e. a statement about what an individual student needs to work on. It is often filled in on a form and can be preceded by or followed with a tutorial.

Action plan
NAME:
Recent work
I feel confident about:
I need to spend some more time working on:
When and how will I do this work?
Future work
My priorities for the next part of the course are:
I particularly want to work on improving:
I think I need to study the following new things:
My teacher can help and support my work by:
Will there be any changes in *how* I do my English language study in the future?

An action plan such as this is not something to do every lesson, but is valuable as a way of reviewing progress after a period of time (e.g. every two or four weeks, or every half term). Make sure that students consider a wide range of skills and systems work (e.g. speaking, reading, writing, listening, grammar, vocabulary, pronunciation).

Technique: Avoid the last-minute rush

When an activity overruns, taking much longer than expected, you will need to have ways to shorten it so that everything can conclude before the lesson's end time.

Try to look ahead to this from as early in the lesson as possible. Keep the end point in mind. If you predict that the activity is likely to overrun, don't wait until the end of the lesson and then cut it off unfinished. Keep making small micro-adjustments to timing, pace and instructions while you work so that the activity will take less time (e.g. stating a shorter time limit than you planned or telling students to do the first five questions, rather than all ten as you had anticipated). By remaining aware and acting preemptively, you can avoid a last-minute shock. It is typically more effective to retrieve time from stages in the middle of the lesson than trying to rush through the closing ones.

Technique: Don't start a new task; extend the old one

If one activity finishes, and it's within about ten minutes of the end of the lesson, think twice before starting a new activity. It's often better to add to or extend the current activity (e.g. introducing a feedback or report stage), rather than starting a completely new stage (which you almost certainly do not have enough time to give instructions for, run and conclude).

What you can do will depend on the specific task that students have been doing, but here are a few examples:

1 Get students to write a new question or two in the style of the grammar or vocabulary exercise they have just finished. These questions can then be passed on to other students to do.
2 Ask students to prepare a report-back (to present either to another pair or to the whole class).
3 Ask students to repeat a speaking task, but changing the roles around.
4 After a reading or listening task, ask students to put away the texts/transcripts and see how much they can remember (or possibly act out).

Technique: Don't draw attention to what didn't happen

It's not usually a great idea to say to students, 'I was going to do something really interesting next, but I'm sorry we have run out of time'. It leaves everyone feeling that their teacher can't plan very well and that something important has been missed. If you run out of time, keep it upbeat, and let students focus on the things they have done which they enjoyed.

Technique: Planning timing from the end

When planning how the lesson ends, you may find it helpful to work backwards from the last moment of the lesson to calculate how long you need for each step. This will give you a clearer idea of just how long before the end you need to conclude the last main activity. For example, here is a backwards plan for the last ten minutes of a lesson.

0 Lesson end.
-1 Tell students that they can pack their bags and get ready to leave.
-3 Set homework.
-4 Tidy up books. Collect work in.
-9 Feedback and questions about the activity.
-10 Conclude discussion activity.

Technique: Have a regular closing stage

With younger learners, you may find that it helps to always do the same thing at the end of every lesson. Students will know what to expect, and the predictability and habit may help to quieten them down and discourage too-early packing up. This stage might include:

- Setting homework.
- Filling in a diary.
- Collecting a new reader from the library box.
- Repeating the 'poem of the week' (or any other text you or they select).
- Singing a song (Scott Thornbury, the series editor, comments that, 'I once took a course in Maori in New Zealand at an Adult Education centre, and every lesson ended with a song which we stood up and sang – there was something sort of reassuring about this, as well as giving a wonderful sense of closure').
- Writing and chorally repeating the 'word of the day' from the board.

Technique: Withholding

Here is a simple technique for discouraging students from packing up early and racing to get out of the door.

Earlier in the lesson, sow the seed of something that will only be revealed right at the end of the lesson. For example, you tell the class a riddle (e.g. 'What is the only word in English that is pronounced exactly the same when you cross out the last four letters?'). Let them think about it and suggest answers, but don't confirm any solution. Tell them that you will let them know the right answer at the very end of the lesson. In the last few minutes of the lesson, remind them of the riddle, let them speculate again – then tell them the answer in the final few seconds of the lesson. (Answer: 'Queue!') Some other ideas:

- A joke. (You save the punch line for the end.)
- A test. (You save the scores for the end.)
- A video clip. (You stop the playback just before the last scene; ask, 'What happened next?' and only reveal it at the end.)
- A story or anecdote. (You don't tell them the ending until the end of the lesson.)
- A puzzle that students work on. (You save the correct solution for the end.) For example, 'Jill is visiting Jack and sees a picture on the wall. She asks, "Who is that?" Jack says, "Sisters and brothers I have none, but that man's father is my father's son." Who is it?' This example demonstrates that a puzzle can be quite complex despite using very simple language! (Answer: 'Jack's son'.)

Techniques: Better fillers

Do you habitually always use the same filler game when you have spare time at the end of a class … and does it always seem to be Hangman? Take a little time to research online or in books for short games that could extend your repertoire, e.g. Ur, P. (2012) *Vocabulary Activities*, Cambridge: Cambridge University Press.

The most useful games are likely to be ones that review and recycle language that has come up in the lesson, or which get students to look back or think back over what they have learnt.

The following are some popular quick games that can be used to revise language from the lesson:

1 Anagrams
On the board, write up a number of anagrams of words from the lesson. Students try to decipher them as fast as possible.

2 Phonemic anagrams
Same idea, but put the words up as mixed-up phonemic symbols.

3 Mixed-up sentences
Similarly, write a sentence that uses a structure from the lesson, but with the words in a mixed-up order.

4 Word clouds
Write several words and punctuation marks in random places on the board. Students see how many good sentences they can make from the items. For example:

(Answers include: 'She is a teacher', 'Are you going to meet the detective?' 'You are going to ask the teacher later', 'Is the detective going to meet a teacher?' 'She is going to ask, "Are you a teacher?"')

5 Back to the board
You invite a student to come to the front and sit facing the class, with his back to the board. You write a word from the lesson on the board so that the class can see it, but the student can't. The class define the word or say synonyms until the student at the front guesses the word or gives up. Also works well as a team game, with game players from the two teams taking turns at the front.

6 Sentence-making challenge

Write up three words, perhaps using noun, verb, noun (e.g. *builder, drop, piano*). Challenge the students to make sentences following these five rules: (1) They cannot add any more nouns or main verbs, (2) They can change the form of the words (e.g. *builder* → *builders*; *drop* → *dropped*), (3) They can add 'small words' such as auxiliary verbs, pronouns, articles, prepositions, question words, adverbs, etc., (4) They can add punctuation, (5) They can use the original three words in any order, repeat them if they wish or omit one or more.

Show an example (e.g. 'The builder has never dropped the piano'); then allow a few minutes' thinking time. Collect ideas together on the board – and enjoy them! There is no correct answer, but sentences might include: 'I dropped the piano on the builder', 'Where's the builder?' 'Under the piano', 'That builder's always dropping my piano!' 'That piano is mine, not the builder's.'

(I got this idea from Scott Thornbury's *Uncovering Grammar*.)

Technique: Pause; don't stop

Some practitioners of the Silent-Way method make a deliberate point of *not* timing their activities so that they conclude, wrap up or reach a natural pause at the lesson's end time. Instead they just stop whatever they are doing when the time runs out, often right in the middle of something. At the start of the next lesson, they simply pick up where things left off. One effect is that the teacher has no need to feel stressed about timing activities, hurrying people up, worrying about fillers and so on. The work is allowed to take however long it needs and allows you to link lessons – one to another, in a natural way.

Questions for reflection

• Do your lessons tend to end elegantly or in a muddle? What small change could make these endings more effective?

10 Closing courses

> At the end of the course, we finished the last exercise; then I said goodbye to them, and they all left. After all the work and time together, it felt incomplete, and I was wishing that I could have marked the day in some more special way.

Aim

To close courses in a memorable way that allows students to look back, recognise their achievements, recall the enjoyable times and become more aware of any emotions associated with saying goodbye.

Introduction

The end of a course is an important transition. Students and teachers will have been together for some time, working, interacting, laughing and enjoying each other's company.

As people move on to new classes, new colleagues or perhaps to very different futures, there can be feelings of pleasure and achievement, as well as some sadness and loss: saying goodbye to friends, realising that a period of one's life is over, wondering what will fill the gap left by the course, nostalgia for the camaraderie of the group. Often these feelings go unspoken or unrecognised.

Some teachers like to mark the end of courses with some formal or even ritualistic activity, to draw people's attention to what is happening and to provide a memorable moment that symbolically closes the time together and allows everyone to look back at what has happened. This is often achieved through a game or activity, perhaps involving the chance to review what has and hasn't been enjoyed and achieved.

In terms of John Heron's (1990) description of group stages (see Chapter 3 Unit 2), this is autumn – the gathering in of the harvest, followed by the harvesters setting off on their different ways.

Technique: Review files and portfolios

If your students have been keeping a diary, file or portfolio through the course, the end provides a chance to look back through it, tidy up, tie up loose ends and finish it formally in some way, perhaps with the teacher signing it off.

1 Ask students to fill in a form you have prepared. This could include a range of questions that ask them to review different aspects of their portfolio.
2 Get students to compile statistics, e.g. a table of all marks and test results through the course, teacher comments over time, etc.

3 Get students to formally write a closing statement of some kind and sign it.
4 Questions on the review form could include things such as:
- Which three pieces of work do you feel proudest about?
- Which piece of work would you like to throw away?
- Does the portfolio show good progress over the course?
- According to teacher comments, which areas have improved over the course? Which areas still need some work?
- Are you satisfied with the presentation of the portfolio? Does it look organised and smart?

Technique: Tutorials

While perhaps inappropriate for the final lesson itself, offering every student a one-to-one tutorial is an excellent way to summarise what they have done and to note what work lies ahead for them in the future. You will probably need a minimum of 10 to 15 minutes for each person, which suggests that you might have to timetable the sessions over a number of lessons towards the close of the course.

Prepare for tutorials by making brief notes on each student yourself and by asking them to similarly fill in a self-evaluation. In the tutorials themselves, get students to speak most of the time, reviewing what they have achieved, as well as looking forward.

Technique: Separate grades and test marks from the goodbye

In some schools, the last day of a course is often dominated by students receiving grades for the course or learning about marks from tests. This naturally affects people's moods and reactions, and gets in the way of celebrating the course in its own right.

Whenever possible, deal with grades and marks in a lesson before the final one, thus freeing yourself up to focus on the course closure in its own right.

Technique: The ball of string

Bring a very long ball of string (or wool) to class. Ask everyone to stand in one large circle, and join it yourself. Tell students that when they get the ball, they should say something good that they remember about the course (e.g. 'I really enjoyed ...'), maybe about an activity, an individual, a shared experience or anything else. They should make their comment relatively concise.

When they have finished what they have to say, the student unwinds a length of string and throws the ball on to another person across the circle *while keeping hold of the string that has been unwound.* This means that the ball will slowly unwind as the activity progresses. It leaves behind a steadily growing network or web around, and among, the class members.

When everyone has spoken, or when the string runs out, make a statement about how the web represents all the links and relationships that people have formed over the length of the course – and how those links will remain, even though we are not all together in the same room. On your command, everyone should simultaneously let go of the string they are holding. It falls to the floor, a visible representation of the ending of the course, and of the continuing links between people.

Technique: Walking the course

You can do this in the classroom, but it will work better in a more open space, e.g. a hall, a playground or even a corridor. Choose a location that allows students to walk from one point to another.

Ask students to all stand at one end of the space. Tell them that where they are standing represents the first day of the course (e.g. 7 September). The other end of the walk represents the last day of the course (e.g. today, 2 July). The distance between the two locations is like a timeline symbolising the duration of the course.

As an example, ask students if they can recall some of the things that happened on the course, and then agree a consensus on where these events might be located on the timeline. They can talk about concrete things that they studied, how the group lived and changed, how they felt themselves – or anything else that is memorable. When students understand the idea, invite them to wander, initially in twos or threes along the line, recalling things that happened at different points, meeting up with other students and comparing notes.

At the end, ask everyone to stand on the line at the spot which is most memorable for them. Compare stories and memories.

Technique: The course museum

Ask the class to imagine that it is thirty years in the future, and they have all come back to their old school for a reunion. Their former classroom has been preserved as a museum. Invite students to meet up, role playing themselves from the future. They should wander round the room, comparing notes and memories about the course and their time together (e.g. 'Do you remember when we looked out of this window and saw …?').

Techniques: Drawing the course

Hand out sheets of large paper (e.g. A3). Tell everyone to divide their sheet into four boxes. Explain that they should think back over the course and select four 'highlights'. These might be to do with work done, things that happened in class, relationships with other students – or anything else that has happened during the life and time of the course. Instead of writing any words, students should now draw a sketch picture of each of the four highlights in the four boxes. Tell them not to worry about artistic ability – just do their best. Allow enough time for the task to be done well; then let students meet up with other people that they will feel comfortable talking to. (This may be a time not to make the pairings/groupings yourself.) Students show their pictures and talk through them. Others can ask questions.

Technique: Handshakes, thanks and gifts

Ask everyone to think of three imaginary presents that they would enjoy giving to others in the class. The gifts should be things that help people to recall nice moments in the course. Emphasise that these presents do not need to be real objects. They could be, for example:

- A photo of the day we all went a bit crazy talking about hairstyles!
- The Monet painting we liked when we read about that art gallery.
- A recording of the song by Lady Gaga (that we listened to in Unit 7).
- The joke about the three doctors from the story on page 121.
- The word 'bumblebee', because for some reason it always makes us all collapse into laughter when our teacher says it.
- A sunny day, because we always felt happier when the weather was good.

When each student has a list of gifts, explain the activity. Everyone will stand up and mingle. The aim is for each person to meet and say goodbye to everyone else in the class, one person at a time. It doesn't need to be a rush. When two students meet, they should shake hands, say 'thank you' to each other (for being in the same class) and then 'give' one of their imaginary gifts to the other person, explaining a little about what it is and why they think the other person will like it. For example, 'I'd like to give you this small green plant because it will go on growing after the course is finished, and it feels like our friendship can continue and grow afterwards as well.'

Technique: Design a ceremony

The last major task of the course can be for the students to devise, script and design a formal or ritual goodbye ceremony for the whole class. Let them plan it and then run it.

Techniques: Getting feedback

It's surprisingly hard to get real feedback from students. It's easy enough to collect bland comments or a general vote that the course was OK, but much harder to get thoughtful, useful comments that will help you to improve what you do. Naturally, students are often nervous about saying things that may be perceived as negative comments to their teachers (especially ones they might meet again and who can mark them down!).

The following techniques might encourage more students to give more useful comments.

1 Formal feedback form

Prepare a series of questions about the course. Distribute this to all students, and allow time for them to fill in their answers. Promise that anything they say will be taken seriously. If you think it will help, make the forms anonymous.

2 Lucky–dip feedback

Distribute lots of slips of paper. Encourage students to write any honest comments about the course on these slips. As they are anonymous, there may be a temptation to exaggerated or silly comments, so you may need to discourage this as far as possible. Collect all the slips in, and review them with a nice drink in the evening!

3 Lucky dip – *live*

This is a 'riskier' version of the idea above. Collect all the slips into a box or bag. Sit at the front, pull one out and read it aloud. You (or the students) can make any comment or reaction they wish to. Continue reading though the slips.

4 Letter to teacher

Ask students to write you a private personal letter or email. Say that you won't mark it or share it with anyone else. (You could offer them a short reply if you wish.) Tell them that they can say anything they want to about the course, including giving you any advice they wish to.

5 Teacher-led self-evaluation

Give your own oral review of the course: what you enjoyed and what you didn't. Include an honest appraisal of those things that you think you could have done better or differently. Invite others to follow your example, and do the same (in pairs, groups or to the whole class, if they are confident enough).

6 Letter to future students

Ask your class to write a letter to the class that will follow them, next course or next year. What do they need to know about the course? What will they probably find difficult? What might be the highs and lows? What advice will they give them? What warnings are necessary? Promise to pass on their letters. (You could promise to pass them on as completely private messages, unread by you, if you feel brave!)

Technique: Keeping the group going online

In the modern connected world, there is no reason why a course-end day needs to mark the end of the group's life. Set up a website, a page on a social-networking site or a Twitter hashtag (i.e. a keyword to quickly reference something) so that everyone can stay in touch over the months ahead. Agree a particular time (e.g. a weekend in three months' time) for a synchronous meeting.

Questions for reflection

- There are lots of ideas here for formal or even ritualistic endings to courses. What might be the arguments for *not* doing anything like this?

Classroom management booklist

Bolton, R. (1979) *People Skills*, New York: Simon and Schuster (A Touchstone Book).

Dörnyei, Z. and Murphey, T. (2003) *Group Dynamics in the Language Classroom*, Cambridge: Cambridge University Press.

Ginnis, P. (2001) *The Teacher's Toolkit*, Carmarthen: Crown House Publishing, Ltd.

Gower, R. et al. (2005) *Teaching Practice Handbook*, Oxford: Macmillan Education.

Hadfield, J. (1992) *Classroom Dynamics*, Oxford: Oxford University Press.

Harmer, J. (2007) *The Practice of English Language Teaching*, Fourth edition, Harlow: Pearson Education/Longman.

Hattie, J. (2008) *Visible Learning, A synthesis of over 800 meta-analyses relating to achievement*, London: Routledge.

Heron, J. (1999) *The Complete Facilitator's Handbook*, London: Kogan Page Limited.

Heron, J. (2001) *Helping the Client, A creative practical guide*, Fifth edition, London: Sage Publications.

Houston, G. (1990) *The Red Book of Groups, and how to lead them better*, Third edition, London: Rochester Foundation.

Jaques, D. and Salmon, G. (2007) *Learning in Groups, A handbook for face-to-face and online environments*, Fourth edition, London: Routledge.

Lewis, M. and Hill, J. (1992) *Practical Techniques for Language Teaching*, Hove: Language Teaching Publications.

Maley, A. (2000) *The Language Teacher's Voice*, Oxford: Macmillan Education.

Nolasco, R. and Arthur, L. (1988) *Large Classes*, Oxford: Macmillan Education.

Petty, G. (2009) *Teaching Today, A practical guide*, Fourth edition, Cheltenham: Nelson Thomas, Ltd.

Powel A. (2009) *The Cornerstone: Classroom management that makes teaching more effective, efficient, and enjoyable*, Longwood, Florida: Xulon Press.

Rogers, C. (1983) *Freedom to Learn, for the 80's*, Columbus, Ohio: Charles Merrill.

Scrivener, J. (2011) *Learning Teaching, A guidebook for English language teachers*, Third Edition, Oxford: Macmillan Education.

Thornbury, S. (2006) *An A-Z of ELT*, Oxford: Macmillan Education.

Tsui, A. (1995) *Introducing Classroom Interaction*, Harlow: Penguin Books, Ltd.

Underwood, M. (1987) *Effective Class Management*, Harlow: Pearson Education/Longman.

Ur, P. (2012) *A Course in English Language Teaching*, Second edition, Cambridge: Cambridge University Press.

Wright, T. (2005) *Classroom Management in Language Education*, Basingstoke, Hampshire: Palgrave Macmillan.

Wright, T. (1987) *Roles of Teachers and Learners*, New York: Oxford University Press.

Other publications mentioned in this book

Atkinson, D. (1993) *Teaching Monolingual Classes*, Harlow: Pearson Education/Longman.

Cowley, C. (2009) *Teaching Skills for Dummies*, New Jersey: John Wiley and Sons.

Kramsch, C. (1985) 'Classroom interaction and discourse options', *Studies in Second Language Acquisition*, **7**, 169–183.

McCourt, F. (2005) *Teacher Man*, London: HarperCollins/4th Estate.

Pullman, P. (1997) *His Dark Materials: The Subtle Knife*, New York: Scholastic.

Roethke, T. (1972) *Straw For the Fire*, New York: Doubleday.

Tuckman, B. and Jensen, M. (1977) 'Stages of small group development revisited', *Group and Organizational Studies*, **2**, 419–427.

Tuckman, B. (1965) 'Developmental sequence in small group', *Psychological Bulletin*, **63**, 6, 384–399.

Wilson, K. http://kenwilsonelt.wordpress.com

Index

Made in the USA
Middletown, DE
08 September 2016